The Interracial Con Game

The Interracial Con Game

by Umoja
(formerly Anon)

TROJAN HORSE PRESS

First Edition
First Printing: December 2011

Library of Congress Control Number:
2011935616
ISBN: 978-0-9822061-2-6

Disclaimer for resemblance to real persons

This book includes political satire and works of fiction. Names, characters, places, and incidents are either the product of the authors' imaginations or used fictitiously. Any resemblance to actual persons, living or dead, business establishments, events, or locales is entirely coincidental. The publisher does not have any control over and does not assume any responsibility for any third-party websites or their content.

Printed and bound Manufactured in the United States of America

Trojan Horse Press
PO Box 245
Hazel Crest, IL 60429

email: info@trojanhorse1.com
website: www.trojanhorse1.com

Cover Design by P. Evans

Dedication

To our beautiful black women, our mothers, wives, lovers, sisters, and daughters. To our strong, courageous black brothers, fathers, and sons, wherever you are, fighting for justice.

And a very special dedication to:

Dr. Frances Cress Welsing
Neely Fuller, Jr.
The Honorable Elijah Muhammad
Malcolm X
Rosa Parks
Marcus Garvey
Gus Renegade

Acknowledgements

This book could not have been written or completed without the ground-breaking works of Neely Fuller, Jr., Dr. Frances Cress Welsing, the Honorable Elijah Muhammad, Dr. Yosef Ben-Jochannan, John Henrik Clarke, Marcus Garvey, Dr. Mwalimu K. Bomani Baruti, Chancellor Williams, Malcolm X, George Orwell, Tony Brown, Jawanza Kunjufu, Carter G. Woodson, James Baldwin, Willard Motley, and many others too numerous to mention. Naturally, we accept total responsibility for any misinterpretations of their works, and any errors that may appear in this book.

A very special thanks to Gus Renegade (C.O.W.S.), Ed Williams (counter-racism.com), D.H., Wendy Williams, R. Parker, J. Wickett, D.B., K. Richardson, D. Robinson, and of all our friends, families, and mentors who shared their special insights, wisdom, and patience with us.

We hope we have done justice to all who inspired us to complete our third book, and have inspired others in the fight for universal justice for all the people on our Creator's planet.

About the Authors

Why the authors use a pseudonym

There is nothing original about the ideas presented here. Wiser minds have come before and will certainly come long after this book was written. The authors are not falsely modest; we are acknowledging we did not invent the wheel.

The authors are not seeking fame. This is not an attempt to be mysterious or provoke curiosity. This is not a gimmick or a perverse, reverse publicity ploy. In today's media-obsessed world, there is too much focus on "show" and not enough on "substance." The authors choose not to participate.

The authors reserve the right NOT to be a distraction to the message. We are the least important part of this book. You, the reader, are more important. Even more important, is what you do with this information.

Every word in this book was designed to inform, provoke discussion, decrease confusion, reduce hostility, minimize conflict, and to promote the kinds of constructive action that are necessary to replace the system of Racism/White Supremacy with a system of universal justice for ***all the people on the planet.***

You may not agree with everything or anything written here. We have presented *our* truths to the best of our ability. If this book inspires you to seek your own truths, the book has been a success.

(The pseudonym, Anon, used for our first book, "Trojan Horse: Death Of A Dark Nation" has been replaced by "Umoja" -- the Swahili word for "UNITY.")

The Purpose of this Book

The *"Interracial Con Game"* was originally written as a chapter in our second book, *"Black Love Is A Revolutionary Act."* However, as our research uncovered the catastrophic effects of sexual intercourse between blacks and whites within a white supremacy system, we decided this topic deserved a separate book.

Using Dr. Frances Cress Welsing's CHESS GAME ANALOGY (example), this book will explain how **interracial sex** is used by the white supremacy system as a weapon of mass mind, body, economic, political, and genetic destruction against blacks (and non-whites).

We will also present historical evidence and personal testimonies that support our controversial and politically-incorrect position by proving the following:

1. Sexual intercourse between whites and blacks ALWAYS creates MORE oppression, degradation, self-hatred, and mass confusion among blacks.
2. The Victims of white supremacy (oppression) MUST MAINTAIN a PSYCHOLOGICAL AND SEXUAL DISTANCE between themselves and their Victimizers. Otherwise, ANY efforts to overcome their oppression will be rendered USELESS.
3. It is IMPOSSIBLE to overcome your oppression when you engage in sexual intercourse with your oppressors. In other words, ***you cannot sleep with white supremacy at night and wake up in the morning and fight it.***
4. Historically, sexual intercourse between blacks and whites has been used by the white supremacy system to create a "buffer class" of non-whites with a white parent who will be programmed to support the system of black/non-white oppression.

Certainly, there are some blacks -- especially those who are sexually involved with whites -- who feel interracial relationships are harmless or feel those unions are a sign of "racial progress." Others may reject our research and logic that proves (in the Authors' opinion) that sex between blacks and whites ***in a white supremacy system DEEPENS the oppression of blacks.***

That being said, the reader is free to agree or disagree with anything or everything written here – and to draw their own conclusions.

Important Note To All Readers

Some chapters in our first two books -- *'Trojan Horse: Death of a Dark Nation'* and *'Black Love Is A Revolutionary Act'* -- have been included in our third book -- *'The Interracial Con Game'* for the following reasons:

1. **NEW READERS** -- To get the most out of this book, it is important all readers understand what the Authors mean when we refer to the system of racism/white supremacy. It has been our experience that some readers are unaware that such a system exists OR that it controls every aspect of our lives as non-whites. Others may believe white supremacists represent a minority of poor whites -- the type that belongs to the Aryan Nation, the KKK, wear tattoos, or burn crosses. ***Nothing is further from the truth.***

2. **TO MAXIMIZE UNDERSTANDING** -- For many readers, the system of white supremacy is a NEW concept – but it is the MOST IMPORTANT concept that any black (or non-white) person will ever understand. Without that understanding, everything else you know will only confuse you. It is CRITICAL that our readers understand how the white supremacy system devastates the lives of black people, so we can make better decisions in RESPONSE to it.

3. **REPETITION IS THE KEY** -- to understanding AND remembering information. More repetition means MORE information will be ABSORBED and RETAINED.

4. **CONSISTENCY:** We felt it is important to be consistent from one book to the next, and the best way to do that was to provide the SAME explanations and definitions in all our books.

5. **HONESTY:** We felt it would be dishonest to rewrite the same chapters and pretend it was new information. We have included the table of contents of all our books on our website and on our Amazon.com pages so our readers will know exactly what they are getting in each book.

Contents

CHAPTERS

Introduction

In a White Supremacy Society...

...Is Black Love Taboo?

Is Seeking Black Love Taboo?

"There was this really attractive black man who started riding the same commuter train I took. Everyday for about a week, we'd steady eyeball each other. Then one day, we wound up standing at the door at the same time and he introduced himself.

Both of us were smiling and talking, not loud or anything, but I noticed this white man staring and frowning at us like we were doing something wrong.

It seems like whites are threatened whenever blacks show any interest in each other, instead of lusting after them. It's like they have to have it all, all the money, all the power, all the whites and the blacks chasing them.

The media's always putting out this negative crap about black relationships, like they can't stand the idea of black men and women being together. I think white people know if we ever come together, we will challenge all this racism out here."

– Sylvia, 31

"I was at the food court across from the street where I live and this 'becky' (a white female) was checking me out hard and wondering why I wasn't interested in her. Then some fine sistas passed and they got my attention as they passed by the becky.

She rolled her eyes at them then looked back at me like I was supposed to lust over her and like all black men are attracted to white women.

I get called racist all the time for turning down white women. I really hurt beck's feelings that day, she was turning red. I noticed that she was with another white chick and a brother." –

-- Darnell, 23, student

***

"Even black people will call you racist if you won't or don't want to date whites. True as well that white people put the tag on us. But I can go you one better, a BLACK MAN told me I was racist, bitter, and prejudiced because I prefer blacks, my own people, over whites. That one NEVER ceases to amaze me."

– Calindra, 31, law student

Is Showing Black Love In Public Taboo?

"A few years ago, I had a very passionate relationship with my ex-boyfriend. We couldn't keep our hands off each other even when we were out in public. We'd hold hands, kiss, hug, but nothing in bad taste.

We were the only black people at this white pizza place. My boyfriend was sitting on my side of the booth like he usually did. When he kissed me, I saw this white female frowning at us.

What kills me is white people kiss in public all the time and nobody says a word, but let a black couple do the same thing, you would think we were making a porno movie.

That's when I started noticing black couples don't show affection in public. Maybe, they think it's something only white people do, or they're tired of getting dirty looks from white people."

-- Winnie, 37, flight attendant

FACT:

During the 'Jim Crow' era -- a racial caste system which operated primarily in the south between 1877 and the 1960s -- black males and females were not allowed to show affection OR kiss in public, because it offended whites.

Is Creating Black Babies Out Of Black Love Taboo?

"The best way to hate a nigger is to hate him before he is born." - Louisiana judge Leander Perez (1970)

"If you wanted to reduce crime, you could -- if that were your sole purpose -- you could abort every black baby in this country and your crime rate would go down. That would be an impossibly ridiculous and morally reprehensible thing to do, but your crime rate would go down." -- former US Education Secretary, William Bennett, Sept 2005

Professor Lombardo, a historian and legal scholar at Georgia State University, and editor of "A Century of Eugenics in America" offers an explanation for a commonly held belief among the white collective: "The fewer black babies we have the better, that's what some people said. They're just going to end up on welfare."

"Black women on welfare have been forced to accept sterilization in exchange for a continuation of relief benefits and others have been sterilized without their knowledge or consent. A young pregnant woman recently arrested for civil rights activities in N. Carolina was convicted and told her punishment would be to have a forced abortion." -- National Council of Negro Women, editorial, 1973

The black infant mortality rate – 13 deaths for every 1,000 births -- is nearly double the national (white) average and higher than in some (so-called) Third World nations, according to the Centers for Disease Control and Prevention.

In 1968, a 13-year-old black female, Elaine Riddick, was raped by a neighbor who threatened to kill her if she told what happened. A social worker deemed her "feeble-minded" and petitioned the North Carolina state Eugenics board to have her sterilized. While she was in the hospital giving birth, the "state" sterilized her "just like cutting a hog," she says. "They killed my kids. They killed mine before they got to me."

"There is a lot of racism going on in the U.S., and it's even been reported that black women are targeted more for unnecessary hysterectomy/castration. This was done to me with no medical basis after going into an emergency room with pain. A minor surgery was all that was necessary, but instead, my healthy uterus, cervix and ovaries were amputated. On top of that, my consent form was falsified. It's unbelievable that this can be done in the United States in 2008."
-- Corinne, 35, teacher

According to the director of obstetrics and gynecology at a New York municipal hospital, "In most major teaching hospitals in New York City, it is the unwritten policy to do elective hysterectomies on poor black and Puerto Rican women...to train residents."

In 1973, two black girls, ages 12 and 14, were declared mentally incompetent by an Alabama physician who sterilized them by deceiving the mother -- who could not read or write -- into signing "x" on the consent forms.

Is Black Love Taboo For Single Black Males & Females?

Some Headlines in Major (White) Media

Could Mr. Right Be White?

Book "Is Marriage For White People?"
Suggests Interracial Marriage

45% Of Black Women
Will Never Marry

Can White Men Fix Black
Women's Relationships?

"Single Black Women, Count Your Blessings"
-- USA Today

"Single Black Women Choosing
To Adopt." -- CNN

Tiger Marries Swedish Nanny

Black Women Should Date Outside Their Race

Why Are Black Women Single More Than
Women Of Other Races?

Is Interracial Marriage The
Solution For Unwed Black Women?

The Consequences of Marriage
for African-Americans

"Single Black Women Being Urged To Date
Outside Race" -- Washington Post

"Marriage Is For White People"
-- Washington Post

"Why successful black women can't find a
good man." -- ABC News Special

Comedian Wanda Sykes
Marries White Woman

Ice-T Loves Cocoa

Is Black-on Black Marriage Dying?

New Book Tells Black Women:
"Don't Marry Down. Marry Out."

Is Promoting Positive Images Of Black Female Beauty Taboo?

On the March 31, 2006 broadcast of his nationally syndicated radio program, white male, Neal Boortz said black congresswoman, Rep. Cynthia McKinney (D-GA), "looks like a ghetto slut" and that her "new hair-do makes her look like an explosion at a Brillo pad factory."

Then Boortz said Congresswoman McKinney's hair looked like "Tina Turner peeing on an electric fence." (As of the printing of this book Neal Boortz is still on the air).

***

In April 4, 2007 white male shock-jock Don Imus publicly referred to six black teenaged girls on the Rutgers University Basketball Team as "...nappy-headed hos..."

Imus was fired then rehired later that year as a richer, more popular personality:

"Citadel Broadcasting Corporation and 77 WABC Radio announced today the return of radio's lone cowboy Don Imus as the station's new morning host beginning Monday, Dec. 3. Imus signed a 5-year deal with Citadel that pays him between $5 and $8 million annually."

"All we ever see are images of Ethiopian women who are starving with a baby hanging on them. Well, I have seen something completely different. One of the temps that used to work in our office was from Ethiopia and I went to an Ethiopian restaurant about 6 months ago.

They are the most beautiful women I have ever seen in my life. But of course these images are not allowed. I could get angry and get started all over again about the absence of beautiful, dark-skinned black women in magazines and movies, but you know the story."

-- Robert, 41, engineer

"I love deep, dark black women with luscious lips, roller coaster curves, and unprocessed hair the way God made her.

I think a big part of the problem is the TV and movies have brainwashed us (black men) to think a black woman has to look white to be beautiful when it's the white girls who want what the black woman's got naturally -- the lips, the butts, the breasts, the smooth skin tone, but you have to be sharp enough to see through the racist hype."

-- Dave, 48, educator

Is Promoting Strong Heterosexual Images Of Black Males Taboo?

Why Does (White) Hollywood Love Black Males Who Wear Dresses?

It's a question comedian Dave Chappelle pondered when he appeared on the Oprah Show in February 2006, shortly after he turned down a $50 million Comedy Central deal, and an offer to wear a dress in a film with black actor, Martin Lawrence:

> "I'm a conspiracy theorist to a degree. I connect dots that maybe shouldn't be connected. Certain dots like when I see they put every black man in the movies in a dress at some point in their career. Why all these brothers got to wear a dress?
>
> This happened to me. I'm doing a movie with Martin, the movie's going good, so I walk in the trailer, and I'm like, man, this must be the wrong trailer, cause there's a dress in here. The writer comes in, and like "Dave, listen, we got this hilarious scene where Martin's sneaking out of jail so he disguises you as a prostitute, and you put this dress on. Naw, I'm not doing that, I don't feel comfortable with that."

As of this writing, Chappelle hasn't appeared on film or TV since 2006. Is this his "punishment" for not allowing himself to be "feminized" and for NOT selling himself (and his soul) for $50 million?

Black Men In Dresses: Comedy Or Conquest?

- Flip Wilson (as Geraldine – the original cross-dressing female)
- Jamie Foxx (as Wanda on 'In Living Color')
- Damon Wayans & David Alan Grier (as homosexuals on 'In Living Color')
- Tyler Perry (Madea Movies)
- Tracy Morgan
- Howard Rollins (deceased, appeared in a dress on a talk show)
- Chris Tucker
- Will Smith
- Eddie Murphy (As Rasputia)
- Kenan Thompson (as Virginiaca)
- Martin Lawrence (As Sheneneh, Big Momma's House I & II)
- Arsenio Hall (In Coming To America)
- Rupaul's reality show (a famous BM drag queen)
- Wayan Brothers (In White Chicks)
- Wesley Snipes (In To Wong Foo With Love)
- Little Richard (who explained his "girlish" persona was designed to keep whites from assaulting him whenever he performed in the South).

Is Black Love Taboo In White Hollywood?

"I asked a white casting director why there weren't more roles for black women to play the love interest of a black man. Do you know she had the nerve to say, 'America is not ready to see love between black men and women.' I was shocked, but I shouldn't have been. The black man is paired with anybody but a black woman in the movies, even "Dancing With The Stars won't put a black man with a black woman!" -- Melody, 27, unemployed actress.

***

"I was part of a writer's panel where a white writer -- who was supposed to be this super liberal -- made a statement that nearly knocked me off my chair. He said they needed more scripts where black males are romantically involved with white females. I was sitting there with two other black women. He was looking right at us when he said it." -- Noelle, 30, black female television writer

***

In blockbuster films like "Hitch" starring Will Smith, black leading men are more likely to be cast opposite a Hispanic actress than a black one, like Eva Mendes in "Hitch;" Zoe Saldana in "Drumline;" and Jessica Alba in "Honey." The blatant dismissal of black actresses as desirable leading ladies is obvious even to Mendes, who asked why she was considered too dark to be paired with a white lead, but just right for an African-American male.

Some black actors have to almost threaten to quit a show or movie in order to get a black actress cast as their love interest. (Eriq LaSalle, Russell Hornsby, etc.). Unless they have a little bit of clout, a black writer/producer takes a risk to suggest casting a black actress darker than Halle Berry who isn't Gabrielle Union or Sanaa Lathan.

Otherwise, white women paired with black men are usually the first and only choice by white men who really hate black men, but envy the alleged sexual prowess of black men. White men have the power to make their sexual fantasies come to life on screen. White men (and white women) prefer to see white women with black men.

I think they hate the fact that they enjoy watching black men and white women together and exact revenge against black men because of this sexual fetish. I'm relaying what I know to be true from my own personal experiences." -- Olivia, 31, unemployed screenwriter

***

Most Hollywood-Produced "Black" Films Usually Fall Into One Of Two Categories:

1. the "good black" female triumphing over the "bad" black male: (The Color Purple, Waiting To Exhale, I Can Do Bad All By Myself, For Colored Girls, Diary of a Mad Black Woman, Precious)
2. the "good black" male triumphing against the odds without the support of black females (The Blind Side, The Pursuit of Happiness, most Denzel Washington and Samuel Jackson movies)

The dark-skinned black female is an endangered species in today's TV commercials. In fact, the vast majority of "blacks" in commercials -- male and female, adult and child -- are the racially ambiguous, light-skinned blacks who have a white parent (the so-called bi-racial blacks).

According to the black "stage" mother of an unemployed child actor (who asked to be anonymous), the mostly white female casting directors prefer the "black" children of white females over the brown and dark-skinned children with two black parents.

***

For the last 5 or 10 years, it seems like every time I see a black man in a TV commercial or TV show he is always isolated from other black people. He'll have nothing but white friends, live with white people, or he'll have a white girlfriend, or a white best friend. He won't know any black people -- which is just the way they want black men to be, think, and act.

It reminds me of the documentaries on the Animal Planet channel where the predators go after their prey by trying to separate a sick or weaker animal from the herd so they can take it down, kill it, and eat it. It makes you wonder, are they trying to tell us something? Like, is the black man the prey and the white system is the predator trying to separate him from the herd so they can kill him?" -- Pamela, 41, unemployed social worker

"In a universe of infinite possibilities, anytime that you see repetition, the same thing happening over and over, the same thing being said over and over, you should pay attention to that, and I think with white people you see a lot of repetition."

-- Gus Renegade, host of C.O.W.S.
(The Context of White Supremacy)
www.contextofwhitesupremacy.com

Is Black Love Taboo In Â White Supremacy Society?

ÂBSOLUTELY

It should be obvious from the real-life testimonies on the previous pages that there are powerful forces at work to break the bond between the black male and female.

If the Authors accomplish NOTHING ELSE with our third book -- The Interracial Con Game -- we will:

1. expose the TRUE (hidden) motives of the white supremacy media that promotes sexual intercourse between blacks and whites

2. demonstrate why sex between blacks and whites in a white supremacy system should be seen as MAXIMUM RACIST AGGRESSION

3. reveal the White Supremacy Chess Game where the main strategy is to DIVIDE and CONQUER the black male and female with the ultimate goal of:

CHECKMATING THE BLACK KING

The White Supremacy Chess Game

Rule #1-1001

White Âlways Moves First

"When two people prove incompatible in marriage and they can't live together, they separate; and the mass of average niggers simply don't "fit" in modern American society.

A leopard doesn't change his spots just because you bring him in from the jungle and try to housebreak him and turn him into a pet.

He may learn to sheathe his claws in order to beg a few scraps off the dinner table, and you may teach him to be a beast of burden, but it doesn't pay to forget that he'll always be what he was born: a wild animal."

-- George Lincoln Rockwell
Founder of the American Nazi Party
-- The Playboy Interview - April 1966

http://www.playboy.com/arts-entertainment/features/george-lincoln-rockwell/george-lincoln-rockwell-02.html

CHAPTER ONE

Dr. Welsing On White Supremacy & The Game Of Chess

In different parts of the country, when I go around and speak, I will ask white people, 'do you want your children to be colored? Do you want your grandchildren to be colored? Do you want your great, great grandchildren to be colored? And they say, no.

So I say, if you don't want that to happen, you have to be engaging in certain, specific behaviors, so that issue of genetic annihilation does not occur. They're (white people) going back to the old way of doing things.

The door opened a little bit and now the door has to slam back, and we (black people) feel that pressure and say, "racism is going on." But the white response would say, "nothing is happening."

The behavioral dynamic of white supremacy is analogous (the same thing) to a chess game. We haven't looked at it in that way before. We looked at it as, everybody holding hands, ring-around-the-rosie, we're in this together, and that's not what's happening.

I'm not talking about hating white people, I'm talking about analyzing the behavior and understanding this so-called game of chess. If we understand the game of chess, you have a white side of the chessboard and a black side of the chessboard.

In the game of chess for the last 100 years, the game has been played where white always moves first. The white side is playing offense/defense. The black side is playing defense/offense.

That's a perfect analogy to white supremacy. White supremacy has to move against non-white people for the purposes of genetic survival. The game of chess is also about checkmating the King. With white moving offensively and then defensively, that means the real issue in the game of chess is about the white King checkmating the black King.

That is perfectly analogous to racism/white supremacy because the primary thrust of racism/white supremacy is it's against all black people, and all non-white people, but it is most specifically against the black male because it is the black male who can cause white genetic annihilation. The game of chess is about the white King checkmating the black King.

If black people say, it's like the game of chess, we didn't understand that before. Now we can play, it's just a matter of tactics and strategy.

Then I go further to look at the chessboard as though each of these vertical columns – we really need nine – one column represents economics, another education, entertainment, labor, law, politics, religion, sex, and war.

You have to play on those nine fronts simultaneously, which is just like playing chess. You don't play on just one column, you have to play and look at all of the columns at the same time.

If we now begin to understand the dilemma of the white minority on the planet, that they are now operating in fear of white annihilation and the intention then being to survive – white genetic survival by any necessary means – then black people can begin to say, 'that means we have to have tactics and strategies for black survival and maximal development.'

In the presence of this continuous onslaught, we will give up completely, begging and pleading. Ninety percent of our energy as black people in this area of the world is being spent begging and pleading. That would be analogous to the person who is playing the black side of the chessboard, begging the white side to let them win.

So, if you're playing the black side of the chessboard and you ask the white side to let you make some points, they ought to take you to the nearest mental hospital. That's not the way the game is played.

***

Frances Cress Welsing (born March 18, 1935 in Chicago, Illinois) is a black psychiatrist practicing in Washington, D.C., and the author of *'The Isis Papers; The Keys to the Colors'* (1991), and the *"Cress Theory of Color Confrontation."*

"If you know the enemy and know yourself, you need not fear the result of a hundred battles.

If you know yourself but not your enemy, for every victory gained you will also suffer a defeat.

If you know neither the enemy nor yourself, you will succumb in every battle."

-- Sun Tzu,
'The Art of War' (544-496 BC)

"If you do not understand White Supremacy (Racism), what it is, and how it works, everything else that you understand, will only confuse you."

Neely Fuller, Jr. (1971)

CHAPTER TWO

WHAT IS RACISM/WHITE SUPREMACY?

"Racism is white supremacy. White supremacy is racism. There is no other form." -- *Neely Fuller, Jr.*

Let's Begin At The Beginning By Defining The Words:

1. **White Supremacy --** a social, economic, and political system based on the belief that whites are superior to non-whites. (the Foundation).
2. **Racism** -- the systematic discrimination (the denial of rights and benefits) by whites against non-whites in all areas of human activity: (1) economics, (2) education, (3) entertainment, (4) labor, (5) law, (6) politics, (7) religion, (8) sex, and (9) war. (the Behavior). ***Racism = Power + Prejudice.***

Q: Why is it called "Racism/White Supremacy?"
A: Because this describes exactly WHO is practicing racism. For one group to practice racism that group must have MORE POWER than another group. Since whites control **ALL** the major areas of human activity in America -- housing, education, health, entertainment, economics, politics, law, and religion -- it is accurate to define all "**racism**" as **"white supremacy."** We must be accurate so the victims of racism do not become confused.

Q: Isn't all racism the same, regardless of who is practicing it?
A: There is only ONE kind of racism: **white supremacy**. White people are the only group in America with the POWER to discriminate (deprive or punish other ethnic groups), and the systems and institutions to maintain the imbalance of power.

For example, rich people are more powerful than poor people. Rich people have the POWER to discriminate against poor people by depriving them of income, promotions, jobs, housing, land, justice, and any other rights – if they choose to do so. Racism is not empty rhetoric (words) or mindless emotion. Racism is social, economic, and political POWER.

In America, whites have the POWER to discriminate against blacks (and other non-whites) by depriving them of income, promotions, jobs, housing, land, justice, and any other rights – if they choose to do so. It doesn't matter that some whites are poorer than some blacks.

In all things and in all places in America, whites are **collectively** more powerful than blacks are **collectively**. This imbalance of (white) power creates the opportunity and the ability to practice racism against non-whites.

Q: Why do you refer to non-whites as "groups" instead of "races?"
A: Because there is ONLY ONE RACE: ***the white race.*** To prove this statement, let's look at the TRUE meaning of "race." In ancient civilizations tens of thousands of years ago (before Europeans inhabited the planet), the world's people identified themselves by bloodline, birthplace, and culture – but NEVER by the artificial construct (concept) of "race."

What is the "black race" in real terms? It does NOT describe the place where black people were born because there is no such place as "black land," (or red, yellow, brown, or white land). Race does not describe a person's religion because there is no such thing as a black, red, brown, yellow, or white religion.

Race does not describe a person's culture (except in false, stereotypical terms), and it does NOT define biology, ethnicity, or nationality. Race does not describe skin color because the so-called "black race" includes people whose complexions range from the palest pink to the purest blue-black. ***Therefore, "race" is a false, manmade concept.***

Q: If "race" is a false concept, why was it created?
A: Race was created for ONLY one purpose: ***to practice race-ism (racism).*** To practice "racism," whites had to separate themselves from other groups of people by artificially creating different "races."

Q: Why was "racism/white supremacy" created?
A: Dr. Frances Cress Welsing, a black psychiatrist and the author of *'The Isis Papers: The Keys to the Colors'* (1991), states that White Supremacy is practiced by the global "white" minority on the conscious and unconscious level to ensure their genetic survival by any means necessary.

Because of their "numerical inadequacy," whites may have defensively developed *"an uncontrollable sense of hostility and aggression" towards people of color, and developed a social, political, and economic structure to give blacks and other 'non-whites' the appearance of being inferior."*

The Authors will add one more reason: Racism/white supremacy was created to allow the people who classify themselves as "white" to economically, socially, politically, sexually, psychologically, and genetically DOMINATE all the people who they classify as "non-white."

Q: Who decides what "race" a person will be?
A: The same (white) people who created the concept of race. If the ONLY purpose of "race" is to practice racism, and whites are the only group or "race" (in a white supremacy system) that can practice racism, then it is logical to assume there is ONLY ONE RACE: ***the white race.***

Q: If the white race is the only race, what are the other 'groups' called?
A: There are three types of people in a white supremacist system:

1. Non-white people
2. White people (Racist Suspects)
3. White Supremacists (Racists)

Q: What is a "Non-White" person?
A: Anyone who is NOT classified as "white." This includes all black, red, yellow, and brown people aka "people of color."

Q: What is a "Racist Suspect?"
A: ANY white person who is CAPABLE of practicing racism against non-whites. Since all whites are able to practice racism in a white supremacy system if they choose to do so, it is correct (and logical) to use the term "racist suspects" to identify whites who do not openly function as white supremacists (racists). This is not a hateful, unjust, or racist statement, but it is a **logical statement.**

Q: What is a "White Supremacist?"
A: A white person (a racist) who practices racism against non-whites. Being a white supremacist has nothing to do with income, title, or status. It does not mean a white person belongs to the KKK, the Aryan Nation, or is covered with Nazi tattoos.

A white supremacist can be a soccer mom, a businessman, or a US Senator if they are practicing racism against non-whites. Another term for a white supremacist is "racist man" and "racist woman."

Q: How can a non-white person determine if a white person is a racist?
A: Non-whites cannot always determine who is a racist, and who is not, because it is impossible to monitor (or judge) all the individual actions and words of any white person at all times. To illustrate this point:

Case Of The Stolen Wallet

There are five people in a room when a wallet that belongs to a sixth person (who is not in the room) is stolen. All five are "suspects" because every person in the room had the ability and the opportunity to take the wallet. This does not mean all five are thieves NOR does it mean all five are not thieves, because any of them could have stolen something at an earlier time.

As it turns out, two of the five people in the room CONSPIRED to steal the wallet by breaking into the sixth person's locker. The other three saw it happen, did not participate in the crime, did not care that the wallet was stolen, and did and said nothing to stop it from happening.

The sixth person – the owner of the wallet -- has no idea who stole it, if anyone saw what happened, or how many participated in the theft. All he knows is has been the VICTIM of a crime because his wallet is missing.

The two people who stole the wallet are guilty of "commission" – they actually **committed the crime**. The three witnesses are guilty of "omission" since they **witnessed the crime, said nothing and did nothing to stop it, and refused to help the victim with the information they had.**

The next day the two thieves treat the three witnesses to lunch, paying for it with the money from the stolen wallet. The witnesses did not steal the wallet but are knowingly or unknowingly benefiting from the theft. The three witnesses are not **legally liable**, but they are **morally liable,** and are correctly viewed as **"suspects" by the victim.**

Racism operates the same way. There are whites who:

- are practicing racism against non-whites at a particular moment
- are not practicing racism at that moment but have practiced it at a previous time, or will practice it at a later time
- are not practicing racism at that moment, but say and do nothing to stop those who are
- are not practicing racism at that moment, but have no problem with other whites practicing racism (don't care)
- are benefiting from the crime of racism even if they are not practicing racism at that moment
- refuse to tell WHO is practicing racism; HOW racism is being practiced; and refuse to help the victims with the information they have
- oppose racism by exposing and opposing whites who practice it

Another Example:

Mr. X, a black management trainee, is looking for an apartment closer to his new job. He calls an upscale rental complex near his office, and asks if they have any one-bedroom apartments.

The rental agent, a young white male, says there are two one-bedroom apartments available, takes Mr. X's name and phone number, and asks him to stop by and fill out an application.

The next day Mr. X stops by the complex after work. A different rental agent, Mrs. W, a middle-aged white female, greets him in the reception area. She says she's sorry, but there are no apartments available.

She suggests he fill out an application so they will have his information on file, and assures Mr. X that he will be the first one she calls when a one-bedroom becomes available.

Mr. X is immediately suspicious, but he fills out an application anyway. On his way home, he replays the conversation with the rental agent. Mr. X has no way of knowing if the first rental agent made an honest mistake, or if he has just been a victim of racial discrimination. His gut tells him it was the latter.

The Crime

When Mrs. W saw Mr. X was black, she used the same line she always used with black applicants. Later, she warns the new rental agent -- who talked to Mr. X over the phone – to never rent to blacks or Hispanics.

The Victim

Like the man whose wallet was stolen, Mr. X is the victim of a crime. The problem is, Mr. X can't be sure a crime was even committed, which makes it more difficult for him to protect himself from being victimized in the future. It is this kind of confusion that wreaks the most psychological damage on black people who run a DAILY risk of being victimized by racism – without being able to prove they were victimized.

The Criminals

Mrs. W is guilty of commission (practicing racism). The new rental agent is guilty of omission because he said and did nothing, and refused to help Mr. X with the information he had (that another white person, Mrs. W, was practicing racism).

It is the ***crime of commission AND omission*** that allows the system of racism/white supremacy to function so effectively. The system does not require all whites to practice racism at all times, but it does require that **the majority of whites say and do nothing when racism is occurring and allow themselves to benefit from the victimization of non-whites.**

Those benefits include better jobs, housing, food, medical care, education, police protection, justice, etc., than non-whites. If the majority of whites were opposed to racism/white supremacy, it would NOT be the most powerful social, economic, and political system on the planet.

It is LOGICAL to assume that the majority (or possibly all) white people have made a DELIBERATE DECISION to do one or all of the following:

- practice racism
- do nothing and say nothing to stop others from practicing racism
- deny racism is being practiced even when they know it is happening
- refuse to help the victims of racism with the information they have

That's why simple-minded thinking is useless when determining which white person is a racist and which one is not. It cannot be determined by a white person's sexual behavior. White slave owners had sexual relations with male and female slaves but they were still white supremacists (racists).

Whites have engaged in sexual relations with black people, but that doesn't mean they are not racists. Whites who have black friends, wives, husbands, or children are still "racist" if they are practicing racism against non-whites. It cannot be determined by observing the words or the actions of a particular white person, who may or may not be practicing racism at that particular time.

It cannot be determined by a random (or deliberate) act or acts of kindness toward a non-white person. Mass child-murderer John Gacy was "kind" to children when he performed in his clown costume. There were slave-owners who were "kind" to their slaves, but not kind enough to stop selling human beings.

AXIOM #1: YOU CANNOT OPPOSE SOMETHING AND KNOWINGLY BENEFIT FROM IT AT THE SAME TIME.

It is LOGICAL in a white supremacist society to assume the **majority of whites** are either practicing racism (the act of commission), or are cooperating with those who are, by saying and doing nothing to stop them, refusing to help the victims of racism with the information they have (the act of omission), and are ***benefiting*** from the practice of racism.

Q: Do non-racist whites benefit from White Supremacy?
A: ALL whites benefit from white privilege in a white supremacy system, even if they are not practicing racism at that moment. It does not matter if they are rich or poor; or whether they admit there is such a thing as white privilege. Anyone who is classified as "white" in a white supremacy system will always have advantages over someone who is not. Just as a black person in a black supremacy system (if one existed) would have advantages over someone who is not black.

Q: Aren't some white people opposed to racism?
A: Only if they are saying and doing something to oppose it. For example, John Brown, a white male, encouraged armed insurrection by slaves as a means to end slavery, and as a result, was charged with treason and hanged. However, that does not mean John Brown did not practice racism at an earlier time OR would not have practiced it at a later time had he lived.

Q: Aren't white anti-racists opposed to racism?

The self-annointed, white anti-racist activist offers little more than LIP SERVICE. They sacrifice NOTHING, take NO risks, and reap MORE financial rewards than the black activists fighting in the (real) trenches.

The white anti-racist actually creates MORE confusion by creating the FALSE illusion that the devastated black masses can be liberated from racism by sitting in a church, auditorium, or conference room listening to a white person -- who is STILL enjoying his or her white privileges -- making anti-racism speeches.

It is UNLIKELY that the same white anti-racist activists who PROFIT from writing books and giving speeches about racism -- have any real desire (or intent) to destroy the same white supremacy system that allows them to oppose it without losing a single 'white privilege.'

There may be whites who are sincere about replacing the system of white supremacy with a system of justice, ***but that number is so statistically small, it is insignificant.***

Q: When a black person mistreats a white person, isn't that "racism/ black supremacy?"
A: No, because black supremacy does not exist. If black people were collectively more powerful than whites collectively, blacks would have the power to practice racism. Logically speaking, that would mean the end of white supremacy.

AXIOM #2: BLACK SUPREMACY CAN EXIST ONLY IN THE TOTAL ABSENCE OF WHITE SUPREMACY. WHITE SUPREMACY CAN EXIST ONLY IN THE TOTAL ABSENCE OF BLACK SUPREMACY. THE TEXTBOOK DEFINITION OF "SUPREMACY" IS:

THE HIGHEST RANK OR AUTHORITY.

THIS MEANS ONLY ONE THING CAN BE "SUPREME" OR OCCUPY THE "HIGHEST RANK" AT A TIME.

If blacks and whites had equal power and resources, there could be no black supremacy OR white supremacy. Our ability (power) to discriminate against (mistreat) each other would be cancelled out, leaving only two options: ***coexist peacefully or destroy each other.***

"What about black people who believe in 'black supremacy?'

You can believe in something like a prisoner believes in being the warden, or thinks he or she is the warden, but that doesn't make it true. There's a difference between being in a position and aspiring to be in a position."

- Neely Fuller, Jr.

CHAPTER THREE

BLACK POWER IN A WHITE SUPREMACY SYSTEM

Q: Aren't "black supremacy" groups like the Nation of Islam racist toward white people?

A: The Nation of Islam is a religious organization, not a black supremacy group. Even if its members so desired, the Nation of Islam cannot be a "black supremacy" organization because "black supremacy" cannot exist at the same place and same time as "white supremacy."

The Nation of Islam cannot be a "racist" organization because it does NOT have the ability or a history of interfering with the rights of white people, or dictating where whites can live, work, shop, play, learn, or teach.

The Nation of Islam does not advocate harming or killing white people. To the authors' knowledge, no white person has ever been attacked, murdered, denied housing, a job, a fair trial, an education, a law license, or any rights by the Nation of Islam, or under the banner of black supremacy.

In fact, every so-called "black supremacist" organization in America was created ***in self-defense*** to white racism. To compare the KKK to any black group is the same as comparing the bully to the person being bullied, who eventually fights back, then calling BOTH of them bullies.

Q: Are you saying blacks cannot be racist toward whites?

A: That's correct. Of course, all people can be hateful or prejudiced. Those terms describe individual behaviors, not systematic power. Racism is the COLLECTIVE behaviors of a group. A white individual within a system of racism/white supremacy has the implicit or explicit support of that system IF they choose to practice racism.

If a poor man robs a rich man at gunpoint that doesn't mean the poor man is more powerful (economically and politically) than the rich man. The poor man is an individual who committed a crime of opportunity. There are no powerful institutions or systems that support his right to rob the rich man, but there are institutions and systems that allow the rich man to rob the poor man – which is why he doesn't need a gun to do it.

A black person who mistreats a white person doesn't mean black people are more powerful (economically and politically) than white people. Never confuse the actions of a black individual (or a group of black individuals) that mistreats someone white as proof that black racism exists.

Their "power" is limited ONLY to what they can do as individuals. There are NO black institutions or systems that support, defend, or finance the right of blacks to mistreat whites.

There are NO black individuals or black organizations that have the power to strip whites of their collective right to live where they want, work where they want, get an education wherever they want, or control what white people do collectively in ANY area of human activity. There are NO black institutions that are more powerful than white institutions. Therefore, blacks do not have the COLLECTIVE POWER to diminish the quality of life for the white collective.

Q: What is collective power?
A: Collective power is the institutions and systems that benefit one group at the expense of another group, and allow one group to dominate another group in all areas of human activity.

For example, when a white policeman shoots an unarmed black man (50 times), his fellow officers, the police chief, internal affairs, the union, the media, the prosecutor, the judge, and the jury will support, defend, and finance that white police officer's "right" to shoot (murder) an unarmed black person. That is ***white collective power***.

It is rare for a white police officer to be punished for using excessive force against a black man, woman, or child. It is just as rare for a black police officer to use excessive force against a white person.

In fact, the authors were unable to find a single instance of a black police officer shooting or killing an unarmed white person in the history of modern law enforcement. This is not surprising but it is absolute proof that the black individual operating within a system of white supremacy cannot mistreat whites even if he or she is wearing a uniform, a badge, and carrying a gun.

Another example of white collective power is the mortgage and real estate industry, which systematically discriminates against black (and non-white) renters, homebuyers, and homeowners by:

- **Red-lining** – denying home loans to minority geographical areas.
- **Reverse red-lining** -- targeting minority areas for fraudulent sub-prime home loans that are designed to self-destruct.
- **Inflating home appraisals** in racially changing neighborhoods to defraud (overcharge) minority homebuyers.
- **Low-balling appraisals** in minority areas to reduce home equity.
- **Refusing to rent or sell** to minorities in certain geographical areas.
- **Raising property taxes in minority areas** to drive minority residents out of desirable inner-city neighborhoods. (gentrification)
- **Exclusion from special financing deals** that are not generally known to the public, and are only offered to a select group of white buyers.

Banks, real estate brokers, appraisers, and mortgage lenders represent INSTITUTIONAL RACISM (power) that is reinforced by the courts, banking, and government (systems).

This does not mean blacks are less likely to abuse power than whites if given the opportunity. It means blacks cannot abuse power that does not exist. The proof: there is no place in America where blacks are collectively practicing racism against whites collectively.

Q: Don't black politicians and corporate executives represent black power?

A: Not necessarily. Having a powerful position does not make a person powerful. For example, shortly after a female employee sued the XYZ firm for sex discrimination, Ms. X and Mrs. Y are appointed to the corporate board. They will be used as proof in the upcoming trial that the XYZ firm does not discriminate against women.

Like most token board members, Ms. X and Mrs. Y are benchwarmers; not policy makers. Their "powerful" positions are an ILLUSION designed to deceive the public and the courts. The black man or woman in a (public) position of power often serves the same purpose: to give the appearance that certain companies do not discriminate.

These blacks may be qualified for their position; however, even the "powerful" black person – regardless of title -- is still controlled by more powerful whites who limit whatever authority or power this black individual possesses.

Q: If a powerful black person mistreats a less powerful white person, isn't he or she practicing black racism?

A: A black person whose power comes from a white institution will not be allowed to mistreat whites – unless he or she is following orders from more powerful whites. In a system of white supremacy, all whites are more powerful than blacks.

A white supremacy system by its very NATURE forbids ALL non-white people – regardless of wealth, status, or position – from victimizing white people. Of course, a powerful black person can – as an individual – harm a white individual. For example, it was well known that OJ Simpson physically abused his white ex-wife, Nicole, but that abuse was limited to what he was able to do as an individual.

Powerful blacks present no danger to the white collective but they can be extremely dangerous to other blacks. They are often rewarded for victimizing black people (doing the dirty work), and are usually following orders from more powerful whites behind the scenes.

If they are not following direct orders, they will abuse other blacks: (1) for profit or career advancement; (2) out of fear of losing status or income; (3) out of fear of being lumped with the "inferior" black masses; (4) because of self-hatred issues, which they project onto other blacks; or (5) out of frustration because they have no real power (over whites).

Even the most "powerful" blacks in America cannot practice black racism because it does not exist. Nor can they be black supremacists because black supremacy cannot co-exist within a system of white supremacy. They cannot practice white racism because they are not white.

They cannot be racists of any kind; but are knowingly OR unknowingly agents (extensions) of the white supremacist system. If anyone disagrees with this premise and believes that blacks can be racist, he or she should be able to answer the following question:

Name one thing that black people – *as a group* -- have stopped white people – *as a group* -- from doing that they had a RIGHT to do? For example, denying them the right to work, own a home, live in a certain area, get a fair trial, an education, or use any public facility.

Affirmative action is not a correct response. Affirmative action is NOT black racism. Black people did not create affirmative action, the terminology, or the where, when, and how it becomes a policy in Corporate America.

Blacks do NOT have the power to implement any just or unjust policies at any white college or university. Whites control, name, legislate, and decide everything that happens within America's institutions of power – including black institutions.

If it can be documented (proven) that black people are COLLECTIVELY mistreating white people COLLECTIVELY in the United States, someone should write a book about it. The truth should be made public, even if it contradicts what is written here. Any corrections would be greatly appreciated in the interest of being as accurate as possible.

Q: What about rich black entertainers and athletes? They don't work for Corporate America. Isn't that "black power"?
A: All black entertainers work for Corporate America in one fashion or another. Corporate America controls everything that happens in the entertainment industry; whether it's the movie, music, television, radio, news, advertising, publishing, or sports industry.

It is impossible to be a successful black (or white) entertainer if you do not have access to movie theaters, chain music and bookstores, comedy clubs, stadiums, ballparks, cable, radio, magazine, and television.

The corporations that control the airwaves, athletic arenas, retail stores, networks, movie, and television studios, distributors, and advertisers are more powerful than all the black entertainers combined.

Money is NOT synonymous with power. Power is NOT a paycheck; even a forty-million-dollar one. The person with the most power is the one who SIGNS THE CHECK. For every black person who is paid in the millions, there are whites behind the scenes making BILLIONS.

Q: If money isn't power, what is power?
A: Power is self-evident. **Power** answers to no one other than God, himself. Power is the ability to determine the status quo and who sits at the top of the pecking order. **Power** is the ability to determine what is news and what is not. **Power** is controlling the financial, political, and educational institutions so *you and your kind* benefit. **Power** is the ability to CONTROL your own images and the images of those who are less powerful than you are. **Power** is the ability to determine WHO goes to jail, for what crime, and for how long. **Power** is the ability to VOTE in an election and STILL HAVE THAT VOTE COUNTED.

Power is other people coming to you to get what they need and you deciding how much they get. Power is the ability to feed yourself without depending on others. **Power** is the ability to generate and produce what you need to survive -- which includes your own infrastructure and necessities: electricity, gasoline, water, housing, food, clothing, weapons, schools, universities, currency, banking, and hospitals – without depending on others for your survival.

Power is the ability to decide what your currency looks like; how much it is worth; and how much it buys; whether it is a gallon of milk or a gallon of gas. **Power** is the ability to determine who lives where, how many of them can live there, and how long they can stay there.

Power is the ability to move populations, and to determine what part of what city will be black and what part will be white. **Power** is the ability to own land that no one can take from you, even with eminent domain, because YOU make the laws. **Power** is the ability to punish a police officer for shooting an unarmed man 41 times. **Power** is the ability to rescue people from rooftops after a hurricane in *less than four days*, and to make sure a "Katrina" never happens in the first place.

Not ONE black politician, poet, activist, entertainer, corporate board member, CEO, businessperson, millionaire, or billionaire had the juice (POWER) to pick up a phone, call the White House, and get ONE black person off the roof after Katrina struck.

Power Is NOT...

...a Mercedes or a Jaguar, a dozen rental properties, a good job in a Fortune 500 corporation, a dozen college degrees, or a Pulitzer Prize. It is not being the biggest rap star or black movie star with the most crossover appeal.

It is not owning the biggest house on the block when the bank still holds the mortgage; the taxing authority can seize it for unpaid taxes; and the government can take the land it sits on by declaring eminent domain. It is NOT owning a black business when the business relies on white suppliers, bankers, dealers, distributors, contracts, and advertising dollars.

This is not intended to demean or diminish the accomplishments of so many distinguished, successful, and talented black people, but it is **time to be honest about our situation.** We cannot afford to keep telling ourselves that the only color "the (powerful) white man" cares about is the color "green." **If that were true, "white supremacy" would be called "green supremacy."**

AXIOM #3: IN A SYSTEM OF WHITE SUPREMACY, COLOR ALWAYS TRIUMPHS OVER CASH (GREEN SUPREMACY).

Color is as fundamental to racism/white supremacy, as reading is to education. There is short-term rich and long-term wealth, and the white supremacists know the difference.

They are long-range strategists who know it is wiser (and more profitable) to pay millions to a handful of blacks in sports, entertainment, and business than to allow blacks to accumulate the tools and capital to generate our own billions.

Q: If blacks are not inferior to whites, why are blacks in such an inferior position, not just in America, but all over the world?
A: There is no way to do justice to such a complex, profound question in one book NOR do the authors pretend to have all the answers. In the Resource Section of this book is a list of authors who have written excellent books on Africa before and after European colonization.

Historical documents and artifacts prove (without a doubt) that Africans were once the most powerful people on the planet, and that all intellectual human endeavors -- the arts, sciences, writing, astronomy, medicine, architecture, and the world's first universities – ***began in Africa.***

Do not mistake the present condition of African people as proof of black inferiority. What is happening on the African continent -- widespread starvation, tribal warfare, political chaos, AIDS, or crushing international debt – is the by-product of European imperialism and white supremacy.

John Perkins, author of the controversial bestseller, *Confessions of an Economic Hitman,* explained how third-world economies were deliberately undermined to gain control of their natural resources and UN votes. Perkins describes in chilling detail, the two primary objectives of an Economic Hit Man:

1. Make huge loans to third-world countries and funnel the money back to US engineering companies in exchange for construction projects that are (deliberately) never completed.
2. Without the promised infrastructures to modernize their countries, the huge international loans go into default, bankrupt their economies, forcing these third-world nations to turn over control of their natural resources and UN votes to their US "creditors."

These third-world nations were robbed of their ability to build the kind of infrastructure that would allow them to eliminate poverty, educate their children, and provide a higher standard of living. They were also deliberately excluded from the technology and information-sharing that occurred freely between non-third-world nations.

The conditions in third-world nations have nothing to do with inferiority, **but everything to do with skin color and white supremacy**.

"...and the People of the River are black people, and the People of the Plains are brown people, and the People of the Mountains are red people, and the People of the Forest are yellow people..."

Chapter Four

A WHITE SUPREMACY "FAIRY TALE"

(TRUTH IS STRANGER THAN FICTION)

Excerpted from an article
by Edward Williams
(www.counter-racism.com)

Looking at how the universe works...we are all people. All of the people in the known universe are only people. Picture that in your mind. Now some people come in contact with other people and say that they are white people.

And you say "OK" because you don't know what they are talking about. Now just because they say they are "white people" instead of calling themselves "people" means they have an agenda.

Wherever you are on the planet the people are identified by where they are located. People of the River, People of the Plains, People of the Mountains, People of the Forest and they may or may not have one word to describe it. Such as the Paoli people where Paoli means "People of the River."

Now...in addition to saying they are white people they also say that you are a non-white person. And you say, "OK" because you still don't know where they are going with all of this. Now... they also say that the People of the River, People of the Plains, People of the Mountains and the People of the Forest are also non-white people.

The white people say that the People of the River are black people, and that the People of the Plains are brown people, and the People of the Mountains are red people, and the People of the Forest are yellow people.

Everyone says "OK" because they still don't know where these people who say that they are "white people" are going with all of this. And over the years the people really buy into the idea of being black or brown or red or yellow...so much so that they begin to become proud of being black or brown or red or yellow and shout each other down about it while the white people are just watching them shout each other down about it.

One day a child comes along and asks, to a white person, *"Why do you say I'm a black person?"* And the white person, while laying on their death bed says, *"It means that you do what I tell you to do and if you don't do it I will shoot you."*

That is what racism (white supremacy) is all about. It means that every person who is not white (non-white) qualifies for mistreatment based on that alone. You don't qualify for mistreatment based on what you do or don't do or because of what you may say or not say.

You are qualified for mistreatment because you are not a white person. Just because you are not a white person. And there are many words or terms that are used to describe the people who are non-white such as:

- colored people
- negroes
- chinks
- niggers
- sand niggers
- spics
- darkies
- black people
- red people
- yellow people
- brown people
- slant-eyed
- darkie
- tribe
- natives
- indians

...and the list goes on and on.

We -- meaning all non-white people -- are just a group of people who are victims of racism (white supremacy). It is time we understand how the white people who practice racism (white supremacy) are the smartest, most powerful white people, and how they view the world, and how they manage people based on their world view. We have to begin to talk like we understand what they are doing.

When someone asks me if I am a black person, I usually say "I am a person who is a victim of racism (white supremacy). I have been known to say that I am a black person and when I do say I am a black person I simply mean that I understand that I have been targeted for mistreatment because I have been identified, by white people, as not being a white person.

Just like the People of the River, People of the Plains, People of the Mountains, and the People of the Forest...targeted for mistreatment.

The End

A Question From A Reader On The Meaning Of "Race"

"In your second book, 'Black Love Is A Revolutionary Act,' pg.130, I understand "race" is a false concept, and why it was created, to be able to group and classify non-white people for the purpose of practicing racism.

I agree race does not describe culture, biology, ethnicity, or nationality. Race does not describe skin color because the so-called "black race" includes complexions from pale to blue-black. My question is how is the white race the only race? If white racists created the concept, can they create reality?" – Thomas D.

ANSWER: That's a good question, Thomas. The first time we heard Mr. Neely Fuller, Jr. say there was only one race -- the white race -- this confused us because it went against EVERYTHING we had been taught about "race." However, once we followed his LOGIC, we realized ***Mr. Fuller was right on the money.***

If "race" was created for ONLY one purpose -- to practice "race-ism" (racism) -- AND white people are the ONLY people who have the POWER to practice "racism," it is LOGICAL to conclude that ***the only race is the white race.***

Can the white supremacists create reality? Think of the white supremacy system as a MATRIX created by the smartest, most powerful white people on the planet to control all the non-white people.

Before white people came into existence, the non-white people made up names for themselves but after white people started oppressing non-whites all over the world, white people RE-NAMED all the non-white people and all the places they came from.

The non-white people DID NOT UNDERSTAND that white people were setting up a SYSTEM that would allow them to mistreat non-white people ***on the basis of color***, so the non-white people went along with it.

COMMON SENSE tells us that the "black race" CANNOT be an accurate description of a people who number in the BILLIONS; who come from all over the world; who have different cultural practices and backgrounds; who speak different languages; who practice different religions; who eat different foods; and have all types of skin tones, hair textures, and facial features. There is one even more compelling reason:

If black people (Africans) were the first people on earth -- and even the smartest white people on the planet say this is true -- then EVERY man, woman, and child on earth DESCENDED from the "black race" -- including white people!

That being said, even though a ***"black race"*** is a false concept, the Authors still refer to ourselves as ***"black people"*** for the following reasons:

1. We are ***black people*** because ***people exist*** -- BUT we cannot be part of a (nonexistent) "black race" because there is ONLY one race: ***the white race.***

2. We have been targeted for mistreatment because we have been classified BY white people as ***black people -- and our mistreatment is a reality.***

3. We are spiritually, historically, genetically, culturally, biologically, emotionally, sexually, and romantically CONNECTED to the people that white people classify as ***"black people."***

We hope we've answered your questions. We recommend you review the previous chapters on Racism/White Supremacy (pp 47-64) until the concept becomes a natural part of your foundation.

We also recommend that you listen to the interviews of Mr. Neely Fuller Jr. with Gus Renegade on the C.O.W.S. (Context Of White Supremacy) -- www.contextofwhitesupremacy.com and visit www.counter-racism.com

The Authors

"(White) People everywhere are looking for what I offer. Most won't agree with me openly, but if you ask them privately, they'd tell you, 'Rockwell has the right idea. White Christian people should dominate.'"

-- George Lincoln Rockwell
Founder of the American Nazi Party
-- The Playboy Interview - April 1966

http://www.playboy.com/arts-entertainment/features/george-lincoln-rockwell/george-lincoln-rockwell-02.html

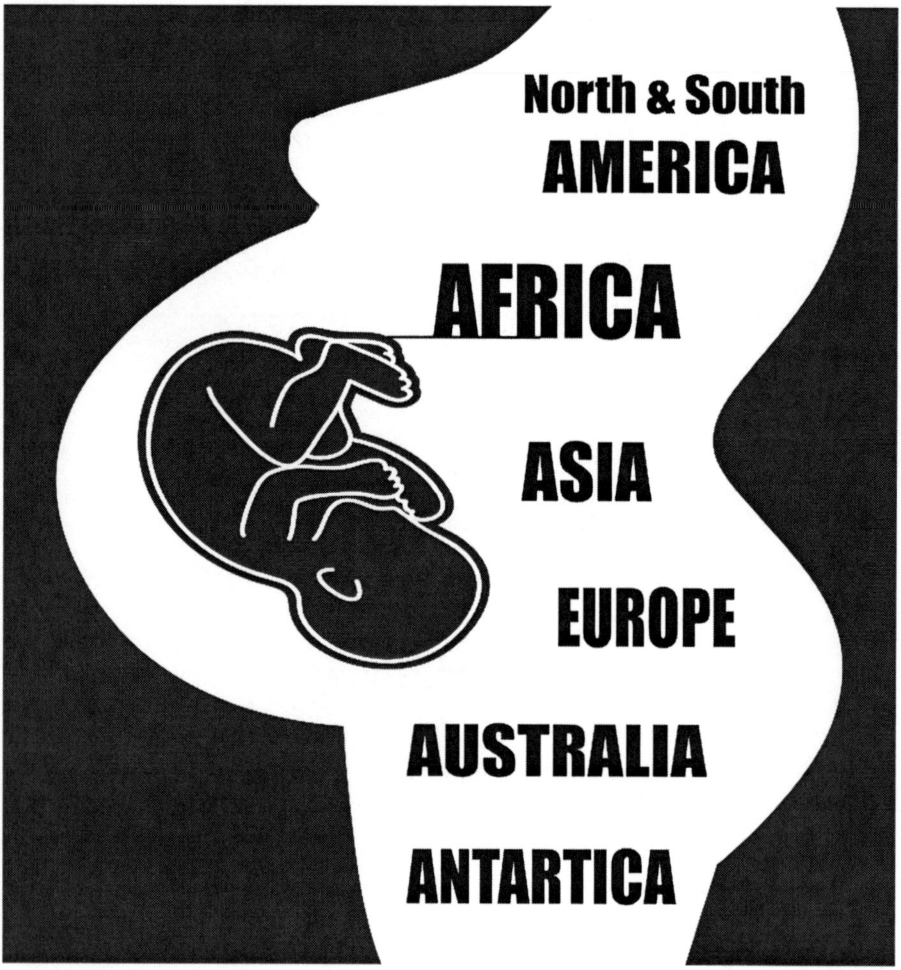
North & South
AMERICA
AFRICA
ASIA
EUROPE
AUSTRALIA
ANTARTICA

The Game Objective:

TOTÂL White Domination

"The only reason white people would want their "genes" to survive is so that they could survive as "white people," and the only reason they would want to survive as white people would be to practice white supremacy (racism).

It has been my observation that white people do not want to survive as white people for the sake of surviving as white people...it is for the sake of being in the powerful position over the other people on the planet.

In other words, being a white person has no value and no function except in the SYSTEM of white supremacy (racism)."

-- Edward Williams
(www.counter-racism.com)

CHAPTER FIVE

GAME OBJECTIVE: TOTAL WHITE DOMINATION

"Whiteness" Is The Foundation Of White Supremacy

White supremacy could not exist without "whiteness." Whiteness could not exist without white people. The only reason white people were "invented" was to allow them to dominate all the people they classify as "non-white."

Some "Whites" Are "Whiter" Than Other Whites

Even whites make a distinction between the "original settlers" -- the white Anglo-Saxon Protestants (WASPS) -- and the European (non-white) tribes that immigrated to America during the 1800s.

For example, when Irish immigrants came to the US, they were not seen as white, and were often given jobs too dangerous for slaves. Slaves were seen as valuable property, while the Irish -- who could not read or write -- were the most despised of all laborers.

In his book, *'How The Irish Became White,'* Noel Ignatiev explained how the Irish were allowed to become "honorary whites" if they agreed to serve as the foot soldiers for the white elites by derailing the progress and freedom of former (black) slaves.

The darker-complected Greek and Italian immigrants also faced rampant discrimination because of their lower caste (mixed-race) status -- but were still given more privileges and status than blacks to cement their loyalty to the white status quo.

This is indisputable PROOF that "whiteness" is NOT a fixed identity but can be "adjusted" on an ***as-needed basis.*** "Whiteness" is a **manmade concept; a code of behavior; and a political IDENTITY** that serves the NEEDS of the most powerful and privileged whites.

Mr. Neely Fuller, Jr. suggests, "economic forms of government such as capitalism and communism were created to perpetuate white domination" and that "the white race is really an "organization" dedicated to maintaining control over the world." ***The Authors agree.***

The value of "whiteness" can be compared to the value of paper money. Paper has no REAL VALUE other than what the most powerful people say it can BUY. "Whiteness" is a CURRENCY that has no real value BUT is used (inflated) by the most powerful people who classify themselves as white to ***dominate all the people they classify as non-whites.***

"I look at the system of racism having come into being consciously because the White population recognized, after they circumnavigated the globe, that they were a tiny minority, fewer that one-tenth of the people on the planet.

And they were genetic-recessive compared to the genetic dominance of people who produce color. They realized that they could be genetically annihilated and White people could, as a collective of people, disappear.

They worked out a system for White survival, which entails dominating all of the Black, Brown, Red and Yellow people on the planet. So racism is a behavioral system for the survival of White people.

Black people must finally understand that White people are playing a White survival game which has to inferiorize the functioning of Black and other people of color."

-- Dr. Frances Cress Welsing

The Cress Theory Of Color Confrontation

Dr. Frances Cress Welsing, a famous African-American psychiatrist and the author of *'The Isis Papers: The Keys to the Colors'* (1991), states that White Supremacy is practiced by the global white minority on the conscious and unconscious level to ensure their genetic survival by any means necessary.

Dr. Welsing contends that because of their "numerical inadequacy" and "color inferiority," white people may have defensively developed "an uncontrollable sense of hostility and aggression" towards people of color, which has led to "confrontations" between the races throughout history.

Repressing their own feelings of inadequacy, whites *"set about evolving a social, political, and economic structure to give blacks and other 'non-whites' the appearance of being inferior."*

The Final (White) Solution: Non-White Genocide

Some blacks think breeding with whites or out-populating whites will eventually wipe out racism but this kind of wishful thinking contradicts today's reality: ***nine percent of the (white) people on the planet are dominating the other (non-white) 91 percent.***

However, IF or WHEN the "white" population numbers falls to an UNACCEPTABLE level where white domination becomes impossible -- whatever level whites decide that is -- certain "measures" will be taken (and are being taken) to reduce that threat.

Non-whites should take NO comfort in a decreasing white population. The more threatened whites feel, the more violently aggressive they will become toward the ***increasing non-white majority*** to maintain their system of white domination.

- *"Depopulation should be the highest priority of foreign policy towards the third world."* -- Henry Kissinger, 1974
- In the 1970s, South Africa developed race-specific bio-weapons to target blacks and Asians.
- In September 2000, the Project for a New American Century published a document in which Dick Cheney described race-specific bioweapons as *"politically useful tools."*
- *"A total world population of 250-300 million people, a 95 percent decline from present levels, would be ideal."* – Ted Turner, Audubon Magazine.

White supremacy is more about CONTROL than it is about COLOR. COLOR is a means to maintain and refine control, in the same way anything else -- like a nose shape or eye shape -- could be used to EXPLOIT the differences between one group and another. COLOR is a TOOL used by white supremacists to justify dominating and exploiting non-whites.

Playing the White Side of the Chess Board

The
United
Independent
White
Supremacy
Conduct
Codebook

Chapter Six

THE UNITED INDEPENDENT WHITE SUPREMACIST CONDUCT CODE (UIWSCC)

What is the ***"United Independent White Supremacist Conduct Code?"*** Let's begin by defining the words, "united," "white supremacist," "independent," and "conduct code."

- **united** -- *being in agreement; made one; joined together politically, for a common purpose, or by common feelings*
- **independent** -- *having the freedom to make certain decisions within the context (environment) and control of a system or society or group*
- **white supremacist** -- *a white person who practices racism against non-whites*
- **conduct code** -- *a set of rules that outline the responsibilities for an individual within an organization or group*

The **United Independent White Supremacist Conduct Code** includes (but is not limited to):

1. ***White Privilege***
2. ***Using Code Words (In A White Supremacy System)***
3. ***The Universal Conduct Code For White Males***
1. ***The "Don't Snitch (On Other White People)***

All four "PARTS" have one thing in common: EVERYTHING that happens in all nine areas of human activity: ***economics, education, entertainment, labor, law, politics, religion, sex, and war*** -- must promote white supremacy and the domination of non-white people.

Wherever white people exist on the planet -- regardless of class, income, education, or location -- the ***United Independent White Supremacist Conduct Code*** **(the UIWSCC)** ***is the rule of the day.***

Some whites and non-whites may doubt this, but the evidence -- which will be presented in this chapter -- clearly speaks for itself. White is ALWAYS in a superior position over black (or non-white) -- no matter what the cost.

Even when it comes to the (modified) Europeanized version of the game of chess, the WHITE SIDE always moves first.

The Psychological Wages Of Whiteness

"It must be remembered that the white group of laborers, while they received a low wage, were compensated in part by a sort of public and psychological wage.

They were given public deference and titles of courtesy because they were white. They were admitted freely with all classes of white people to public functions, public parks, and the best schools.

The police were drawn from their ranks, and the courts, dependent on their votes, treated them with such leniency as to encourage lawlessness. Their vote selected public officials, and while this had small effect upon the economic situation, it had great effect upon their personal treatment and the deference shown them.

White schoolhouses were the best in the community, and conspicuously placed, and they cost anywhere from twice to ten times as much per capita as the colored schools. The newspapers specialized in news that flattered the poor whites and almost utterly ignored the Negro except in crime and ridicule.

-- "Black Reconstruction in America" (1935)
by W.E.B. DuBois (1868-1963)

UIWSCC PART 1
WHITE PRIVILEGE

"At least I ain't a nigger!" -- Michael Richards (Seinfeld's "Kramer") taunting blacks in audience at a L.A. comedy club. (2006)

It was a revealing comment from Michael Richards, who later claimed he was not a racist. However, when Richards used his "skin color rank" as the ultimate weapon to beat down his non-white opponents, he *knew* he had something that black people (niggers) will *never* have in a white supremacist society (like America) – regardless of their wealth, position, or title: ***white privilege.***

The FIRST PART of the UIWSCC is 'White Privilege.' For the best definition of white privilege, the Authors will defer to an expert on the subject: *a white person.*

"The whole idea is to grapple with the difficult issue of racism by looking at it from a fresh viewpoint - the viewpoint of what I, as a white person, am given, unearned, simply because of the color of my skin in contrast to what other people are deprived of unfairly because of the color of theirs." – Donna Lamb, Communications Director for Caucasians United for Reparations and Emancipation (CURE), a white organization that supports reparations for descendants of slaves.

While (some) whites deny the existence of white privilege, their flimsy denials quickly evaporate whenever they are engaged in a conflict or competition with a non-white person. The belief that a white person should (always) triumph over a non-white person, usually surfaces when:

1. A black person is hired or promoted over a white person.
2. A black person is more affluent than a white person (unless the black person is an entertainer or athlete).
3. A white authority figure takes a black person's word over a white person's.
4. A black authority figure attempts to dominate them.
5. A black person beats the (white) system (OJ Simpson verdict).
6. A white person is treated (or mistreated) in a way usually reserved for black people.

Suddenly, all is not right with the (white) world. Either there's an assumption that the black person did something illegal or unethical to be in a "superior" position over a white person, or there is a blatant refusal to acknowledge the superior position of a black person.

"A white salesman rings my doorbell and asks to speak to the homeowner. I'm standing there in a pair of old shorts and house slippers. Do I look like a damn butler? I knew right then what time it was. I decided, no matter what this white man was selling, even if he was giving it away for free, he wasn't stepping one foot inside my house." – A black, fifty-something attorney from an affluent suburb of Virginia.

This is a common experience for many affluent blacks. A black person who drives a luxury car or lives in an expensive home is often perceived by (some) whites of obtaining them through immoral or illegal means, such as welfare fraud or drug dealing. The assumption is: *"How can this black person afford something that I – as a white person – cannot afford?"*

This perception is based on the fear of losing something (white privilege) that most whites deny even exists. White privilege also surfaces in the workplace whenever a white employee is told to perform a menial task that is usually reserved for black employees:

"You ain't working me like a nigger." -- A white male, 23, employee said after his supervisor told him to move some heavy boxes.

Black students attending predominantly white colleges and universities are regularly regarded with suspicion and scorn. The assumption on the part of (some) white students and faculty is: *"This unqualified black is here because of reverse discrimination policies that penalized a more qualified white applicant who really deserved this spot."*

Even when the educational or financial backgrounds of these black students is unknown (they usually aren't), the negative stereotypes persist. After graduation, the degrees of black graduates are routinely dismissed as "dumbed-down affirmative-action degrees," or "affirmative-action things."

In the minds of (some) whites, blacks have not earned whatever they have; do not deserve whatever they get; and wouldn't have anything at all had it not been for the (misguided) generosity of whites.

Some prominent whites have gone as far as stating that blacks should be grateful they were "rescued from the jungle" and enslaved for 400 years so they could live in the greatest country on earth.

"America has been the best country on earth for black folks. It was here that 600,000 black people, brought from Africa in slave ships, grew into a community of 40 million, were introduced to Christian salvation, and reached the greatest levels of freedom and prosperity blacks have ever known." -- Pat Buchanan: "Slavery Best Thing Ever to Happen to Blacks"

The obvious (and false) assumption is that America would still be the same great country even WITHOUT our ***400 years of free slave labor***, ingenuity, inventions (which helped to modernize the nation), literature, art, music, science, and medicine.

Perhaps, black people should be thanked for "rescuing" white America from an almost certain, mediocre, colorless, and less prosperous existence.

White Privilege Means Whites Pay Less For Cars, Homes, And Credit

Reverse Red-Lining & Subprime Mortgages

In 2002, President George W. Bush pledged to "increase the number of minority homeowners by at least 5.5 million families." On cue, a bloodthirsty mob of banks, mortgage companies, finance companies, and various predatory lenders descended upon the same black and Hispanic communities they had previously shunned, and began targeting residents and the elderly with sub-prime mortgages that were designed (from the start) to self-destruct.

Even when blacks and Hispanics qualified for cheaper prime mortgages, they were steered into expensive loans loaded with higher interest rates, penalties, and hidden pitfalls.

- *"If you're white they overlook the fact that your credit score is a little too low, or you have one extra late payment," said Barbara Rice, a community organizer at the Massachusetts Affordable Housing Alliance, a nonprofit advocacy group.*
- *According to the Center for Responsible Lending, African-American borrowers with prepayment penalties on their subprime home loans were 6 percent to 34 percent more likely to receive a higher-rate loan than if they had been white borrowers with similar qualifications." (SOURCE: Racial disparities with subprime mortgages: A Study by Center for Responsible Lending (June 2006)*

A car is the second biggest purchase for most Americans. Black and Hispanic consumers pay thousands more in higher interest rates and other hidden costs when financing a car than whites.

> ***"Car buyers' suits charge racial bias in lending.*** *Rogers, who is black, is among 15 local plaintiffs who claim auto-financing companies discriminate against car buyers based on race. Their five lawsuits, filed against the financing companies of Ford, General Motors, Toyota, Honda and Nissan allege that the lenders allow dealerships to inflate interest rates without telling consumers. "If you compare blacks and whites with the same credit risk, blacks pay more," says Gary Klein, one of a team of attorneys representing black car buyers in the lawsuits.*

"It is standard practice, unfortunately, at many dealerships and many financing companies that they can make more money on blacks and other minorities," says Remar Sutton, author of "Don't Get Taken Every Time: the Insider's Guide to Buying or Leasing Your Next Car or Truck."

"The markup usually is higher for black customers than for white customers, according to a Nashville lawsuit. Debby Lindsey, a business professor at Howard University, analyzed thousands of loans from GMAC and NMAC and concluded that blacks paid more in dealer markup than whites paid."

Discriminatory Lending Practices Not Limited To Car Loans

- *Blacks and Latinos are denied access to* ***credit and financial services*** *at a much higher rate because of their credit scores, according to a recent study by the University of Denver Center for African American Policy.*

- *Credit card companies offer residents of black communities a lower credit limit than residents with the same profile from white neighborhoods, an economist at the Federal Reserve Bank of Boston has found.*

- *In his report, "Credit Card Red-lining," Ethan Cohen-Cole studied the* ***credit reports*** *of 285,780 individuals. Blacks moving from an 80%-majority white neighborhood to an 80%-majority black neighborhood reduced their credit by an average of $7,357 – even when their employment, incomes, and payment history remained the same.*

- *The Seattle Post-Intelligencer newspaper discovered* ***payday loan companies*** *target black areas and the military, charging as much as* ***400 percent on a two-week loan.*** *In addition, payday lenders are exempt from most state usury laws that limit what the maximum interest rate on loans."*

The difficulty blacks and Hispanics experience in obtaining bank loans – even when their credit history is comparable to whites – makes the short-term payday, car title, or finance company loan the only alternative in a financial emergency.

Cooking Up Credit Scores

Credit scoring is nothing more than a black box that takes our information and spits out a number. Since this process cannot be monitored, or verified as to its accuracy or fairness, we are left to assume the worst.

If American financial institutions systematically practice racism against non-whites, it is logical to assume that "skin color" and "ethnicity" are some of the prime ingredients that go into "cooking up" our credit scores.

White Privilege In Entertainment

"Mr. Trump, it's not 'The Apprenti, it's 'The Apprentice.'"

In December 2005, Dr. Randall Pinkett became the first black person to win first place in Donald Trump's *"The Apprentice"* reality-TV show. Dr. Pinkett was the only Rhodes Scholar 'Apprentice' in the history of the show with five degrees: a Bachelor of Science in Electrical Engineering from Rutgers; a Master of Science in Electrical Engineering from the MIT School of Engineering; a Master of Science in Computer Science from Oxford University in England as a Rhodes Scholar; a Master of Business Administration from the MIT Sloan School of Management; and a PhD from the MIT Media Laboratory, in the history of the show.

Despite Pinkett's impressive credentials and masterful performance on *"The Apprentice,"* his victory was almost stolen before a live audience of millions of viewers. When Trump asked Dr. Pinkett if he was willing to share first place with the runner-up, Rebecca Jarvis (a white female), Dr. Pinkett's controversial (and correct) response was:

> *"Mr. Trump, I firmly believe that this is 'The Apprentice,' that there is one and only one apprentice, and if you want to hire someone tonight it should be one. It's not 'The Apprenti,' it's 'The Apprentice.'"*

After Pinkett's respectful but firm refusal, Mr. Trump looked properly chastened because he had just revealed his racial bias on national television. Pinkett's self-respecting response created a firestorm of resentment from the white press and angry (white) viewers, who booed, boo-hooed, and blasted Pinkett for choosing "selfishness over selflessness."

It was illogical (and racist) to expect Dr. Randall Pinkett – a **competitor** in the most competitive reality show in television history -- to suddenly become ***non-competitive***. Certainly, selflessness is not one of the qualities that made Donald Trump one of the most admired businessmen in America.

Yet, a black man was condemned for doing exactly what Mr. Trump would have done under the same circumstances: *rightfully claim his prize.* Dr. Pinkett's real crime was not selfishness; it was his refusal to do what all black people are expected to do in a system of white supremacy: submit; be subordinate to the demands and expectations of white people; and sacrifice themselves (share his prize) to rescue a white damsel in distress.

Fair-minded viewers understood that asking the first black winner to share his prize was Trump's gaffe, not Pinkett's. Dr. Pinkett had every RIGHT (and every obligation) to resist a double standard that would have cheated him out of being the one and only winner.

The resentment from the white media and (some) white viewers can be explained with two words: ***white privilege.*** In other words: *"It ain't right for a non-white (nigger) to win over a (superior) white person, and that's why you should share your prize, Pinkett (nigger)."*

In the face of this black man's victory over a white person, white privilege reared its ugly head. That is the bottom line.

Black Success And White Resentment

"Please, I'm blacker than her mother." – Meadow, teenage daughter of mobster Tony Soprano, referring to a black classmate. (HBO's Sopranos)

After "Meadow" learned of a black classmate's early acceptance into an Ivy League school, she and a white male classmate sullenly assumed skin color was the reason for the black classmate's acceptance to a prestigious college NOT academic performance. In addition, since the black classmate's mother did not fit Meadow's stereotype of what a black woman should be, Meadow decided she wasn't "authentically black."

White Perception Is More Powerful Than Black Reality

"I couldn't get over the fact that there was no difference between Sylvia's restaurant and any other restaurant in New York City. I mean, it was exactly the same, even though it's run by blacks, primarily black patronship," said radio and TV commentator Bill O'Reilly, about his trip with Al Sharpton to the famous Harlem restaurant on his nationally syndicated radio show.

"There wasn't one person in Sylvia's who was screaming, 'M-Fer, I want more iced tea.' You know, I mean, everybody was -- it was like going into an Italian restaurant in an all-white suburb in the sense of people were sitting there, and they were ordering and having fun. And there wasn't any kind of craziness at all." (September 2007)

Perhaps, O'Reilly's words were not meant to be taken literally, but the fact that he saw nothing wrong with saying them publicly speaks volumes about the power of **perception VS reality**.

It's hard to believe Mr. O'Reilly has never met any educated or sophisticated blacks in his profession. Yet he just *"couldn't get over the fact"* that the black diners at Sylvia's (a black establishment) weren't screaming, *"M-Fer, I want more iced tea!"* at their waitresses.

Certainly, there are loud, ignorant blacks, just like there are loud, ignorant whites in New York City, yet no one – including Mr. O'Reilly -- would make the mistake of thinking all whites behaved a certain way.

Much of the credit for the negative stereotypes of blacks belongs to a mainstream media that (deliberately) rewards and promotes black entertainers who portray foul-mouthed buffoons, clowns, criminals, and whores, instead of the wide range of humanity blacks represent: mothers, fathers, sons, daughters, doctors, lawyers, chemists, architects, educators, students, cooks, clerks, firemen (and women), police officers, postal workers, and some extraordinary, but mostly average, imperfect human beings.

White Privilege And The Legal System

The OJ Simpson Verdict And White Privilege

The 1995 acquittal of OJ Simpson was not the first time a defendant was acquitted of murder, but it was the first time in American history that a black man was acquitted of allegedly murdering not one, but two whites. After the verdict was announced, many whites were shocked and outraged, while many blacks were overjoyed.

The unthinkable had finally happened: a black man (a nigger) accused of murdering two whites had leveled the uneven playing field of white privilege by having enough "green privilege" to hire a dream team of the best trial lawyers money could buy.

Guilty Until Proven Guilty

The OJ Simpson "not guilty" verdict led to frantic calls from politicians, talk show pundits, law enforcement, and (white) citizens for a drastic overhaul of the criminal justice system. Some of the proposed changes:

1. Allow non-unanimous jury verdicts.
2. Create a verdict system with three possible outcomes: guilty, not guilty, and not proven.
3. Set a minimum time limit for deliberation (because the four-hour Simpson verdict upset many people).
4. Allow juries of less than 12 people (overturning the tradition of a 12-person jury).
5. Change the venue rules to create a jury that is more "racially balanced" (eliminate predominantly black juries).
6. Use professional jurors. Train and pay people to be jurors, so they will have job experience and a "big picture" view by overturning the constitutional right to a "jury of our peers."
7. ***Repeal the sixth amendment*** (eliminate juries altogether!)

Ironically, the same justice system that has railroaded thousands of innocent black men and women into prison was suddenly called into question because it failed to convict ONE black man (a nigger) accused of murdering two whites.

A legal system that allowed a black man (a nigger) to get a taste of the best white privilege his millions could buy was more than the white collective could stomach. *(Simpson is currently serving 33 years for armed robbery and kidnapping for allegedly stealing his own property).*

Murderous Spouses And White Privilege

Charles "Chuck" Stuart -- Boston, MA

On October 23, 1989, **Charles "Chuck" Stuart** murdered his pregnant wife, Carol, then told police that a **black gunman** forced his way into their car at a stoplight, robbed them, shot Charles in the stomach, then shot Carol in the head. Carol Stuart died that night.

Their son, Christopher, died 17 days after his father discontinued his life support. Boston police searched for black suspects, abusing the civil rights, using stormtrooper tactics, and racial profiling of blacks in Boston. On December 28, Stuart picked a Willie Bennett, black man, out of a lineup.

The case against Bennett came to an abrupt close when Stuart's brother, Matthew, identified Charles Stuart as the killer. Matthew admitted he saw his brother shoot his wife and then shoot himself to support his false story.

Police discovered Charles Stuart had been involved in an affair and was having financial difficulties. On January 4, 1990, Stuart jumped from the Tobin Bridge to his death. He left no suicide note.

Susan Smith -- Columbia, SC

On October 25, 1994, **Susan Smith** drove her auto into a lake while the children slept in their car seats. The case gained worldwide attention because Smith initially reported to police that she had been carjacked by a **black man** who drove away with her sons still in the car. Nine days after a heavily publicized investigation and nationwide search, Smith confessed to drowning her children.

Charles Stuart and Susan Smith assumed their "whiteness" would guarantee their innocence if they accused a black man (a nigger) of committing the crime. And they were almost right. Ironically, if we were able to ask Charles or Susan if they used *white privilege* to get away with murder, both would probably deny such a thing existed.

Black VS White Justice

Those who compare these cases with blacks who have (allegedly) falsely accused whites should be reminded that the white defendants went free – regardless of the evidence – 99% of the time.

To believe blacks have the same opportunity as whites to get justice when whites control the police, the media, the courts, the appointment of judges, the laws, the district attorneys -- even the DNA analysis labs -- is illogical and ludicrous.

It is just as illogical to believe wealthy and politically powerful white families wouldn't use their influence (power) to "persuade" law enforcement officials to destroy or falsify evidence to assure a dismissal of all charges against their sons.

At the opposite end of the economic, political, and racial spectrum, there are thousands of cases where law enforcement planted or fabricated evidence against black defendants to ensure a conviction.

American Justice: Tulia, Texas-Style

In 1999, in a dusty town that boasted a population of around 5000, 40 black men and women in Tulia, TX were sent to prison by the Dallas County District Attorney's Office during a fake drug scandal. The "defendants" were pressured to plead guilty even though no large sums of money, illegal drugs, drug paraphernalia, or illegal weapons were found.

However, the trials of the first defendants by all-white juries, which resulted in long sentences despite the lack of evidence, made most of the untried defendants plead guilty in exchange for shorter sentences.

The "drugs" used to convict the black defendants were later discovered to be chalk not cocaine, a fact that the police and prosecutors were aware of. After the cases were legally challenged, most had already served several years in prison.

The recent wave of overturned convictions of falsely imprisoned black men freed after DNA evidence confirmed their innocence is ABSOLUTE PROOF that the American justice system is inherently racist and unjust.

We Can (Logically) Draw The Following Conclusions:

1) If blacks can be convicted on the basis of skin color (regardless of the evidence), it is logical to assume that whites can be acquitted or never charged on the basis of skin color (regardless of the evidence).

2) If evidence can be falsified by police and district attorneys to CONVICT black defendants, then it is logical to assume evidence can be falsified to ACQUIT white defendants -- ***in a white supremacy system.***

White Privilege Builds Generational Wealth

> *"Money can be earned by anyone. REAL WEALTH is created by passing it from one generation to the next." -- Umoja*

Stolen Life Insurance And Investment Opportunities

Life insurance is designed to: (1) to replace the lost income of a deceased parent or spouse, (2) pay funeral costs, and (3) to leave a financial legacy for future generations. Up until the late 1970s, blacks were not allowed to buy policies or freely invest in the stock market.

- *"As late as the 1960s...company rate books unabashedly warned 'Negroes and Indians need not apply' for coverage." ("What's Wrong with Your Life Insurance" by Norman F. Dacey)*

- *"At one time, life insurance in the African-American community became known as 'burial insurance.' African-Americans were only allowed to buy a small policy for burial expenses, and this is how it was marketed to them.*

- *Yet many times, their Caucasian counterparts, who had the same type of insurance policy, paid less, and were offered more coverage."* ***(African Americans and Life Insurance, Dereck L. Smith JR, LUTCF Secure Heights Financial, Inc. Financial Advisor.***

- *"The practice of charging African Americans as much as 35% more for life insurance than white policyholders is not a new one." (Black Enterprises, June 2002 by LeAnna Jackson).*

White Privilege Creates A Generational Curse Of Black Poverty

White privilege allows whites to pass along intellectual and real property, real estate, investments, insurance proceeds, businesses, quality educational opportunities, social and professional contacts, access, and exposure to a higher standard of living.

These things create the emotional, social, and professional confidence and quality of life that creates **WHITE GENERATIONAL WEALTH**.

The reverse is true for millions of black mothers and fathers who have been systematically and historically prevented from accumulating AND passing along established businesses, intellectual properties, employment opportunities, land, houses, and social contacts -- all of which creates a **GENERATIONAL CURSE OF BLACK POVERTY** that is passed from one black generation to the next.

"If you really understand racism and white supremacy, it's a sign of insecurity. People that are secure, are comfortable with differences.

Only insecure people have to rationalize, because I'm different from you, then I'm better than you. So I don't allow those whites who are racist, who believe in white supremacy, to put their insecurities on me.

If we were inferior, there would be no need to discriminate, which means that the people who are insecure, that believe in racism/white supremacy, they know if African-Americans were given the same opportunities, we would succeed.

-- Dr. Jawanza Kunjufu, educational consultant and author of 'The Conspiracy to Destroy Black Boys'

"Invalidation is in the language that racist man and racist woman have crafted to exchange information about their system and refine their code.

One of the main words that I harp on consistently on this program gets to the crux (the heart) of it: "valid" is a synonym for "fair."

It's in the language of their (white people's) language, is about invalidating anyone who is not white. Valid is fair, white. Everything else – reject pile."

I would say, unfortunately, they have equated white with normal. Victims, you should have in mind that they have equated normal with racist. Racist – white – normal – are all the same. Unfortunately, I have concluded those are the parameters we are working with. That's the way racist man and racist woman are thinking."

-- Gus Renegade, host of the C.O.W.S. (Context Of White Supremacy), an internet blogtalk radio program - www.context

UIWSCC PART 2

USING CODE WORDS IN A WHITE SUPREMACY SYSTEM

The SECOND PART of the UIWSCC are *"Code Words"* that create the (false) APPEARANCE of inferiority in non-white people, allowing racist man and racist woman to confuse and demoralize their victims.

Code Words For Whites

1. **Mainstream, Mainstream America, and Main Street** – standard (white) values, (white) institutions, and (white) individuals that are defined as the most normal.
2. **All-American** – wholesome and normal (white) institutions, values, and people.
3. **Lower class** – lower-income whites. Poor whites are never referred to as the "white underclass" because white skin privilege guarantees that poor whites will always have more status than poor non-whites.
4. **Middle Class** – the assumed status of most whites, regardless of income.
5. **Middle America** – (white) individuals whose values and lifestyle are considered the most normal.
6. **Fair --** pleasing to the eye; honest; clean; pure, *white or light-skinned.*
7. **Mom and Apple Pie** – the most wholesome (white) Americans.
8. **Regular** – normal as opposed to abnormal or undesirable. Often used to describe (white) facial features in popular fiction. For example: "*... the deep tan of his skin hinted some Indian or Negro blood but the regularity of his features gave lie to this.*" (from the novel "Lila" by Curtis Lucas, © 1955).
9. **Patriotic** – a term that usually refers to (white) US citizens, especially those who support US foreign policies (and aggression) against third-world nations, even if those actions are unjust.
10. **Taxpayers** – (white) US citizens whose taxes support the government.
11. **The Civilized World** – First World people, Europeans, whites.
12. **Person** -- a human being, individual, partnership, or corporation that is recognized by law as having rights and duties.

13. **First World** – new term (created by whites) to refer to the U.S., Western Europe, Japan, & Australia (where non-whites are in the minority and occupy an inferior position). "First" signifies most important, i.e., superior.

14. **Second World** – new term (created by whites) that refers to the Soviet Union, Eastern Europe, China, and Turkey.

15. **Citizen** -- An inhabitant of the US who entitled to the rights, privileges, and protection of their government, distinguished from legal and illegal immigrants and refugees. A naturalized person (immigrant or refugee) who goes through a formal process of naturalization, owes allegiance to a government, and is entitled to protection from that government.

16. **Suburban** – a code word for whites, regardless of income or location, used by the mainstream (white) media and advertising industry.

17. **Gentrification** – when city officials allow affluent people (usually whites) to displace poorer (usually black) inner-city residents from desirable inner-city neighborhoods by raising taxes and declaring imminent domain.

18. **Reverse Discrimination** – a term used by whites who claim affirmative action gives special preference to (unqualified) non-whites over (qualified) whites.

19. **Eurocentric** – a world view and perspective that assumes white people, white culture, and white values are superior to non-white people, culture, and values. Eurocentrism is practiced throughout the world, even in countries where non-whites are the majority.

20. **Evacuee** – a citizen who has been evacuated from a dangerous place OR removed from a place of residence for reasons of personal security.

21. **Pro-Life** – individual and/or organized opposition to the abortion of (white) babies for religious and/or political reasons (such as the declining white birth rate.)

Code Words For Blacks (And Non-Whites)

1. **Nigger** – a racial slur created by whites to describe blacks and other non-whites, i.e., Arabs are often referred to as "sand niggers."

2. **Negro** – a (made-up) word used from the early 1900s to the late 1970s to describe American-born blacks -- obviously from "Negro-land."

3. **Colored** – any non-white person; a person of color.

4. **Underclass** – blacks who occupy the lowest possible rung of the socio-economic ladder.

5. **Urban** – a code word used by the media and advertising industry for blacks, regardless of income or location.

6. **Inner city** – a predominantly black area of a city, regardless of income and education.

7. **Diversity** – implies the token inclusion of "minorities" (non-whites) in white corporate, educational, social, and government environments, usually for appearance's sake.

8. **Articulate** – an "unusual" black person who is able to express themselves intelligently as opposed to the black "norm" (who is not). An example is the comment former Senator Joe Biden (D-DE), made about former Illinois Senator, Barack Obama, in 2007: *"I mean, you got the first mainstream African-American who is articulate and bright and clean and a nice-looking guy."*

9. **Ebonics** – describes the type of "black English" spoken by (some) black children and adults. Note that no "word" has been created to describe the speech patterns and mispronounciations of English by poor or uneducated whites (to the authors' knowledge).

10. **Overpopulation** – refers to the increasing (and undesirable) populations of non-white people.

11. **Third World** – a term that describes people of medium to dark complexions in Africa, Middle East, Central, Latin, and South America, South Asia, North Korea, Saudi Arabia, and Oceania. The word "Third" versus "First" implies the inferior status of the darkest-skinned people on the planet.

12. **Fourth World** – a (new) term that describes the indigenous people (non-white natives) living within colonized countries, such as American Indians (Moors) and Aborigines from Australia. Again, this term minimizes people of color.

13. **Afrocentric** – a lifestyle and/or perspective that is decidedly pro-black but not necessarily anti-white. Afrocentrism -- in self-defense -- challenges the myth (lie) that African people are inferior and redefines African people and their contributions from a more accurate historical perspective.

    Afrocentric blacks identify with the black collective and support those things that benefit the black collective. Afrocentrism does not promote hatred of whites, and has no historical legacy of victimizing white people. It is important to note that this philosophy might not exist if racism/white supremacy (Eurocentric) did not exist.

14. **Tribe** – more than two non-whites occupying a specific geographical area at the same time. Note that whites are never referred to as "tribes."

15. **Natives** – describes the non-white original habitants who have been colonized (conquered) by European imperialists. (Not surprisingly, the word "native' is never used to describe indigenous whites.)

16. **Aborigines** – a term created by the invading English around the 17th century, meaning "first or earliest known." It describes the original, dark-skinned inhabitants of the Australian continent and nearby islands.

17. **Indigenous** – a term created by whites for (non-white) people who inhabited a geographic region before Europeans "discovered" and colonized them.

18. **Non-white** – anyone who is not classified as "white."

19. **People of color** – anyone who is not classified as "white."

20. **Exotic** – a non-white, usually a female, who is part white and is, therefore, considered more physically appealing. For example a "Eurasian" (Asian and Caucasian) female is usually described as exotic and attractive. The official definition of exotic: "Somebody or something unusual and striking; an exotic species; *a person or thing that is foreign or unusual."* Whites are never described as "exotic" even though they represent the (exotic) minority on the planet.

21. **Minority, minority group, minorities** – non-whites living within a larger white population. (It is worth noting that whites are a "minority" of the world's population).

22. **Barrio** – a Hispanic (non-white) neighborhood.

23. **Oriental** – a politically incorrect term for Asians and Asian Americans, Pacific Islanders, Eskimos, etc.

24. **Baby's Momma** – a word popularized by the mainstream media that stereotypes and dehumanizes single black mothers as nameless breeders (animals) -- a concept that originated during slavery.

25. **Baby's Daddy** – a word popularized by the mainstream media that stereotypes and dehumanizes single black fathersas nameless studs (animals) -- a concept that originated during slavery.

26. **Ho** – a word popularized by black male rappers and the mainstream media to stereotype (degrade) young black women as naturally promiscuous and immoral.

27. **Dawg (dog)** – a word used by unconscious black males to stereotype themselves as animalistic, oversexed, and immoral. Popularity of the word among black males is due to collective low self-esteem and a false view of manhood.

28. **Ghetto** – a low-income black or brown neighborhood. Never used to describe poor white neighborhoods.

29. **Ghetto fabulous (ghetto rich)** -- low or moderate income (black) people whose lifestyle is above and beyond their financial means.

30. **Refugee** – defined by the UN Convention as *"a person (non-citizen) who is outside her or his country of nationality and who is unable or unwilling to return."*

31. **Wilding** – a (new) word used to describe the alleged rape & assault of a white female jogger in NYC's Central Park by several black youths in the late 1980s. Other (animalistic) terms used by the mainstream (white) press to describe the black male defendants: a pack, predators, animals, preying, and wolves.

    Several years later, after the black males were convicted and serving their sentences, DNA evidence and an unexpected confession from the real Central Park rapist cleared them of all charges. Not surprisingly, the mainstream media was largely silent and unapologetic for crucifying – and convicting before trial – these young black males.

Code Words For "Pro-Black" And "Anti-Black" Whites

32. **Liberal** – a word that is used to reassure (deceive) blacks into thinking that a particular white person, policy, or organization that is supportive of the rights of blacks as a group. Also used as a coded word by other whites to imply that a particular white is a "nigger-lover" (aka traitor).

33. **Conservative** – a word that is used to alarm (frighten) blacks by implying that a particular white person, policy, or organization is hostile to blacks as a group (is racist). Also used as a coded word to (falsely) imply that a particular white person is a "nigger-hater."

34. **Bleeding-Heart-Liberal** – a code word used by whites to describe a white person who makes excuses for the (naturally) bad or criminal behavior of "niggers."

35. **Law-and-Order** – a code word that is used to reassure (con) the white collective that a particular political candidate will be hard on "niggers," especially niggers who break the law.

"Here's what white privilege sounds like: I'm sitting in my University of Texas office, talking to a very bright and very conservative white student about affirmative action in college admissions, which he opposes and I support.

The student says he wants a level playing field with no unearned advantages for anyone. I ask him whether he thinks that being white has advantages in the United States. Have either of us, I ask, ever benefited from being white in a world run mostly by white people? Yes, he concedes, there is something real and tangible we could call white privilege.

So, if we live in a world of white privilege – unearned white privilege - how does that affect your notion of a level playing field? I asked. He paused for a moment and said, "That really doesn't matter." That statement, I suggested to him, reveals the ultimate white privilege: The privilege to acknowledge that you have unearned privilege but to ignore what it means."

-- Robert Jensen, white male professor,
University of Texas

UIWSCC PART 3

THE UNIVERSAL CONDUCT CODE FOR WHITE MALES (IN A WHITE SUPREMACY SYSTEM)

The THIRD PART of the UIWSCC is "The Universal Conduct Code For White Males (In A White Supremacy System)"

The system of white supremacy is a male-dominated "brotherhood," where much is GIVEN, ***but much is also expected*** from the most privileged people on the planet: *white males.*

Not only are white males programmed to feel superior to non-whites and females; they are programmed to believe they MUST BE superior. This means white males -- who are **LESS THAN 5 PERCENT** of the world's population -- are burdened with the unenviable task of trying to dominate the other **NINETY-FIVE PERCENT**.

The white male's racial isolation isn't due just to the billions of black, red, yellow, and brown people who (rightfully) oppose his unilateral and unjust domination; it also comes from a lifetime of faulty programming under the patriarchal system of white supremacy.

To maintain the white male status quo, there is an unofficial, unspoken, and unwritten code of conduct that white males are expected to follow from the cradle to the grave:

- A white male is superior to all females and all people of color.
- A white male should be professionally, economically, and educationally superior to all women and all people of color.
- White males created everything worth creating on the planet.
- A white male should never be in a subordinate (inferior) position to a woman or any person of color.
- A white male should rebel against the authority of anyone who is not white and male, because they have no right to have any authority over him in a white supremacy system.
- A white male should never willingly take orders from a non-white or female person unless ordered to do so by another white male authority figure (who is really in charge).
- A white male is the biggest victim in America due to reverse racism, and should view affirmative action, civil rights, and women's rights as an attack (threat) against the white male.

- A white male should not share any more information than necessary, except in the performance of his job or business.
- A white male should suppress any sexual or romantic interest in non-white women, in particular brown or dark-skinned black women, unless it is out of eyesight of other whites, in particularly, white females.
- A white male should view any relationships with non-white women as temporary sexual flings.
- A white male should never let his guard down around people of color, especially males, and should avoid close friendships with men of color.
- A white male should restrain his desire to be "cool" lest his white peers label him a "wigger" or worse, a "nigger lover."
- A white male should always assume: a black male is "slick" (if he is confident); "articulate" (if he is well-spoken); and up to no good if women (especially white women) find him attractive.
- A white male should view the black male as a sexual predator who cannot control himself around white women.
- Never treat the "inferior" black female as if she is equal or superior to the white female.

***

The pecking order in a white supremacy system places the white male in a superior position over women and people of color, and programs the white male to assume this is ***the natural order of things.***

Q: Do you practice white supremacy?
A: "Yes I do. The question is not am I a racist, the question is how am I a racist.

"Racism/white supremacy and democracy are one and the same . . . in this country, they are joined at the hip."

Mr. Jacobson agreed that for white people to practice white supremacy all that one needs to know is:

1. Who is white/who is non-white
2. White people mistreat non-white people

-- Matthew Jacobson, white male, Professor of American Studies and History, Yale University, admitted Racist/white Supremacist, on The C.O.W.S Internet Radio Program (Sept 2009)

Don't
Snitch!

UIWSCC PART 4
'DON'T SNITCH!'
(ON OTHER WHITE PEOPLE!)

Don't Snitch -- Example #1

The *"Don't Snitch"* code works is apparent in the 2011 interview of Dr. Barbara T., on the C.O.W.S. internet radio station (www.contextofwhitesupremacy.com) on June 12, 2011.

Dr. T. is a white female and the author of a book that explains how *"well-meaning white people"* often practice *"silent racism."* In addition to writing a book, Dr. T has led numerous focus groups informing other whites about racism BUT she could not (or refused to) explain exactly HOW white people practiced racism (!)

JUSTICE (CO-HOST, age 12): Who teaches you how to practice racism/white supremacy?

DR T: My parents first, and then my teachers in school, and my friends, and the media.

JUSTICE: What makes you a racist/white supremacist?

DR T: Not understanding how racism works.

JUSTICE: How do you practice racism/white supremacy everyday?

DR T: I don't know.

JUSTICE: Could you at least name three ways?

DR T: No, I can't. That's part of the problem.

JUSTICE: What's part of the problem?

DR T: Not being able to see it.

JUSTICE: See what?

DR T: Pardon me?

JUSTICE: See what?

DR T: To see how racism operates in my life, personally.

JUSTICE: Gus, I might be incorrect, but I think she's practicing racism.

GUS (the Host): What is she doing?

JUSTICE: First of all, she's using terms that I don't understand. Second, she said something right before the other question, that I thought that she was practicing racism/white supremacy.

GUS: Well, I highly suspect Dr. Trepanier is practicing racism/white supremacy and I suspect she's aware of this. I could be wrong, but she said she's not aware of how the system works. She has written a book, a very sophisticated book. An in-depth study of how the system works. That is a huge contradiction. She studied this for 15 years and worked with different organizations. This does not seem accurate to me.

JUSTICE: I agree. My next question is, what are a few specific ways that your children practice racism/white supremacy?

DR T: I don't know what they do. (Pause). You know what, Gus? This is not working. This is not a good fit. I don't know what you thought. I've been as honest as I can be in my book. I don't know where the disconnect is between you and me, but this is not going to work. I'm sorry if I disappointed you, and disappointed your listeners and Justice, but I'm going to have to end the interview because I can't go on.

GUS: I am not disappointed at all. This is what I expect—

DR T: You're thrilled to death.

GUS: This is what I expect from racist man and racist woman. Exactly what I expect – from a well-meaning white person.

DR T: Okay, then.

JUSTICE: Could I get in one more question?

DR T: Sure. (sounding reluctant)

JUSTICE: I watched a video where you were explaining how all white people practice racism/white supremacy. You mentioned that you experienced greater resistance from other white people that are more racist and further up on what we call the racist continuum. Who do you know that is more racist, practicing racism/white supremacy better than you, further up on the racist continuum?

DR T: Well, I'm not going to say people by name, but I think that on the political spectrum, there are conservatives that want to change some of the civil rights legislation and I think that's more racist, and I don't know if that's where you're getting at or not but I don't think this conversation is going anywhere. I'm very sorry but I'm going to leave it now. I'm really disappointed and I know you're disappointed, I think you're disappointed – you say you're not – because you probably wanted to get a white person on here and embarrass her and you've done a good job of it.

GUS: You feel embarrassed? What do you feel embarrassed about?

DR T: (louder and upset tone) I feel embarrassed, I feel used, you read my whole damn book, and you knew who you were getting on this show.

JUSTICE: Good grief.

GUS: (surprised laughter): Now, I'm surprised. I'm not disappointed, I'm surprised.

DR T: Well, I'm really happy I could surprise you, I'm just...well...

GUS: What did we do?

DR T: You can say anything you want to say, you can say I'm stupid, you can say anything you want to. I don't care. All I know is I've done the best I can to write a book about racism from the well-meaning white person's perspective, and I understand that you don't think there is such an animal, but I give up! Okay? I give up! So, goodbye! (HANGS UP).

GUS: Man!

JUSTICE: That's what we should expect from white people.

***

(AUTHORS' COMMENT): It is difficult to understand how a white person (or any person) can write a book, conduct research, and inform others about something he or she "can't see" and doesn't understand.

That being said, the Authors totally disagree with the (false) premise that a white person can practice "silent racism" AND be a "well-meaning white person" at the same time.

This is as logical as saying a burglar can practice "silent burglaries" and still claim he is an honest person. Certainly, his victims would NOT agree that the criminal who burglarized their homes was a "well-meaning person."

*Once it was revealed ON-AIR that Dr. T was practicing racism, she attempted to transform herself into the (white) victim of Justice, the **12-year-old** co-host of the C.O.W.S. internet program. It is common for racist woman to resort to hurt feelings or (crocodile) tears to derail any constructive (or honest) discussion of racism.*

It is LOGICAL to assume that a "well-meaning" white person who practices "silent racism" is simply practicing a more REFINED (and dishonest) form of racism/white supremacy.

Don't Snitch -- Example #2

This is an excerpt from an interview with an admitted white female supremacist, Ferrell Winfree, on the C.O.W.S. internet blogtalk program in 2009. Throughout her two-hour interview with the host, Gus Renegade, Ms. Winfree insisted most white people don't think about being white.

WINFREE: The fact that most of those in power, the everyday man, woman, that gets up, goes to work, cooks supper, makes their children do their homework, it never occurs to them that they have any power at all.

They use the power without ever thinking about it, which is, of course, one of the greatest privileges of white supremacy is the fact that you can take advantage of it and not even think about it or be aware of it.

In that sense, that the system is there, Gus, and that we do take advantage of it, yes, but whether or not the majority of my people, and when I say my people, I'm talking about those classified as being white, the majority of my people would deny, number one, that they have any power until it is brought in front of them and discussed, and isn't often done, because they don't have to think about it and it is not brought to the forefront of their minds."

GUS: I wanted to clarify for myself and our listeners, for the purpose of this interview, are you in agreement with the definition for white supremacy being a system of people who classify themselves as white, and are dedicated to mistreating and/or abusing and/or subjugating everyone they say is not white? Are we in agreement?"

WINFREE: The only thing I'm in disagreement with the word that whites are dedicated, because like I said, the majority of them, it never occurs to them that they have the privilege so it's not something that they will get up in the morning and say, okay, today, I must make sure that I take advantage of being white, and to me that's the idea that comes from the word 'dedicated.'

Most of my people don't think about it...and I'm not talking about people in authority, I'm talking about the majority of people who are classified as white. When I do seminars, one of the things that I ask is, ok, those of you who are classified as white, what did you like about being white?

And most of the time until we're through with the seminar, and we ask that same question again, there's this blank look on their face, because they have never thought about it.

GUS: Interesting...I wanted to ask, do you think under the system of racism/white supremacy, do you think it is logical for any non-white person to think that white people are not aware of what it is to be white in a system of white supremacy?
WINFREE: I believe the majority of my people, they have no contact with people of color and no real concept of what it would be like to be in the shoes of the person of color and be in this system.

I believe that the majority of white people are not conscious of this system itself. Which again, is one of the greatest privileges is that we don't have to think about. Our lives are advantaged by the system. It has been going on so many hundreds of years that we don't think of it.

The fact that we don't have to worry about race when we apply for a job, or applying for a loan for a mortgage, or sending our children to school, knowing that they're not going to read in that history book negative things about how this country was established, that was near genocide of one people, and the enslavement of another, they don't think about the fact that their children in most places are not going to have to listen to that.

***

(AUTHORS' COMMENT): It is illogical to believe that white people in a white supremacy system do not know they are white, just as it is illogical to believe that a rich person in a capitalist system does not know he is rich.

A rich person does not have to get up every morning, look in the mirror and say, "okay, today, I am rich" to know they are rich. All they need to know is they have luxuries and privileges that poor people do not have.

When a white person in a system of white supremacy refuses to admit they are white to a non-white person, OR explain how other whites function as racists, they are practicing racism by withholding important and accurate information from the VICTIMS of racism.

It is a contradiction to say white people KNOW they do not have to worry about (their) race when they apply for a loan or mortgage (like non-whites) AND at the same time say white people are "not conscious" of being white in a system that gives whites more privileges than it gives non-whites.

It is also illogical to think that the white supremacy system could function so efficiently on a 24-7, 365-day BASIS, any time and anywhere whites come into contact with non-whites WITHOUT the vast majority of white INDIVIDUALS supporting and maintaining that system.

The White Supremacy System is supported and maintained by:

- *the white loan officer who charges black applicants a higher interest rate for a loan than white applicants with the same credit rating and income*
- *the white police officer who racially profiles black drivers for driving in the "wrong" (white) neighborhood*
- *Mr. and Mrs. Ted and Jane Smith who sit on the local school board and vote to give white schools more funding than the black ones*
- *the white parents who meet every year to continue the tradition of a 'whites-only' high school prom in their integrated high school*
- *the white receptionist who throws the job applications from black jobseekers in the circular file (trashcan) after they leave her office*
- *the white female housewife who sits on a jury and votes to acquit three white policemen who pumped 41 bullets into an unarmed black male*
- *the white janitor who sits on a jury and decides that the dark-skinned, black male defendant is (always) guilty before he hears a single piece of evidence*

> *"While appearing on the Larry King Live show (December 9, 2010), Wesley Snipes talked about his tax evasion conviction and his upcoming prison sentence. The host, Larry King, read aloud a statement from one of the jury members who admitted that there was 'one juror hat had said they knew Mr. Snipes was guilty right when they first saw him during the jury selection."*

It is the SYSTEM made up of millions of ordinary and average white INDIVIDUALS that maintains the system of white supremacy -- the same whites Ferrell Winfree claims "do not think about being white."

***

(INTERVIEW CONTINUED)

GUS: Just to clarify that, you did say for a non-white person it would be difficult to think that white people in a system of white supremacy are not aware of what it means to be white, and are not aware that we're in a system where the people classified as white dominate and abuse the people classified as not white?

WINFREE: Yes.

GUS: As a victim of white supremacy, I have asked many white people, and Mr. Tim Wise and many other white people have all conceded it would be difficult, if not illogical, if they were non-white, to think that white people are not aware of the system of white supremacy.

And I have seen a lot of non-white people, they say that white people are ignorant, that that is one of the problems of racism/white supremacy, that white people are ignorant.

I feel it is very dangerous in the system of white supremacy for the victims to reference the white people as "ignorant;" that they are doing this because they're ignorant. And I've seen many of the consequences of that, that the victims of WS remove culpability (blame) from white people. They are no longer held responsible for the system of white supremacy because the non-white people think they are ignorant and I think that's a major error on the part of non-white people. Do you have a view on that?"

WINFREE: The only thing I have hope for is more and more I'd be able to make my people, to cause my people to be aware of this system in the hopes that they will try to stop this system as it is now. The danger that's there, I believe, for your people to think it's a matter of ignorance... because it's the system that needs to be talked about, that needs to be recognized, the system that subjugates millions of people."

***

*(AUTHORS' COMMENT): The definition of the word "ignorance" is: **"a lack of knowledge or awareness."** Anyone who is acting deliberately and willfully to mistreat other people IS NOT acting out of ignorance. It is illogical to believe that white people are NOT "aware" that they are mistreating black (and non-white) people when they are practicing racism. It is also ILLOGICAL to state that the "system" is the problem, NOT the people who CREATED, MAINTAIN, and BENEFIT from the system.*

White supremacy = white people
white people = the white supremacy system

The white supremacy system did NOT create white people; white people created the system of white supremacy.

***

GUS: I wanted to bring up Mr. Neely Fuller, Jr. and I spoke to you before about him. Mr. Fuller has been quoted as saying white people cannot be ignorant about racism/white supremacy. Do you think that statement is true?

WINFREE: I have a great deal of respect for him. I read some of his work. I met him briefly once, but again I have to come back with almost 70 years of living in this system, in this society, a society that subjugates, and again, I say this over and over, most of them have never thought of that. And I say it again, they don't think about it.

GUS: One thing that I tell non-white people when having conversations with any suspected racist in the system of white supremacy, is be diligent in making sure you get a clean answer to your question. I'm not sure I got a clean answer to my question. My question, Mr. Fuller says, white people cannot be ignorant about racism/white supremacy. Do you think that's true, or do you think that's false?

WINFREE: I think he is mistaken.

GUS: Ok, thank you for that answer.

WINFREE: Please understand that I make that statement with great respect for the work that he does. But, I'm not sure that during his lifetime has had the opportunity to meet those people that I'm talking about because they're not going to be listening to black radio stations. They're not going to be going to seminars where racism is discussed, they're going to be getting up in the morning, shaving. Race has not occurred to them.

***

(AUTHORS' COMMENT): It is illogical and frankly, ABSURD, to think that Mr. Fuller -- who was born in 1929; is 82 years old as of this writing; and has lived through the Great Depression AND Jim Crow (legal segregation) has not had an "opportunity" to meet (a ton of) white people -- including those who have NEVER, ever listened to a "black radio station" or attended a racism seminar.

Obviously, Ms. Winfree is reluctant to admit that the majority of her (white) people are well aware of their white status in a white supremacy system.

In the Authors' opinion, this is another example of a "well-meaning" white person who refuses to "snitch" and deliberately withholds important and accurate information from the VICTIMS of racism.

***

Don't Snitch -- Example #3
(The Penalties For Breaking The White Code Of Silence)

Blue Eyes, Brown Eyes, And (False) White Innocence

In her famous "blue-eyed/brown-eyed" exercise in 1968, Mrs. Jane Elliott, a white schoolteacher, divided her third-grade class into two groups: the brown-eyed children and the blue-eyed children.

The brown-eyed students were given extra recess time, second helpings at lunch, and praised for being more intelligent than the blue-eyed students. The blue-eyed students were forced to wear crepe paper armbands; were not allowed to drink from the same fountain as the brown-eyed children; and were told they were not as good as the brown-eyed students.

"The brown-eyed people are the better people in this room," Mrs. Elliott told her class. "They are cleaner and they are smarter."

By the end of the first day, the brown-eyed children could do schoolwork they had been unable to do before. The blue-eyed students became withdrawn and made mistakes on the same classwork they had been able to do. On the second day of the exercise, Elliott had the brown-eyed and blue-eyed students switch places. After the exercise ended, the children had to write essays about what they had learned about discrimination and what it felt like.

"I think these children walked in a colored child's moccasins for a day," said Mrs. Elliott.

Mrs. Elliott's two-day experiment confirmed what many black educators and parents had always suspected: that black underachievement is a DIRECT REFLECTION of a white supremacy system that teaches black inferiority from cradle to grave.

After only EIGHT hours of "inferiority programming" in the classroom, the blue-eyed children began to BEHAVE as though they were inferior to the brown-eyed students.

When word spread of Mrs. Elliott's experiment, she was invited to appear on the Johnny Carson show. Following her appearance, hundreds of irate (white) viewers called in and wrote letters to the show, most of which read like the following:

"How dare you try this cruel experiment out on white children! Black children grow up accustomed to such behavior, but white children, there's no way they could possibly understand it. It's cruel to white children and will cause them great psychological damage."

What the letter writer didn't say (and didn't have to) was he or she understood that racism causes "great psychological damage," but it was all right (normal) to damage ***black children.*** The local (white) community's response to Mrs. Elliott was equally telling. Teachers at her school shunned her; her children were harassed and assaulted; and her father's store was boycotted, forcing him into bankruptcy.

Don't Snitch -- Example #4

In 1992, Jane Elliott appeared on the Oprah Winfrey show and conducted the following experiment without the knowledge of the studio audience:

Before the audience was seated in the studio, they were divided into two groups: the blue-eyed people and the brown-eyed people. The show's producers immediately escorted the brown-eyed people to their seats and offered them donuts and coffee in clear view of the blue-eyed people who were treated rudely and forced to stand for two hours.

By the time the blue-eyed audience members were seated in the studio, they were furious. Mrs. Elliott poured gasoline on the fire by saying their unruly behavior was proof that blue-eyed people were less intelligent and more violent than brown-eyed people.

Even after Mrs. Elliott revealed that the entire audience had been part of an experiment on racism, most of the blue-eyed audience members continued to rant and rave about the way they had been treated. Mrs. Elliott calmly reminded them that being mistreated for two hours was nothing compared to dealing with racism on a daily basis.

For the first time in their lives, the blue-eyed audience members got a taste of real-life racism, and discovered that being mistreated for having the wrong eye (or skin) color was an infuriating and demoralizing experience. Most fiercely resisted the message because it would mean the loss of their imaginary "innocence" and "ignorance" about the cruelty and realities of racism.

It is logical to assume the white people who fought Mrs. Elliott's lesson the hardest, were most likely, the most guilty of practicing racism themselves.

The hostility Jane Elliott experienced from other white people for SNITCHING on white people completely contradicts ***the lie of white innocence (and ignorance) about racism.***

The reactions of other whites in both experiments are UNDENIABLE PROOF that whites are well aware of how racism is practiced and the damage it does to its non-white victims – because they objected to being treated IN THE SAME RACIST MANNER. These reactions also PROVE that a white person who "breaks the white code of silence" will be PUNISHED.

Neely Fuller Jr. On The Average White Person by Age 16

(Excerpted from an interview with Mr. Fuller, Jr. by Gus Renegade on the internet blogtalk program, C.O.W.S. (Context Of White Supremacy)

GUS: Ariela Gross, a professor at the University of Southern California wrote a book on white supremacy called, *'What Blood Won't Tell,'* and analyzes how white people practice racism, and how they have changed the rules about who gets to be a white person.

One of the things she highlights is to be a white person, you are expected to be informed about racism. You are expected to know the rules of how you're supposed to function as it relates to other white people and non-white people. That is expected of you. You cannot be ignorant of those rules.

Mr. Fuller, I have heard you say white people cannot be ignorant about racism, and if you are, you will get into trouble with other white people. Could you share your view on that study?

FULLER: Every white person by the time they're sixteen, they know all the rules. They've picked it up by osmosis, just by being around people and observing and listening and being around the dinner table when political talk is going on.

The little white girl, the little white boy who's sitting there, he's six years old but he hears his white grandfather sitting up there talking about that blankety-blank Obama, and all the rest of those heathen niggers, are ruining the society, and on and on and on.

He's six years old, and by the time he's fifteen, he's well-schooled, and he hasn't said a word to anybody. By the time he gets ready to go to school, he knows the fundamentals, and by the time he gets to eighth or ninth grade, he's got it down pat.

Now and then, he'll make some mistakes. He'll choose a black buddy or something like that, they'll be on the football team, and all like that. But for the most part, he knows the rules.

He knows where the line is and he's not supposed to cross it cause when he does, he'll be crossing his grandfather, who's still sitting on that porch, rocking back and forth.

'Now, boy, you know better than that. Okay, you be nice and kind to the people, don't call them names, but after all, don't forget you're white, that means something. I didn't go through all the wars, fighting, for you to wind up being like them.

It's alright for you to be around them, laughing and talking, but you're a different species altogether, and don't you forget it. How do you think we got all that we got? By being like them? Look at them.

Drive through where they live. Look at the way they act. Do you think that's an improvement? They (white boys) go out and check it out, and they say, no, I'd rather behave. There's something to being white.

You get a lot of things out of being white that you don't get if you're black. They see that. They ain't blind. Are you in a better position being white or in a better position being black, anywhere in the world?

And every white person, a 30-year-old white person doesn't know that? Even if they are blind, they know that much. I mean, a blind white person don't even know what a black person looks like, if somebody told him he's white, he knows what that means. That's a much better position. Cause he's listening. He's got ears.

***

Dr. Frances Cress Welsing On What White People Say When No Black People Are In The Room

Dr. Welsing during an interview on C.O.W.S. with Gus Renegade, Mar 2009:

> *"When people who classified themselves as white ask me, Dr. Welsing, what can I do to solve the problem of racism/white supremacy, I say tell black people what white people talk about when there are no black people around. What's the conversation like when there are no black people around?*
>
> *I had a professor at an American university, a white female professor several years ago say to me, 'Dr. Welsing, I hate to admit it, but on all social occasions where white people are together and there are no black people, we're talking negatively about black people. And the assumption is, every white person present agrees with the discussion.*
>
> *And I said, well, I understand that because what the discussion is about even though it is not discussed in the terms that I have used, ensuring white genetic survival.*
>
> *When white people – people who classify themselves as white – are talking negatively about black people they are talking about maintaining the system of racism/white supremacy. And if they're talking negatively about black people, they are giving themselves justification for the mistreatment of black people.*
>
> *And so, when black people don't understand this, and a white person goes to bed with a black person, and a white person doesn't say, 'this is what we say about black people when there are no black people around, the person who has classified themselves as white, is keeping very important, strategic and practical information from black people, and saying, 'I love you' – but I can't love you and at the same time not give you important information.*
>
> *See, on the job where they might be white people and black people working together, the white person is in on the fact that white people are being paid more than black people, so the white person, a white male approaches a black person to have sexual relations, or a white female approaches a black male to have sexual intercourse, I say the white person is always the one making sexual overtures.*
>
> *Imagine a black man deciding he's going to speak to any white woman of his choice. All she has to do is say, 'help! rape!" and he'll be lucky if he continues to live that day. So, she has to make the overtures. The white male makes the overtures.*

All kinds of overtures on the part of people who classify themselves as white, male and female, sexual overtures to people of color without revealing what white people talk about when no black people are around.

When a white person says, 'Dr Welsing, how can I help?' And I say simply tell black people what white people talk about when no black people are around.

And I have never had a white person say, other than this one person I mentioned but she didn't exactly what was said, she said we were talking negatively but didn't reveal the details of the discussion. I have never had, 'Well, let me tell you, this is what we talk about, and this is what we're going to do.

And it becomes the sexual activity in the system of racism where it crosses the racial line becomes deception. As Neely Fuller, Jr. has said, the first level becomes tackiness, trashiness, and then becoming terroristic – which is what many black men have experienced in the workplace.

If a white female approaches a black man and he acts like he is not interested, she begins an attack on him. So he ends up getting in trouble, and maybe losing a job.

***

If a white person is UNWILLING to "snitch" on other whites, how can he or she say they are opposed to racism?

Imagine a mother or father who sits by silently while their son or daughter sticks a metal fork into an electrical outlet. Now, imagine the white mother or father of a black/non-white child who REFUSES to tell their child the TRUTH about racism, and how to protect themselves from OTHER white people who are practicing racism against them.

How can a white parent CLAIM to love their black child (or spouse, friend, or lover) when their loyalty to the ***United Independent White Supremacist Conduct Code*** -- the only TRUE religion of racist man and racist woman -- is stronger than their loyalty to their non-white child, spouse, lover, or friend?

This is the MOST IMPORTANT question ALL blacks (and non-whites) should ask themselves before engaging in ANY kind of personal or sexual relationship with a white person.

"We know what we've done to (non-whites). And we know what we've put in your head over 500 years. We know how to utilize that. We know how to take advantage of that. We even know how to have a (non-white) black friend.

We know the dynamics of who is in control. We know where your place is. We know where our place is. The greatest deception we caused is that your people believe us. I have done such a good job, they don't even know that I've done this to them."

-- Ferrell Winfree, white female, admitted Racist/white Supremacist, on The C.O.W.S Internet Radio Program (2009)

Playing the Wrong Side of the Chess Board

Integration was the worst thing that could have happened to black people.

You can't "integrate" into a culture that despises you.

You can't "integrate" when you have to ask (beg) for everything you need.

That's not integration, that's subjugation.

And if you don't know the difference between being equal and wanting to be equal, you never will be.

Umoja

Chapter Seven

THE CURSE OF BLACK SKIN AND WHITE EYES: THE WHITE-IDENTIFIED BLACK

"It is impossible to achieve equality when one group has the power to deny rights to another group. Until we understand that distinction, we will not understand the difference between tolerance and acceptance." -- *Umoja*

What Is A "White-Identified" Black?

A black person who views the world through a "white lens," and judges most or all events, people, places, actions, and things from a **white perspectiv**e.

What Is The "White Collective Perspective?"

The beliefs, opinions, behaviors, and value systems of whites as a group. The **white collective perspective** is based on what is normal, desirable, and beneficial for white people collectively. An example is the Rodney King beating case. In spite of VIDEOTAPED evidence of police brutality, an all-white jury decided *collectively* that what benefited the white police officers benefited white people collectively. That perceived "benefit" resulted in an acquittal.

Had it been the other way around – an unarmed white male beaten by black police officers -- it is certain that an all-white jury would have convicted the black officers. The white collective would have (correctly) viewed an unarmed white person's beating by black policemen as potentially dangerous to ALL white people collectively – because that meant it could happen to ANY white person. The white collective would have acted in their collective best interest by punishing the black officers.

In a racially divisive society (like America), it is NORMAL for the white collective to set standards that benefit their group, and affirms their self-worth as white people collectively. This does not mean all white people think the same, or share the same perspective in all things.

What Is The "Black Collective" Perspective?

The black collective operates on a similar principle; that black people collectively (should) view most or all events, people, places, actions, and things from a perspective that assumes whatever benefits or harms a black person benefits or harms all blacks collectively. This does not mean all blacks think the same, or share the same perspective in all things.

From the black collective perspective, the beating of an unarmed black man by white police officers would have been (correctly) perceived as harmful to ALL black people – because the same thing could happen to ANY black person. Therefore, a black jury would be more likely to convict the white officers.

The OJ Simpson trial is another example of how the white collective and the black collective perceive their self-interests differently. The white collective assumed OJ Simpson was guilty (even before any evidence was heard), while the black collective saw Simpson's acquittal as justice for all blacks, not just Simpson.

This does not mean all blacks believed that OJ was innocent, or that all whites believed OJ was guilty. An individual may not agree with the group perspective on any or every issue, but it is undeniable this kind of group mentality exists within a racist society.

It is NORMAL for the black collective to set their own standards, according to what benefits black people and affirms their self-worth as black people. However, due to black-inferiority programming, which was accelerated by the integration and assimilation into a black-hating white culture, the black collective often acts against its own self-interest without understanding why they are doing it.

It also explains most of the black collective's self-destructive behaviors. This inferiority programming is the main reason many blacks refuse to identify with the black collective -- because ***it is the black collective***.

AXIOM #4: A GROUP WHOSE COLLECTIVE ACTIONS PENALIZES THEIR OWN GROUP (AND REWARDS ANOTHER GROUP) IS SELF-DESTRUCTIVE AND SELF-GENOCIDAL.

For this reason, the white-identified black is a liability, NOT an asset, to the black collective. Before we go further, let's define what a white-identified black is NOT.

What A White-Identified Black Person Is Not

This is not a condemnation of blacks who are often unfairly labeled as not "black enough." All (or most) blacks are white-identified to a smaller or a greater degree, because we were raised in a white-supremacist culture (America). It is the degree of white-identification that determines the degree of the problem.

Being white-identified does not mean you prefer Beethoven to Beyonce, or Madonna to Master P. It is not about our tastes in food, music, art, or literature. It is not about the way we dress; wear our hair, walk, talk, sing, or dance.

It is not about our level, income, or education, or the type of work we do. It is not about being smart, or educated, or speaking standard English, or several languages that makes us white-identified.

ALL people – regardless of race – have a wide range of talents, interests, skills, and tastes, and are capable of enjoying a wide range of things for the simple sake of enjoyment. Black people are not monolithic (the same), nor are all white-identified blacks the same.

What Is A 'White-Identified' Black?

A white-identified black person is a black person who views the world through a white perspective ***even when*** it conflicts with his or her own self AND group interests. A white-identified black pursues interests, activities, and relationships ***primarily because white people are associated with them*** – and often avoids or looks down on certain people, places, and things ***primarily because black people are associated with them.***

White-identified blacks can be found anywhere, at every income level, from the most exclusive gated community or Ivy League campus, to an inner-city housing project. How a black person sees black people, talks about black people, treats black people, feels about being a black person, and treats white people determines ***the degree*** of white-identification.

White Supremacy Is The Foundation For The "White Perspective"

The white collective perspective is based on the following principles:

1. white is superior to non-white
2. white life is more valuable than non-white life
3. white people created everything worth creating
4. white is the most normal (the standard) for ALL human beings

If white is the most **normal**; black **must be the most abnormal**. For those who doubt that this white standard exists, there is one INDISPUTABLE piece of evidence that can be found in every medicine cabinet in America: **the 'flesh-colored' Band-Aid.** In other words, the "normal" color for human flesh is the color closest to the skin color of white people. What does this say to the non-white person? ***That their skin color is NOT normal because they are NOT as human.***

AXIOM #5: BLACK NORMALCY CANNOT EXIST IN A SYSTEM OF WHITE SUPREMACY.

White-Identified Blackness = Psychological Suicide

By viewing the world through "white eyes," white-identified blacks are in the unenviable position of embracing their own inferiority and abnormality, and have no choice but to be anti-black – and ANTI-SELF.

If the white-identified black is observed interacting with whites or blacks, he or she will eventually reveal their OWN racial bias and inferiority complex by the things they say or do.

Their confusion comes from trying to straddle the precarious line between the black world and white world, by serving two opposing masters at the same time: **white supremacy and black normalcy.**

It is ***unnatural and perverted*** for a race of people to adopt a perspective and a set of standards that does NOT benefit their group AND denies their own NORMALCY and self-worth as members of that group. Unfortunately, this kind of distorted thinking is exactly what has led to the personality disorders and self-hatred issues that plague the black population.

Curing The 'Disease' Of Black Abnormalcy

If whiteness is the norm; blackness must be the disease. The ONLY cure is the assimilation of (inferior) blacks into a (superior and normal) white value system in order to reduce their "black abnormalcy." This fear of being "abnormal" is the main reason some blacks become assimilated (white-identified), so they will be **"normal"** by white standards. Unfortunately, white-identified blacks will never be as normal as white people because they will **never be white**.

By accepting the (false) premise that white is the most 'normal,' the white-identified black is confirming his or her own genetic and intellectual inferiority.

The white-identified black person will never admit to being white-identified, but will do anything to avoid being perceived as too "black." When pro-golfer Tiger Woods created a new term -- "**Cablinasian**" (coined from the words **Ca**ucasian, **Bl**ack, American-**In**dian, and **Asian**) – to describe his racial heritage, some people wondered why a man with a black father and an Asian mother would put "Caucasian" first in the racial pecking order.

Ironically, despite Woods' attempt to racially reclassify himself, he is still known as a "black golfer." In a white supremacist society, non-whites cannot racially reclassify themselves. Those who choose to forget this fact will be abruptly reminded.

A blatant reminder occurred in 2008, when a solution was proposed by Kelly Tilghman, a white female sports anchor, for younger golfers who wanted to challenge Tiger's title as the world's No. 1 golfer. She suggested that they, *"Lynch him in a back alley."*

Tiger's response: *"Kelly and I did speak. There was no ill intent. She regrets saying it. In my eyes, it's all said and done."*

The real question is not whether Tilghman had ill intent; it's whether the word "lynching" would have been used to refer to a white golfer. It is similar to Fuzzy Zoeller's comment at the 1997 Masters tournament when he called Tiger *"that little boy"* and told him not to serve *"fried chicken or collard greens."*

The irony is these blatant "racial reminders" make the white-identified black more uncomfortable than the whites who had an unfortunate slip of the tongue. White-identified blacks are quick to forgive these kinds of comments because they are desperate to reassure whites that they are not "angry" blacks – even when they are being mistreated.

This kind of behavior is more common for black males than black females, since showing anger is taboo for black males who want to succeed with the white public.

The downside of allowing racist comments to appear innocent is the black masses -- who do not have millions of dollars to insulate themselves from everyday racism – are expected to suffer the same racist treatment without protesting:

> *"Look at that black XYZ celebrity. He doesn't make a big deal out of a harmless comment about lynching (niggers), so why should you (an ordinary nigger) get upset?"*

A columnist for a major sports magazine also casts some doubt on the wisdom of Tiger's response:

> *"Woods doesn't have to become a civil-rights spokesman, but he could have at least acknowledged that he understands the meaning of the word, and how powerful and hurtful it remains."*
>
> *-- Farrell Evans, Writer-Reporter, Sports Illustrated*

Their desperate desire to distance themselves from themselves (and their despised blackness) is the emotion that drives many white-identified blacks to deliberately seek out a white or Asian spouse to rid their offspring of the racial 'abnormalities' that exist within themselves. This is why it is critical to recognize the symptoms of black denial and self-hatred, so their "disease" will not infect us.

The Poisonous Effect Of White-Identified Black Celebrities

White-identified black celebrities are extremely dangerous to other blacks because they VALIDATE black inferiority/white superiority by the kinds of lifestyle and romantic choices they make.

These "successful" white-identified black celebrities are more likely to be rewarded by the white supremacy system with lucrative book deals, talk shows, movies, and TV shows ***because they are the best advertising white supremacy can buy.***

Their fame, awards, and desperation to be embraced by the white elite and the white collective sends a DEADLY MESSAGE to the black masses -- especially to black youth: ***if you want to be rich and successful, be less black.***

The white-identified black person is the ADULT victim of the black doll/ white doll experiment. White-identified blacks understand how tragic it is for the little black girl or boy to pick the white doll as the nicer doll, but cannot see how damaged they must be to do the SAME THING.

If blacks are "inferior," how does the white-identified black exempt him or herself from the same judgment?

Some white-identified blacks adopt external gimmicks to maintain the illusion (and delusion) of "black pride" -- like wearing African clothing, coconut beads, dreadlocks, and talking incessantly about the "black struggle," all while imitating, (secretly) identifying with, sexing, and loving ***white.***

Because white-identified blacks usually get more crumbs from the "white" table than their black-identified peers, they are convinced that their external achievements (and white validations) are proof of their internal self-esteem, when in reality, it is just the opposite.

Wealth, fame, status, titles, material things, or wearing dreadlocks and African clothing, have nothing to do with **SELF-ESTEEM**. However, **SELF-ESTEEM** does require RESPECT for the truth:

AXIOM #6: A NON-WHITE PERSON CANNOT BE EQUAL TO OR THE SAME AS A WHITE PERSON IN A WHITE SUPREMACY SYSTEM.

To maintain the level of self-deception and denial needed to maintain their (false) white identity, the white-identified black person must create even more delusions (lies) as to their TRUE status as a black person (a nigger) in a white supremacy system.

This is why white-identified blacks are more vulnerable to the emotional devastation caused by racism -- because they don't think they will ever be victims of it.

Chapter Eight

THE COLOR OF SUCCESS

Miranda is a senior software programmer for a Fortune 500 company and earns a six-figure salary. She drives a luxury car, lives in a downtown condo just blocks from her job, eats out twice a day, and is always stylishly attired. Five foot-six, and attractive; Miranda maintains her trim 140-pound frame by exercising three times a week at the pricey health club in her apartment building.

Miranda avoids interacting with the black copy clerks, messengers, and secretaries at her firm since she has nothing in common with them. She has a handful of black friends and associates -- all Ivy League grads like herself -- who work for other Fortune 500 firms.

She attends most company functions, and occasionally joins her white coworkers for happy hour at the bars near their office. She dated a white consultant for a few weeks the previous year but they went their separate ways after he said he "wasn't looking for anything serious." She hasn't met anyone since, and is dateless most weekend nights.

Miranda has dated only a few black men over the last fifteen years; but after one or two dates, they never called again, which led her to assume black women of her caliber intimidated black men.

This was confirmed (in her mind) after one black jerk said, at the end of their first and only date, that if he wanted to date a white woman, he'd find a real one. Miranda took that as a compliment. If Mr. Right turned out to be white, she was okay with that.

The truth is, Miranda feels more comfortable around whites, which is why she lives in a predominantly white area. She grew up in a predominantly white neighborhood and attended predominantly white schools where she had been one of a handful of blacks. She hadn't stayed in touch with her black classmates, and only occasionally wondered what had become of them.

Although Miranda's midwestern city is one of the most segregated cities in the nation, she swears she has never personally experienced racism, except for the occasional white ignoramus who disliked blacks. Shoot, there were plenty of blacks she didn't like herself!

She refuses to be manipulated by all that "brother" and "sister" crap blacks use as a crutch. All blacks had to do to overcome white misgivings and negative stereotypes, was to be more prepared and work harder than their white peers. It was just that simple.

Either a person was up to the challenge, and if they weren't, they had no one to blame but the person in the mirror. If they succeeded, the rewards were well worth it. Her impressive career was proof.

More proof was the retirement party three weeks ago for the black vice-president of public affairs. The company bigwigs went all out for McCabe. A rented hotel ballroom, a catered five-course meal, a six-piece jazz band, balloons, and champagne. Miranda had never seen anyone -- let alone a black man -- get such a royal send-off. It definitely beat a 30-year pin from the post office.

When Miranda announced to a small group at the retirement party that she was a proud, card-carrying Republican and had never once voted Democratic, she was secretly pleased by their surprised reactions.

It was a prudent career move, she added, since the firm's biggest client was a staunch Republican. The truth was, Miranda despises being typecast as a black Democrat. She hated the patronizing way the Democrats threw out an occasional ham hock to get the black vote. Just what had Democrats done for black people like her lately?

What was even more aggravating was the way the Republican Party ignored the thousands of blacks who thought the way she did. People who were educated, successful, intelligent, and understood the value of an unregulated free market, free trade, and minimal government regulation. Her lifestyle and stock portfolio was living proof of how well it worked.

When the firm eliminated an entire division last year – mostly blue-collar jobs -- Miranda saw nothing wrong with it. Every company had the right to find cheaper labor, even if that meant outsourcing jobs. Management had an obligation to maximize profits for the company and for stockholders—like herself. Any workers who were displaced had to find new jobs. *It was just that simple.*

On the day Miranda receives an outstanding job review, the firm announces plans to cut another 10,000 jobs to boost profitability. Since the firm employs over 61,000 workers worldwide, Miranda isn't too worried, but assumed the people junior to her should be.

Miranda is the only black person in her department, but that small detail hardly causes a wrinkle in her powder-smooth forehead. After chatting with a Human Resources manager, a black woman she was only marginally friendly with, Miranda discovers that she is the only one in her department with a Master's degree.

It feels good to know her job is secure; not that she ever doubted it for one second. Miranda feels appreciated at the firm, gets along well with her coworkers and boss, and always gets excellent performance reviews. She is confident they see her as an equal and a valuable team member.

The following Friday pink slips are handed out in her department, and there is one with Miranda's name on it! Her entire department is being downsized, and the rumor is their jobs are being outsourced to India. No explanations or apologies were issued with the separation package that included three months severance pay.

Miranda packs her belongings in boxes under the watchful eyes of a security guard. She is furious, humiliated, and profoundly confused because she never saw the hammer coming.

A few weeks after she was laid off, Miranda runs into one of her former coworkers, Beth, an accountant who still works for the firm. She tells Miranda that the programmers in Miranda's department were transferred to other branches.

Miranda is stunned. Why wasn't she offered a job when she had the most experience? And why didn't the sister in Human Resources warn her? The look of pity on Beth's face stops Miranda cold before the questions slip out.

Then Beth says something that catches Miranda completely by surprise. She says Miranda should file an EEOC suit against the firm. Two of the senior black accountants in Beth's area were laid off while she and three of the least experienced accountants were shuffled into different jobs. Miranda didn't ask if the three were white. She didn't have to. Beth was.

Eight months after losing her job, Miranda is still unemployed. The few job offers she receives pay a third of what she used to make. Miranda refuses to consider them but is too proud to pound the pavement for a new job, even after her unemployment benefits run out.

Eventually, the headhunters stop calling. A year later Miranda is still unemployed, 35 pounds overweight, and is taking medication for depression. Her savings are exhausted so she is forced to give up her condo and move back home to live with her bewildered parents.

An Epidemic Of Mirandas

Miranda is a classic case of the white-identified black professional. She did everything right. She went to college, graduate school, remained childless and single, and associated with the "right" (white) people. Miranda's false sense of security allowed her to be blind-sided and her career permanently derailed.

There are tens of thousands of male and female Mirandas in America, some of who were raised in predominantly white environments; attended predominantly white schools; and their closest friends and romantic partners -- if they were lucky enough to have any -- were white.

It is understandable that these blacks identify with whites, however, this is a problem for three reasons: (1) They are NOT white, (2) They will NEVER be white, and (3) They believe they are equal to whites (which is never true in a white supremacy system).

White-identified blacks are often fooled by the ease in which they sometimes move about in predominantly white settings. In reality, they are such a small minority, they pose no threat (or competition) to whites.

Unfortunately, white-identified blacks can't tell the difference between tolerance and acceptance. They are so determined to fit in, whites find their admiration and imitation flattering, and thus allow them to be in their company -- as long as the black person **remains white-identified**.

Since most white-identified blacks believe whites are the ONLY people who can validate them, they will do whatever it takes to get white approval and distinguish themselves from the (unwashed) black masses, even if that means reinforcing racial stereotypes against other blacks (and themselves).

Miranda believed the extravagant retirement party for the black vice-president was proof that blacks were equals at her company. She didn't know McCabe had been forced into premature retirement, or that the firm used the bad economy as an opportunity to eliminate the affirmative action positions -- including hers -- created to secure government contracts.

Miranda didn't know about the countless humiliations McCabe had suffered at the hands of his white colleagues. She didn't know that the day after his first promotion a decade ago, McCabe came to work the following morning and found his desk had been moved into a small closet by the white supervisors who resented sharing their office space with a black man.

She never knew McCabe's eternal smile, which earned him the (dubious) nickname of "Smiley," had almost cost him his health and his marriage.

The male and female Mirandas do not understand (or accept) that ***skin color always overrides*** education, degrees, professional credentials, cars, clothes, white lovers, and white spouses when it comes to the CORE pecking order in a white supremacist society.

That's why, when they encounter racism, they have a tendency to ignore it unless they are forced to deal with it. They interpret this denial as confidence and strength, but it is just the opposite. *Denial is the height of weakness.*

The Good Black Is The Most Delusional Of All Blacks

Despite the mountains of overwhelming evidence to the contrary, 'good blacks" like Miranda believe MORE education, degrees, designer clothing, fancier homes, addresses, manners, cars, white spouses, and biracial offspring will accomplish what Michael J. with all his millions failed to do: ***Erase the imaginary stigma of being black.***

'Good blacks' refuse to accept that no one – least of all, a white supremacist – respects any black male or female who is willing to do anything, say anything, be anything, or betray anyone to belong to a club that doesn't want them as a member.

A Healthier, Black-Loving Perspective

The psychological opposite of the "white-identified" black is the **black-identified black**. The black-identified individual sees the world as it really exists and does not blame black people for being the victims of racism. Since they are NOT in denial about racism, they are seldom caught completely off guard because they keep their expectations at a reasonable and realistic level.

They understand that getting along with whites in the workplace does not mean whites see blacks as their equals. This is why most black-identified blacks seldom pursue friendships or relationships with white coworkers outside of work — to the relief of their white coworkers -- and rely on black males and females for their psychological, emotional, and romantic needs.

"The Negro is like a man on a luxury commuter train doing ninety miles an hour. He looks out of the window, along with all the white passengers in their Pullman chairs, and he thinks he's doing ninety, too.

Then he gets to the men's room and looks in the mirror—and he sees he's not really getting anywhere at all. His reflection shows a black man standing there in the white uniform of a dining-car steward. He may get on the 5:10, all right, but he sure won't be getting off at Westport."

-- Malcolm X (1925-1965)

The White Side Plays (Hardball) OFFENSE

Tales From the (White) Relationship Battlefield

"Have you seen what single women have to pick from as partners? I am tired of dating losers, and unemployed, little whiny, mommas-boys." -- Genny, Jacksonville, FL

"A lot of women avoid marriage because they have to take care of the children and the housework, work a 9-5, and wait hand and foot on a husband. Why should they do it? It's a life sentence, and I'm on my 23rd year." Susan, San Antonio, TX

"Why get married, get loaded down with debt, bratty, ungrateful kids, and a wife who nags, complains, every day. Stay single, you keep control of your time, money, sex, without worrying that one day, some judge is going to take everything you earned away from you." -- Lloyd, Westbury, New York

"Women have figured out they don't need a man to have a successful, happy, peaceful life. Life lasts too long to put up with an annoying man, or woman, for that matter." Jan, Corvallis, Oregon

(video responses from a survey polling white viewers on the virtues of single VS married life)

CHAPTER NINE

THE INTERRACIAL CON GAME

From CNN specials, sensationalized "black relationship" articles and books, degrading "black" movies, and Internet articles by black authors seeking fame and fortune at any cost, blacks are BOMBARDED by a barrage of negative (and false) information about black-on-black love. On the heels of all this "bad news" comes the media-manufactured cure: *interracial relationships.*

What the mainstream media DOES NOT EXPLAIN is how whites -- with a 50% divorce rate – can be the CURE for what ails the romantically frustrated black male and female?

Americans – regardless of ethnicity, class, income – are plagued by divorce, broken homes, missing and murdered spouses, domestic abuse, emotionally traumatized children, incest, cheating spouses, closet homosexuality, and babies born outside of a two-parent, committed marriage.

Married-with-children white senators and governors are stepping down in disgrace after their homosexual affairs are publicly exposed. More than half of white American women and men are single or divorced, and the men MOST LIKELY to seek a mail order bride from China and Russia are white males.

The explosion of dating ads, websites, and professional "match-making" services aimed at the romantically frustrated single WHITE population reveals the cleverly disguised TRUTH (revealed by the poll on the previous page):

Blacks aren't the ONLY ones having relationship problems.

In spite of this TRUTH, **black-on-black love** is relentlessly demonized by the mainstream media, while interracial (white/black) relationships are promoted as the superior alternative for blacks. Some blacks see the blatant promotion of interracial dating for blacks as a sign of "racial progress" but the message "interracial is better" ***is NEVER aimed at the white population***, nor are whites encouraged to uplift blacks as a "superior alternative" to whites.

Contrary to popular belief -- especially among the black collective -- ***the LEAST COMMON interracial marriage in America is between blacks and whites.*** The MAJORITY of the tiny minority (less than 9%) of whites who marry non-whites marry Asians and Hispanics.

Despite these facts, **black/white interracial dating** has caused MORE bitterness between black males and black females than any other relationship issue, including adultery, divorce, child support, and domestic violence, which leads to a crucial – and self-respecting -- question:

(Note: the following "White Female Supremacist" excerpts were taken from an article (supposedly) written by a white female white supremacist. The authors could not verify the identity or existence of this particular white female, but found the excerpts useful in exposing the mindset and motivations of the racist white female who has sexual intercourse with black males.

* * *

"White Supremacy must embrace Interracial Sex. The fatal flaw of past white supremacy was segregation and Apartheid. By outlawing and preventing Interracial Sex, it led to more pure blacks being bred.

Sex is the second most powerful tool after political/social repression of non-whites. Britain, France, Spain and Portugal conquered non-white colonies first with deception, second with military force, and finally through Interracial Sex."

-- White Female Supremacist (Der Kosmonaut, 1972)

Why are black males and black females fighting so bitterly over the TINY number of whites who are interested in marrying us?

What is the real agenda behind the INTERRACIAL CON GAME? 'Debunking the Top Ten Interracial Myths' should provide some answers -- and some long overdue food for thought.

THE CON

Debunking The Top Ten Interracial Relationship Myths

NOTE: For the purposes of this chapter, "interracial" refers to the most divisive interracial combination in Black America: blacks and whites.

MYTH #1: Black male/black female relationships are more dysfunctional than white male/white female relationships.

Comparing black relationships to white relationships in a white supremacy society – as if all things were equal -- is as logical as comparing black poverty to white poverty; black schools to white schools; or apples to elephants.

FACT: The black family (and the black male/black female relationship) was systematically DESTROYED by over 500 years of institutionalized slavery, racism, and racist media stereotypes. **The white family was not.**

FACT: Black couples have the SAME pressures white couples have **in addition** to the social, psychological, and economic pressures of being black in a racist society. **Whites are NOT penalized for being white; they are rewarded at the expense of non-whites.**

FACT: Blacks are continually bombarded with propaganda about the (superior) benefits of interracial relationships. **Whites are NOT.**

FACT: Black males and females are pitted against each other by the white supremacy system via the economic, educational, social, political, legal, and law enforcement systems that penalize ALL non-whites. ***White males and females are NOT.***

FACT: After African traditions were destroyed during slavery, the ONLY relationship role model for former slaves was the white male/white female relationship.

What TRUTH does all the above reveal about the quality of white male/white female relationships?

"Some people say they date people from another race because they don't see color, and that's the way it is for me.

I also think it's refreshing for a white woman to be with a black man; that adds something to the relationship...

There's more openness, more of a feeling that you don't have to conform to everything society tells you... If I were white, I thought I could be a little happier. I wanted to be white because I was black, and black was never the right color."

-- Dennis Rodman, former NBA ballplayer

MYTH #2: Love is "color-blind."

Unless an individual is LEGALLY BLIND, it is impossible to NOT see the skin color of another individual. It is common for blacks and whites who date interracially to deliberately shun romantic partners of their OWN ethnic group. Yet, most will passionately insist they didn't "choose" to fall in love because "love is color-blind" (even if they are not).

Just because a relationship was not "planned," does not mean our choice of a partner was an accident. Most people would not "accidentally" fall in love with a 400-lb, blind paraplegic, even if that person had all the other qualities they were looking for.

Certainly, a black person who chooses one white lover after another is NOT color-blind, but is **color-obsessed**, acting out a skin color fetish where white skin represents something (superior) that black skin (including theirs) does not. Some blacks date or marry whites exclusively even when they secretly or openly dislike whites in general. The same is true of whites who date or marry blacks exclusively even when they secretly or openly dislike blacks in general.

It is just as common for whites who date and marry blacks to have few to no black friends, and to avoid socializing with blacks of the SAME SEX for fear their black partner will come to his or her senses, and go "back to black" (where even the white person deep down knows they belong).

Most interracial couples are so uncomfortable talking honestly about racism or facing the racial hang-ups that brought them together in the first place, that just initiating a discussion about racism/white supremacy is enough to send them scurrying into deep denial – or out of the room altogether.

They prefer to ignore the 800-lb gorilla (white supremacy) even when it is standing with one huge foot on their (and our) collective necks. If an interracial couple cannot deal honestly with their own racial issues, they will simply spread their sick confusion to their non-white children and any black person within their area of psychological contamination.

In fact, the need (to pretend) to be "color-blind" is actually an ADMISSION of *color obsession*, and a big RED FLAG that the white person making that false claim is probably practicing racism. The black person who claims to be "color-blind" -- even while they are being VICTIMIZED because of their skin color -- clearly illustrates his or her white-identified, confused mindset.

Otherwise, why deny the ability to see color unless color has some negative associations -- or provokes feelings of guilt or shame?

It is possible (but unlikely) for whites and blacks to be attracted to each other where skin color fetishes, racial and sexual stereotypes, and self-hatred issues played NO major role in their initial attraction, but eventually that interracial couple will have to face the harsh realities that are IMPOSSIBLE to ignore in a white supremacy society:

Color Always Matters.

A Bratter and King study in 2008 found White/White and Black/Black marriages have the same divorce rates;

Black husband/White wife marriages were twice as likely to divorce as White/White couples and Black/Black couples, and had higher divorce rates than Black wife/White husband marriages.

(SOURCE:http://docs.google.com/viewer?a=v&q=cache:1NZ6fP5sycEJ)

MYTH #3: Interracial couples are more committed than black or white couples because they have to be.

It is difficult to prove the "commitment" argument, when the divorce rate for interracial marriages is higher than same-ethnic group marriages. According to the 'Bratter and King' Study (on the previous page) the marriages MOST LIKELY to end in divorce were black husband/white wife marriages. Assuming this study is correct, here are some possible (but unscientific) reasons:

- Many black male/white female couples marry at younger ages, based on societal and sexual stereotypes like the black male sexual prowess ("swagger"), or the perceived social status of white females. It is common for young (immature) interracial couples to rebel (get revenge) against social customs, white society, or white parents (black parents are seldom the targets). However, once reality intrudes on the fantasies that brought them together, these marriages often collapse.
- Lower-income black males are usually limited to marrying lower-income white females, since the majority of middle and upper-income white females prefer white males. These interracial marriages have the added strain of financial difficulties and pressures from family and society in general.
- The highly protected status of the white male (in a white supremacy society) makes him less likely to be penalized for his romantic choices.
- Black females who marry white males tend to be educated with equal or greater status, education, and income. These couples also tend to wait longer to get married, giving them greater financial stability and life experience.
- White males are more particular about the quality and compatibility of the black females they marry (she must be white-identified). The black female must bring more to the table since her "black-ness" is NOT seen as an asset -- UNLIKE the black male who is usually less concerned about the quality of white female he marries because her white-ness is automatically seen as an asset, and she often only needs to bring her "white-ness" to the marital table.
- Since all females and non-white males have been PROGRAMMED to submit to white male domination, it may be easier for the black female to submit to her white husband than a (powerless) black one. It does NOT matter if the black wife has a dominant personality; she is still submissive to white supremacy. The reverse may be true in a black husband/white wife couple.
- Unless the black male is already white-identified, he may eventually resent (and rebel against) his more powerful AND privileged white female partner, who expects him to submit to her white reality and value system. It does NOT matter if that black male abuses that white female; at all times and in all places, she is the most powerful person, and at any given time she can pull the plug on him -- and their relationship.

"Now we come to the importance of bi-racial children for the White Supremacy Project.

First, lighter babies are produced. The children of black males and white females will be educated to hate blacks.

They will be raised in all-white settings. The children will date and sex whites. Finally, these children will marry and have kids with whites. Their offspring will turn white.

It is possible for black males to have sex with white females and have no impact on the white population. When the kids of interracial unions are raised by whites, the numbers will be regained.

The end result is the white population increases, the black population decreases. From the black male perspective, interracial sex is a form of racial suicide."

-- White Female Supremacist (Der Kosmonaut, 1972)

- If the white female's MAIN reason for marrying a black male is rebellion, curiosity, sex, money, or to enrich her genetics by having more melanated children (producing color), she is more likely to divorce the black male after her "mission" has been accomplished, or the thrill has worn off.

MYTH #4: More interracial sex and breeding -- "the browning of America" -- will eventually end racism.

This belief is anti-historical wishful thinking, and ignores the 400-year legacy of American slavery and the REALITIES of the global white supremacy system.

One only has to look at Brazil and other Latin American countries with a large population of **non-whites who have a white parent (NWWP)** to see the white minority STILL rules the black and NWWP majority who are stuck at the economic and educational bottom.

In South Africa, there were (and still are) separations between the ruling white class, the oppressed black class, and the "coloureds" **(NWWP)** who get a few more crumbs than blacks. Even in America, a small white minority controls the white AND the non-white majority.

> *"In the UK (United Kingdom) interracial marriage has created a lot of confused black people who think they are white -- until some white person calls them a "nigger" and then they are shocked." – Michael, 37, health care worker, UK*

It is the **QUALITY**, not the quantity (of numbers) that counts the most. If the majority of the (non-white) population are (deliberately) deprived economically and educationally, the majority will lack the resources OR the will to resist oppression by the (white) minority.

The Smaller The White Minority, The Greater The Need To Oppress The Non-White Majority

When the white minority is greatly outnumbered, they will feel MORE threatened and MORE determined to do whatever they deem necessary -- no matter how cruel, wicked, unjust, or immoral -- to maintain their economic, educational, and political DOMINATION over non-whites.

More non-white children with a white parent (**(NWWP)** in America will NOT reduce OR eliminate racism, just like the election of the first identifiably "black" president in 2008 DID NOT reduce racism. In fact, Obama's election has INCREASED overt racism and resentment from the white collective.

The non-white person with a white parent **(NWWP)** ***historicall***y has been used by the white minority as a "buffer" between privileged whites and oppressed non-whites because he or she is MORE likely to promote white supremacy than OPPOSE it since their "white side" offers more privileges.

The Children Born Of Black Male/White Female Unions:

Since the majority of sexual relationships between blacks and whites involve black males and white females, and the majority of these unions will not last, most non-white children with a white parent and a black parent are more likely:

1. to be raised by single white mothers
2. to have a closer, more sympathetic bond with the white side of their family, in particular, white females
3. to be estranged or hostile toward their black fathers
4. to be white-identified (seek white validation)
5. to distance themselves from the black side of the family
6. to resent their "mixed" heritage
7. to be "pro-white" and "anti-black"
8. to breed with whites (or other non-whites with a white parent)
9. to produce offspring (children and grandchildren) that will look "white" and who will be able to merge ***undetected*** with the white population.

The Children Born Of Black Female/White Male Unions:

A similar situation occurs when the mother is black and the father is white because white males usually marry black females who are white-identified. This almost guarantees that the children born into those unions will prefer white friends, lovers and spouses. As a result, the so-called "browning" soon becomes more beige, then whiter by the 2nd or 3rd generation.

Contrary to the "melting pot myth," MORE interracial breeding between blacks and whites actually LENGTHENS and STRENGTHENS the reign of white supremacy; destroys black genetics; destroys any possibility of building a black economic/business base (BLACK POWER); and reduces the black population – the main reasons the white supremacy system promotes interracial sex for blacks.

Are Black People Enemies OR Allies of White Supremacy?

The future generations spawned from these black/white unions will produce people who are classified as "white" who will be more fertile, resulting in an INCREASE in overall white fertility, which will possibly extend the life of **White Supremacy** and **Black Oppression.**

Therefore, the black male or female who breeds with a white male or female represents the single biggest threat to black liberation and the biggest non-white ally of racism/white supremacy.

"The melting pot of the races began around the northern perimeter. The end result was always the same:

The Blacks were pushed to the bottom of the social, economic and political ladder whenever the Asians (meaning whites) and their mulatto offspring gained control.

This scheme of weakening the Blacks by turning their half-white brothers against them cannot be overemphasized because it began in the early times and it became the universal practice of whites, and is still one of the cornerstones in the edifice of white power..."

-- Chancellor Williams, "Destruction of Black Civilization -- Chapter II: Ethiopia's Oldest Daughter: Egypt. pg. 61."

Aboriginal Bathurst Island men

Interracial Sex Between Whites and Non-Whites = The Systematic Destruction Of Non-White People

Aborigines make up about 2% of Australia's population but they suffer disproportionately high rates of imprisonment and ill-health." (SOURCE: 'Aboriginal children 'starving,' welfare workers say' by Phil Mercer, BBC News)

The ORIGINAL (native) people that once populated Australia have become a micro-minority on their own continent due to European colonization and INTERRACIAL SEX with whites, which led to the genetic, cultural, and psychological destruction of the Aboriginal people.

This dynamic has played out for hundreds of years, whenever non-whites and Europeans cross paths, from North America Latin America, the Fugi Islands; Africa, South Africa, the Australian to Haiti and Hawaii.

Interracial sex between whites and non-whites ALWAYS leads to non-white educational, economic, and political oppression; the genetic destruction of non-white populations; and MORE not LESS racism. The proof: the original Australian Aborigines who once populated Australia are now less than 2% of the population.

Native Americans from the Cherokee, Cheyenne, Choctaw, Comanche, Iroquois, and Muscogee tribes -- Photos date from 1868 to 1924

The Non-White Genocide Scoreboard:

- 100 million people for North American Indians (blacks)
- 18 million for the area north of Mexico
- 28 million from the African Holocaust

"In 1910, the total population of North American Indians was about 400,000, down from about 18 -19 million in 1492." -- David Stannard in 'American Holocaust'

"The Indian was thought as less than human and worthy only of extermination. We did shoot down defenseless men, and women and children at places like Camp Grant, Sand Creek, and Wounded Knee. We did feed strychnine to red warriors. We did set whole villages of people out naked to freeze in the iron cold of Montana winters. And we did confine thousands in what amounted to concentration camps." — The Indian Wars of the West, 1934

Native Americans And The Interracial Sex Connection

The 2009 U.S. Census estimates the Native American population -- that once numbered in the tens of millions -- is currently ***only one percent of the 307 million people in America.***

Native Americans marry whites at a higher rate (56%) than any other non-white population in the U.S. If this sad trend continues, the Native American people will eventually ***breed themselves out of existence.***

"I wish to be acknowledged not as Black but as white...who but a white woman could do this for me? By loving me she proves that I am worthy of white love. I am loved like a white man. I am a white man.

Her noble love takes me onto the road of self-realization – I marry white culture, white beauty, white whiteness. When my restless hands grasp those white breasts, they grasp white civilization and dignity and make them mine." – 'Black Skin, White Masks,' Frantz Fanon (1952)

Frantz Fanon, a trained black psychiatrist, wrote about the feelings of dependency and inadequacy that Black people experience in a White world.

As a result of the inferiority complex programmed into the minds of the black male, he will try to appropriate and imitate the cultural code of the colonizer (and his oppressors).

(Unfortunately, Fanon fell prey to his own diagnosed illness: he married a white female).

MYTH #5: Black males are "forced" to date/marry white females because black females are defective (inferior).

This is the MOST divisive (and hurtful) myth because it automatically implies that black females are so INFERIOR in character and appearance, that a black male seeking an attractive, quality mate is FORCED to date outside his race. Since the majority of black males marry black females, this racist myth -- like all interracial myths -- fails the ultimate test of LOGIC.

"The (defective) black female made me date outside my race."

A popular black radio talk program was debating the pros and cons of interracial dating. A 30-something black male caller, Bill, admitted he only dated white women. When the host asked him why, Bill said, *"Black girls rejected me in high school because I was too dark."*

Tom, a white male, told a similar tale when he was interviewed by a computer industry publication. He recalled being shunned and ridiculed by the pretty, popular girls in his high school because, *"I was a short, skinny nerd."*

Tom's best friend, John, was Asian-American, and just as unpopular with the handful of Asian girls at their high school who preferred white males. *"Instead of dating, John and I spent most evenings and weekends on our passion: writing and debugging computer programs."*

In their freshmen year of college, they wrote a program that was purchased by a major software firm. After graduation, Tom and John started their own software company, and today, both men are millionaires. Both men are also married, with children.

Tom married the same blonde, cheerleader-type that rejected him in high school. John married an Asian beauty contest winner. Do Tom and John remember being the two most unpopular "nerds" in high school? Absolutely. Did that experience make them want to 'get even' by rejecting all the women in their race? ***Absolutely NOT.***

Bill's reasons for having a 'Jim Crow' (whites-only) dating policy was NOT caused by any TEENAGED black girls who rejected him in high school; it was caused by his black inferiority complex -- which may explain why Bill is on his third interracial relationship in five years: ***because he is dating white females for the wrong reasons.***

Bill's need to blame black females for his OWN behavior is PROOF he knows his behavior is incorrect. Otherwise, there would be NO need for Bill to blame black females OR anyone else.

Unlike Bill, Tom and John had not been programmed to dislike themselves or their own ethnic group -- so they had no need to condemn OR reject their female mirror images.

"Now, you integration-minded Negroes are trying to force yourselves on your former slave master, trying to make him accept you in his drawing room; you want to hang out with his women rather than the women of your own kind...

Because only a man who is ashamed of what he is will marry out of his race. There has to be something wrong when a man or woman leaves his own people and marries somebody of another kind. Men who are proud of being black marry black women; women who are proud of being black marry black men.

This is particularly true when you realize that these Negroes who go for integration and intermarriage are linking up with the very people who lynched their fathers, raped their mothers, and put their kid sisters in the kitchen to scrub floors."

-- Malcolm X being interviewed by Louis Lomax (1963)

Black Male Homosexuals NOT Immune to "Jungle Fever"

The same (self-hating) dynamic is at work for the homosexual black male who PREFERS homosexual relationships with white males -- ***despite the rampant racism within the white homosexual community.***

According to Keith Boykin, a "homosexual rights" advocate/columnist who frequently writes about the black homosexual community, some black male homosexuals refuse to date black males.

Referring to a black male acquaintance, Boykin writes: *"He did not want to date a black man. He wanted a white man instead. To catch his eye, a black man would have to be twice as gorgeous and twice as successful as an average white man."*

Ironically, the self-hating homosexual black male who discriminates against other black males is often reluctant to talk about his sexual encounters with white males. Looking back, he may realize that he was just a sexual object to the racist white male, and feels degraded by the sexual contact.

Even this "realization" may not deter the most self-hating homosexual black male from seeking white partners because they represent the ONLY source of white validation he so desperately needs. This irrational, self-destructive mentality is common among blacks infected with "jungle fever."

Revisiting Dennis Rodman's "explanation" for dating interracially:

> *"Some people say they date people from another race because they don't see color, and that's the way it is for me. I also think it's refreshing for a white woman to be with a black man; that adds something to the relationship...there's more openness, more of a feeling that you don't have to conform to everything society tells you...if I were white, I thought I could be a little happier. I wanted to be white because I was black, and black was never the right color."*

***

If we flipped Rodman's contradictory script to explain why some black male homosexuals only "date" white males, it might read something like this:

> *"Some people say they date people from another race because they don't see color, and that's the way it is for me. I also think it's refreshing for a white man to be with a black man; that adds something to the relationship. There's more openness, more of a feeling that you don't have to conform to everything society tells you...if I were white, I thought I could be a little happier. I wanted to be white because I was black, and black was never the right color."*

Perhaps, "the (defective) black female" excuse should be expanded to include "the (defective) black male homosexual made me date a white male" excuse.

"White females engaging in Interracial Sex is White Supremacy with a Human Face. The white female has more trust and credibility among black males than the white male does. The white female can get away with racism and racial oppression against the black male, without arousing the anger and bitterness in black males that white males do.

The black male loves, lusts after, and desires the white female. The WF will f*ck and breed with Niggers but she is well aware of her whiteness. WF sees herself superior to BF. Indeed WF knows that her power over BM is her white skin. WF knows that if she didn't have white skin, BM would not be interested in her.

BM does not want his children to face racism and discrimination. BM desires to have white kids. He knows that's impossible but wants to have white grandchildren and white descendants.

Finally for BM, IR Sex is a desperate attempt to be white. Still, no matter how many WF he f*cks, he remains a Nigger to the day he dies. His attempt to do so is simply a form of racial suicide.

-- White Female Supremacist (Der Kosmonaut, 1972)

MYTH #6: White females are "more supportive" than black females.

"White women treat they man like a king and black women feel like they ain't gotta do that shit." – rapper "Slim Thug" in a 2010 Vibe magazine interview

"It's like a white woman told me once....black women treat their men like property; white women treat their men like people even if they don't always agree." – BiggLoc, black male poster on black website

These comments are not nearly as surprising as the impressive number of black males who have first-hand knowledge of the way white females treat white males ***behind closed doors.***

However, just for argument's sake, if Slim Thug is correct when he says, *"white women treat they men like a king..."* why is the white husband/white wife divorce rate over 50%? How would Slim explain the even higher black husband/white wife divorce rate, which is HIGHER than the black husband/black wife divorce rate? (see Bratter and King study, page 138).

If the white female is MORE supportive than the black female, and black husband/white wife couples have a HIGHER divorce rate than black husband/black wife couples, there can be ONLY be one logical conclusion: ***the black male must be the least supportive partner.*** It is this kind of (false) logic that illustrates the dangers of black people stereotyping other black people.

Black Males Who Sing The Praises Of White Females

Certainly, any black male who has been SUPPORTED by a black mother, sister, aunt, or grandmother for the ***first eighteen (or more) years of his life*** -- but dares to uplifts white females above black females -- is suffering from terminal memory LOSS at best -- or is at the very worst, ***a dishonest, dishonorable, and ungrateful individual.***

Black Males Who Use Interracial Relationships As A Weapon

The threat of having an interracial relationship has become the weapon of choice for the (powerless) black male to control (or punish) the "uppity" black female. He is powerless to limit her educational or economic opportunities. He is powerless to imprison her OR make her a social outcast, but he can REJECT her romantically and make a public spectacle of himself while doing it.

Some black males resent black females for their alleged independence, because it makes them feel they are the only men in America who are NOT in a superior position over their women. Some may resent the black female's unwillingness to "submit" to him as an "inferior" person, because they naively believe the white female willingly submits to the white male.

However -- if white females WILLINGLY SUBMITTED to white male domination, there would be NO (white) women's liberation/ feminist movements against white male sexism, and there would definitely be no white females having sex with black males.

Since the "white females are more supportive" myth is one of the most DIVISIVE (and false) interracial myths, it is time to DEFINE what a "supportive" female is VERSUS one who is not.

Is "Supportive" Sharing White Wealth With Black Males? Rich White Females Do Not Marry Rich OR Poor Black Males

With a few exceptions, wealthy white females DO NOT date OR marry black males. Since most marriages occur between people of the same ethnic and socioeconomic background, this is not surprising. ***However, there is ONE glaring exception: rich and famous black males.***

Rich and famous black males are the MOST LIKELY GROUP in America to marry DOWN. Some well-known examples are the stripper and flight attendant wives of Montel Williams; the nanny wife of Tiger Woods; the waitress wife of OJ Simpson; and the receptionist wife of the late Michael Jackson.

What is NOT surprising is once the former working-class white wives divorce their rich black husbands, they usually take their newfound wealth back to the white community and into the arms of a white male.

When the authors attempted to flip that particular script, we failed to turn up a single example of a rich white female who married the black male equivalent of a stripper, nanny, waitress, or receptionist; or a rich white male who married a black female stripper, waitress, babysitter, or receptionist.

We were also unable to find an example of a rich black female who married the white male equivalent of a stripper, nanny, waitress, or receptionist. To add insult to financial injury, rich black male celebrities are almost always excluded from the dating and marriage pool of rich white females, who overwhelmingly date and marry white males.

Perhaps, these affluent white ladies feel that marrying a black male of any economic, educational, or professional status is still "marrying down." Unlike their poorer white sisters, rich white females have no financial incentive to trade their "whiteness" for the wealth of a white-status-seeking black male.

Is "Supportive" Transforming A Black Actor (Like Denzel) Into A Tom Cruise, Richard Gere, or Brad Pitt?

While white females, individually, might occasionally admire a black male actor (like Denzel), they overwhelmingly **PREFER** white males as their **sex symbols. Even popular black actors (like Denzel) are NEVER chosen as the sex symbols of the white female collective.**

Every black actor who has become a "sex symbol" owes his success to his first and ONLY real fan base: *black females*. Sadly, all too many black male "sex symbols" show their GRATITUDE by dating and marrying anyone BUT a black female.

Is "Supportive" Seeing Black Males As The Social And Romantic Equals Of White Males?

A 20/20 Survey On Interracial Dating

In 2006, on ABC's 20/20 TV program, host John Stossel did a special on the book, *'Freakonomics,'* which revealed the following about interracial dating: white women overwhelmingly preferred white males while dating online (97% of the time). To get the same responses from a white female that a white male would receive:

- A Hispanic male had to make $77,000 more than a white male
- An unattractive male had to earn $150,000 more than an attractive male
- A Black male had to make $154,000 more than a white male
- An Asian male had to make $247,000 more than a white male

The conclusion: the VAST majority of white females preferred white males when seeking a SERIOUS partner for marriage and reproduction.

> *"They (black women) resent our taking their men. But in truth, black sisters, we're after the sex, not the ring, and these guys aren't the marrying kind anyway." – Susan C. Bakos, 'A White Woman Explains Why She Prefers Black Men.'*

Is "Supportive" Pulling A Brother Up the Corporate Ladder?

Thanks to affirmative action, white females are rocketing up the corporate ladder, while black males are falling off in record numbers. Black males – regardless of education and experience – have the highest unemployment rate in America -- even higher than illegal immigrants who do NOT SPEAK ENGLISH. In contrast, white females are the MOST LIKELY people in America to be employed even compared to white males.

According to the US Labor Department, the biggest beneficiaries of affirmative action programs were white females, who ALSO represent some of the most VOCAL opposition to the same policies that opened employment doors for ***qualified black males***.

The number of white females holding executive positions in Corporate America with the ability (power) to hire and fire employees has skyrocketed, but few use that power to ***employ or promote black males.***

Unfortunately, these cold, hard FACTS have done little to dispel the myth of the ***"supportive white female"*** among the black male collective who conveniently ignore one more FACT:

It's SEXISM – not RACISM – that makes the upwardly mobile white female HOT around her starched white collar.

Is "Supportive" Accusing Black Males Of Crimes They Didn't Commit?

A (very) incomplete and infamous list of white females who FALSELY accused black males of crimes they didn't commit:

(1955) Carolyn Bryant, white female, accused Emmett Till, 14, visiting relatives in Money, Mississippi, of "whistling" at her. Till was beaten, tortured, and murdered by a mob of white males, who were acquitted by an all-white jury (of males AND females) even after admitting they killed Till to *"make an example of him."*

(1994) Susan Smith, white female, drove her auto into a lake while the children slept in their car seats, initially reporting to police that she had been carjacked by a black man. Nine days later, after an intensive, heavily publicized nationwide search, Smith confessed to drowning her children.

(1996) Elise Makdessis, white female, who prosecutors alleged had conspired with her (white husband, Eddie), to file a false sexual harassment lawsuit against the Navy. Earlier, it was claimed that Elise made two videotapes in which she accused several coworkers at the Oceana Naval Air Station (Virginia). One of the accused was Quincy Brown, 37, a black male employee.

Prosecutors alleged that Elise and Eddie Makdessis lured Brown to their apartment to have sex with Elise, during which Elise asked to be tied up after the sex act. Eddie later claimed to police that he was knocked unconscious, and awakened to find Brown raping and stabbing his wife. He said he shot Brown in self-defense then called 9-11.

After a ten-year investigation, Eddie Makdessis, was arrested and charged with the murder of his wife. Prosecutors alleged at his trial that after Brown and caught Brown with his wife, shot Brown to death and stabbed his wife to death.

Prosecutors claimed that Makdessis's plot to get insurance money by first murdering Brown, killing his wife with a knife, washing the knife, than planting it in Brown's hand. On March 2006, Makdessi was convicted of two counts of first-degree murder and sentenced to life in prison. Makdessi is planning an appeal.

(2007) Amanda Knox, white female American exchange student in Italy, was convicted in the 2007 stabbing death of her British roommate, Meredith Kercher. Knox initially tried to pin the blame on a reggae club owner, Patrick L., a black male, who was arrested for murder but released after his alibi checked out.

(2008) Ashley Todd, white female Republican, claimed that was assaulted by a black male "Obama supporter" who carved a backwards "B" on her face. She later admitted she had fabricated (LIED) and had assaulted herself.

(2009) Bonnie Sweeten, white female, claimed two black men had abducted her and her nine-year-old daughter, after a fender-bender, and stuffed them into the trunk of a black Cadillac. *"It's a terrifying thing for a community to hear that two black men in a black Cadillac grabbed a (white) woman and her daughter,"* said Bucks County District Attorney, Michelle Henry.

It was later discovered that the "abduction" was a hoax and that Sweeten had fled to Disney World with her daughter. Sweeten, was later indicted for allegedly stealing $700,000 from her employer, a Bucks County law firm.

(2010) Jill Quigg, a white female, actress, was charged with burglary, after she and a white male accomplice allegedly broke into a neighbor's apartment, and blamed the crime on a black man.

(2011) Unidentified white female, a Catholic nun, falsely reported being raped by a 6'4," 250 lb. black male but later recanted her story, which she created to cover up a sexual relationship with a non-white male.

How many black males have been convicted AND/OR executed after being falsely accused by white females? (The authors were unable to find a single case of a black female who blamed a black male for a crime she committed).

Is "Supportive" Championing the Civil Rights Of Black Males?

Since only a tiny minority of white females get involved in civil rights issues, it is safe (and accurate) to state that the main issues that negatively impact black males -- unemployment, police brutality, unjust incarceration, inferior schools, and murder-by-cop -- receive little to no support from influential white-female-headed organizations OR from powerful, high-profile white females.

White females also make up the MAJORITY of white jurors who convict black males with little or no evidence, OR acquit white policemen who are accused of beating or murdering unarmed black males.

If young white males were dying at the same rate as young black males -- that EVERY powerful white-female-headed organization in the nation would be using ALL their financial and political "muscle" to solve the problem.

Is "Supportive" Pursuing Sex with Black Males Under The Guise Of Pursuing Justice?

It is common for the anti-racism-activist white female to be sexually involved with black males, which leads to an obvious question: ***What is the true agenda of the 'anti-racist' white female activist? Justice or sexual intercourse with black males?***

> *"Anti-racist" white female author, Dr. Tochluk, revealed a personal story during an interview on the C.O.W.S. internet radio show in August 2010. After a particular black male refused to date her because she was white, she said: "At that time I could not see why the injury to black women was important, or more correctly, I did not want to care about what this man saw and what black women would feel. I could not grasp why what someone else thought about our potential relationship made a difference."*
> **(SOURCE:** *www.contextofwhitesupremacy.com)*

Rosa Parks (1913 – 2005), "the first lady of civil rights", and "the mother of the freedom movement." Nine months before Parks refused to give up her seat, 15-year-old Claudette Colvin refused to give up her bus seat on the same bus system. Rosa Parks' act of defiance -- and her involvement with civil rights leaders, like Dr. Martin Luther King, Jr. -- help to launch the national civil rights movement.

Is "Supportive" Opposing The Practice Of Racism?

In September 2010, the National Federation of Republican Women (NFRW) held its annual fall Board of Directors meeting in Charleston, S.C., called "The Southern Experience."

South Carolina Senate President, Glenn McConnell, dressed up as a confederate soldier, flanked by two grinning black males dressed as "slaves." Since there was no PUBLIC CONDEMNATION of the racist spectacle by this well-heeled group of professional, educated WHITE FEMALES, it is reasonable AND logical to assume they NOT only found African slavery a source of entertainment, it is quote possible some actually long for a return to the "good old days."

Is "Supportive" Raising White Children Who Will Oppose The System Of Racism/White Supremacy?

If white females are the mothers, civilizers, teachers, and the transferrers of values for white children, are they teaching them to oppose white supremacy OR to continue practicing it to maintain their white privileges?

Would raising anti-racist white children be the ULTIMATE FORM OF SUPPORT by the white female?"

The "Unsupportive" Black Female"

The flip side of the "supportive" white female is "the unsupportive black female" who raised, loved, nurtured, provided for, protected, and financed the college educations of black boys, often without the assistance of their fathers.

The ***"unsupportive" black female*** is the **WORKHORSE OF EVERY BLACK ORGANIZATION** from churches, homeless shelters, and food pantries to black grassroots organizations and national foundations.

The ***"unsupportive" black female*** marches, protests, petitions, donates, and devotes countless BLACK-WOMAN-HOURS to assist, defend, finance, and **SUPPORT THE RIGHTS OF BLACK MALES**.

An ***"unsupportive" black female*** college student is credited (by some) with starting the petition that launched a national movement for the **Jena Six** – six black teenaged boys from Jena, Louisiana who were being railroaded into prison for a simple schoolyard fight in 2006.

The majority of people who descended upon Jena, a small dusty Louisiana town, arrived in cars, buses, and planes to rally around six black boys THEY DIDN'T KNOW FROM A HOLE IN THE GROUND were ***BLACK -- not white, Hispanic, or Asian females.***

Black children are dying on the streets of America on a daily basis, YET the response from the "supportive" white female is SILENCE -- even from those with non-white, black children.

"I am 54 years old and I remember the luxury car commercials and the messages were always the same: buy this Cadillac, and you'll be a successful man with high status, and you'll be popular with blonde white women!

As a little boy I could never figure out why there was always a white woman with blond hair sitting in the passenger side of the car.

Naturally, when we consider that our black fathers and grandfathers watched those commercials at least ten times a day before they became grown men, we see that this "formula" for success and status was still ingrained into the black man's psyche and subconscious."

– Frank, 54, sales representative, Memphis, TN

MYTH #7: Black males prefer white females because they are more attractive than black females.

At the risk of sounding cruel, it is OBVIOUS to even the casual observer of the typical black male/white female couple that beauty (or even average attractiveness) is NOT a requirement when it comes to white females.

In the mind of a white-validation-seeking, low-self-esteemed black male, a white female will always be superior to a black female, regardless of the black female's beauty, intelligence, accomplishments, or attitude. A black female cannot give him the kind of (white) validation he so desperately craves because she has no more status than he has.

To the self-hating, white-validation-seeking black male, adding a black female to his romantic equation is too much black (self).

The Value Of White Females To The Low-Self-Esteemed, Status-Seeking Black Male

According to Dr. Levin (a black psychiatrist), some black males find it hard to connect with the black female because she *"serves as the symbol of his failure."*

For the white-status-seeking, low-self-esteemed, non-white male -- be he black, Hispanic, Native American, or Asian -- the white female is a highly visible human passport of acceptance into the white world and a "soothing lotion" for his wounded pride and ego.

The physical attractiveness, intelligence, or accomplishments of his white female "prize" are less important than her white status, which explains why the majority of rich black males who marry white ***almost always marry down.***

There is a very long list of marriages between wealthy black males and typically unaccomplished, undistinguished, and often unattractive white female waitresses, receptionists, flight attendants, strippers, and nannies, who bring little to the marital table other than their youth (fertility) and white skin.

By "possessing" a white female, the status-seeking, low-self-esteemed black male can IMAGINE he is the equal of the most powerful and most privileged male in America: ***the white male.***

> *"If I were white, I thought I could be a little happier. I wanted to be white because I was black, and black was never the right color."*
>
> *-- Dennis Rodman, former NBA Player*

If white supremacy was transformed overnight into a "system of purple supremacy," and the most privileged females had PURPLE SKIN, they would be the most beautiful and most desirable females in the world to the low-self-esteemed, status-seeking, NON-PURPLE male.

Speaking about an interview with Ms Fairy Tale, a black female who said she was "glad" she had a "relationship" with a white man, Reneathia Tate, author of "Pieces of a Puzzle (1997), writes:

"Black females will talk (or even brag) they had sex with black males to everyone, particularly other black females like myself.

But she (Ms Fairy Tale) really did not want to remember or talk about all of her experience (particularly the sex part) with this white man.

Ms. Fairy Tale, like most black females (who had sex with white men), had a vague feeling that they were either robbed or raped after these terrible experiences."

Myth #8: Black females are "too loyal" to black males to have sex with white males.

The Biggest Sex Secret In Black America: *Black Females Having Sexual Intercourse With White Males*

Black females often condemn black males who date or marry white females, but some are just as guilty of the same "crime:" *talking black and sleeping white.*

The white male's shameful history of rape, economic exploitation, and degradation of black females drives some black females to hide their sexual affairs with white males from "prying eyes."

Black females know many whites and blacks (especially black males) assume a black female who is having sexual intercourse with a white male is either prostituting herself (exchanging sex for money, favors, or material things), or is being sexually exploited by the white male (whoring for free).

The black female who sexually submits to a white male (or a series of white males) often discovers she is "involved" with a racist who has no intentions of making a serious commitment and who dislikes blacks in general. Her biggest fear is being duped into the role of a "white man's whore" – and in most cases, her fears are justified.

In fact, most interracial "relationships" between black females and white males are simply a CONTINUATION of the same (white supremacy) sexual exploitation/power dynamic that began during slavery: *the (inferior) black person submitting to the will (and sexual exploitation) of the (superior) white person -- which often includes verbal and physical abuse.*

For this reason, some black females often look back on sex with white males with much shame and regret, and may be EXTREMELY RELUCTANT to admit any prior sexual involvement with white males.

Many black females resent black male/white female relationships because the white female has a stronger "hand" (more power) and is treated with more respect in the black/white sexual power dynamic than the black female.

It is possible for a black female and a white male to be attracted to each other for the same reasons any man or woman is attracted to each other, but "love" is seldom the emotion that fuels the SECRET SEX RELATIONSHIPS between black females and white males (or black males and white females).

The (Inferior) Position of the Black Female in the Interracial "Dating Game"

Logically speaking, if the lightest female is the most superior in a white supremacy system, the darkest female must be the most inferior. Following this LOGIC, the black (and non-white) male who is seeking white acceptance and status will see the black female as the last LOGICAL choice.

The rejection of black females by black and non-white males reflects MORE on their low self-esteem -- courtesy of their white supremacy programming -- than it does on the true desirability of the black female.

Black Females Who Date White Males Exclusively

The black female, due to her (artificially created) inferior position, may seek alternative forms of validation if black males collectively do NOT validate her worth.

For some black females, an interracial relationship with a white male ***offers the ultimate white validation*** -- and serves as proof to her bruised and battered ego -- and to the rest of the world -- that she is NOT the worthless, undesirable creature that white society (and some black males) have made her out to be.

Her uniquely beautiful racial characteristics are often seen as "exotic" by her non-black admirers, making her feel MORE APPRECIATED than she is by the males in her own community.

The dark and brown-skinned black female who does not fit the "black?" beauty standard (light skin, long hair, European features) may pursue a relationship with the white male for the same reason the DEVALUED white female -- who does not fit the white beauty standard -- seeks a relationship with a black male: ***to be validated as an attractive, desirable woman.***

Their motto – *"it is better to be 'exotic' than disregarded altogether"* – should be a clear warning to the white males and black males who oppose interracial dating by the women of their race.

Black Females Who Refuse To Date Non-Black Males

Overall, black females are **LESS likely to date outside their group** than Asian, Hispanic, Native Americans, and white females. Some "detractors" claim this is due to the black female's lack of "appeal" BUT the simple and well-known FACT is: ***most black females prefer black males.***

The hyper-masculine, soulful image of the black male makes it difficult for non-black males to compete in the sexual or romantic arena for the attention of black females -- something non-black males are well aware of.

A significant number of black females -- especially the black female who understands the connection between racism and interracial sex -- shun interracial relationships despite a shortage of black males to marry. They would rather live their lives as a single female than give in to the racist media's interracial PROPAGANDA that "white is better."

The less confused, black-identified black female knows that as long as white supremacy exists, having interracial sex with white males (or females) makes her PART of the problem, NOT part of the collective solution.

And the authors wholeheartedly agree.

MYTH #9: Black females are jealous of white females.

This accusation is often leveled at black females by white females and by black males who are sexually involved with white females. However, **the true emotion** is NOT jealousy; it is **resentment** -- the same resentment any woman would feel if she was unfairly stereotyped and ***rejected by the men of her own group***.

In reality, the ***"jealous black female"*** is the MOST TOLERANT of interracial relationships, and is the person MOST LIKELY to welcome a black male/white female couple to her home.

She is the LEAST likely to disown OR shun a son, grandson, father, uncle, nephew, or neighbor who dates or marries outside his race -- unlike white males and females who are the MOST LIKELY to disown or shun a son or daughter who brings a non-white (especially a black) partner home.

The ***"jealous black female"*** is also the MOST likely to CONTINUE supporting black male entertainers who DO NOT DATE OR MARRY black females, UNLIKE many black males who stopped supporting Halle Berry after her on-and-off-screen sexual relationships with white males. It is a certainty that any white entertainer who refused to date white people would lose the support of their white male AND female audience.

There is one more thing the ***"jealous black female"*** is LESS likely to do: covet the men and babies of another group as her own -- UNLIKE the white female who has a ***well-deserved reputation*** for COVETING (stealing) and claiming black males AND black babies as her own.

It seems that the "jealous black female" may be the LEAST "jealous" when compared to white females, white males, and black males.

MYTH #10: A white person in an interracial relationship CANNOT be a "racist."

This myth is the most deceptive and the most dangerous of all **Ten Interracial Myths** because it gives the interracially-involved black male or female a false sense of security, making them LESS LIKELY to recognize racism and less ABLE to protect themselves ***even when their white partner is practicing racism against them.***

"I was on the Topix message board, reading messages from white women who are with Black men. These women kept insisting that Black women were all jealous of them, and that they were better for Black men than Black women were. There was one woman who was so rabidly racist, it was ridiculous. She was married to a Black man, had Black children, and insisted the only reason her kids came out right is because they were half-white instead of all-black." -- JJ, white female blogger

The "Darker" Side Of Interracial Sex

IR Sex more than anything else will solve the Nigger Question once and for all. More than civil rights and race equality legislation, and more than affirmative action.

Why must White Supremacy embrace IR Sex? The fatal flaw of past white supremacy was segregation. By outlawing and preventing IR Sex, it led to more pure blacks being bred. Separating whites did not erase Niggers.

Second, racism has created a self-hatred among BM that is unsurpassed by the most ardent white racist. IR Sex is the ultimate expression of Nigger self-hatred. BM hates his race so much that he refuses to f*ck and mate with BF. Finally, sex is the second tool after political/social repression of domination. Britain France, Spain, and Portugal conquered colonies first with deception, second with military force and finally through sex.

How does IR Sex lead to racial genocide? Let's take a look at Canada. Whites conquered the First Nations natives first by encouraging them to f*ck and breed with whites. When First Nations natives refused to do so, Canada created the Royal Canadian Mounted Police to defeat them militarily. The children of WF and Native fathers grow up white, most go on to marry whites, and their kids are white. First Nations natives in Canada were given two choices of extermination: The bullet or white sex.

-- White Female Supremacist (Der Kosmonaut, 1972)

Note to the Reader:

"Darker" refers to sexual intercourse OR any sexual contact between "darker-skinned" blacks and "lighter-skinned" whites.

No negative references to the word "darkness" or "dark people" are intended.

"Belly-warmer" was a term used during slavery to describe an African female slave who was used as a temporary sexual toilet by a slave trader or slave-owner.

For example, in the movie, "Roots," a white crew member on a slave ship asked the captain, "Will you be needing a belly warmer tonight?"

(Translation: Did the captain want to RAPE one of the female slaves that night?)

Are Black Females Being Groomed To Be Modern-Day White Men's Whores (And Belly Warmers?)

In 1944, Recy Taylor, a black 24-year-old mother and sharecropper, in Abbeville, Alabama was kidnapped and gang-raped by seven white men as she left church with her friends.

After the horrendous assault, Taylor reported it to the Montgomery branch office of the National Association for the Advancement of Colored People.

A then-unknown Rosa Parks, an NAACP investigator and anti-rape activist, was sent to investigate. Recy Taylor's brutal gang rape led to a nationwide campaign to bring awareness to the rape of black females by white males.

This was a courageous act on the part of both women and their supporters during the the violent era of legalized segregation.

Chapter Ten

A SHORT HISTORY OF THE RAPE OF BLACK FEMALES

Prior to 1972, rape was a capital crime that was punishable by death. ***More than 90% of the executions for rape involved black males*** who had allegedly raped a white female BUT statistics showed the vast majority of rapes in the U.S. involved white males raping black and white females.

About 5% of executions for rape involved a black male who had allegedly raped a black female, and approximately 2% of executions for rape involved a white male who had allegedly raped a white female.

A white male has never been executed for raping a black female in the history of the U.S. -- because white males raping black females was not (and still isn't) considered a crime...despite the overwhelming evidence...

US Senator Strom Thurmond, a white male and a staunch segregationist, never publicly acknowledged his "illegitimate" black daughter, Essie Mae Washington-Williams, while he was alive.

*Ms. Washington-William's mother, Carrie Butler, a black maid who was only 15 at the time she gave birth, led many to believe she was **the victim of rape**.*

***

According to the book, 'At the Dark End of the Street,' by Danielle L. McGuire, this was a tragically common fate for many black female children and women in the Deep South who had no legal protection against the sexual violence of white males.

"I was in the process of researching the 1959 gang-rape of Betty Jean Owens, a black college student at Florida A&M University in Tallahassee, Florida when I kept coming across similar cases of white men attacking black women throughout the Deep South.

It seemed as if every front page of every black newspaper between 1940 and 1950 featured the same story: a black woman was walking home from school, work or church when a group of white men abducted her at gunpoint, took her outside of town, and brutally assaulted her."

-- Danielle McGuire, author of 'At the Dark End of the Street: Black Women, Rape, and Resistance.'

Long before Rosa Parks was hailed as the "mother of the civil rights movement," she wrote a detailed and harrowing account of nearly being raped by a white neighbor who employed her as a housekeeper in 1931.

***

Two white police officers kidnapped and raped Gertrude Perkins, an African-American woman, in 1949. An all-white, all-male grand jury refused to indict the policemen.

***

Was It The Evidence Or The System Of White Supremacy?

(1987) Tawana Bradley, a 15-year old black female, accused six white men, some police officers, of raping her. After missing for four days, she was found unresponsive in a garbage bag near an apartment where she had once resided.

Her torn clothing was burned and her body had been smeared with feces. After hearing the evidence, a grand jury ruled that Brawley had NOT been the victim of a sexual assault, and that she had lied.

It was later rumored that one of the accused men had committed suicide after the story became public (the authors were unable to confirm this). Tawana Bradley, her parents, and supporters still maintain to this day that she told the truth.

Alton H. Maddox, Jr., Bradley's black lawyer, lost his law license "indefinitely" due to his "conduct" in the Brawley case – an unusual and excessively harsh decision against a criminal defense lawyer for simply doing what ALL lawyers are bound by LAW to do: ***defend his client.***

(2006) Crystal Mangum, 27, a black female student at North Carolina Central University, accused three white Duke University students, members of the Duke Blue Devils men's lacrosse team, of raping her at a party held where she had been hired as an exotic dancer. Prosecutor Mike Nifong mounted a vigorous offense against the white males from prominent white families after the case made national headlines.

Nifong's case fell apart after the defense attorneys for the white male students reported that a "private" DNA lab allegedly discovered that none of DNA found in Magnum's body belonged to the accused players -- insinuating that she had been sexually active with multiple, unknown males prior to her stripping at the party (aka -- a typical black whore who could not be raped). Based on further "investigation," the rape charges were dropped.

Nifong was disbarred, making him the first prosecutor in North Carolina history to lose his law license for prosecuting a case.

(2007) Megan Williams, 23, accused six white males and females, of holding her hostage for a week, raping her, stabbing her, and forcing her to eat animal feces.

Two years later, after a series of "encounters" with law enforcement, Williams "recanted" her story, despite credible evidence and photos taken at the time that indicated she had been severely injured and traumatized as claimed.

Did Williams tell a bald-faced lie? Or was this poor, young black female pressured by the legal system to change her story? Unfortunately, we may never know the whole truth.

(2011) Nafissatou Diallo, an African female immigrant who accused Dominique Strauss-Kahn, an influential French politician and the head of the powerful International Monetary Fund (the IMF) of sexually assaulting a maid in his $3,000-a-night Manhattan hotel room.

> *"The wire service said the woman gave this account to police: Strauss-Kahn emerged from the bathroom naked, chased her down a hallway, and pulled her into a bedroom, where he began to sexually assault her. She said she fought him off, but then he dragged her into the bathroom."*

Almost immediately, Ms Diallo's personal reputation was called into question even more so than the accused Kahn. In the end, she suffered the SAME FATE ALL black female victims face when they accuse powerful white males of rape.

Ms Diallo was portrayed in the white press as an HIV-infected, scheming liar and an incompetent blackmailer. The mainstream media callously ignored the vaginal bruising she incurred during the encounter with Strauss-Kahn, and traces of Strauss-Kahn's semen that were found on her work uniform. They also downplayed Kahn's reputation as a:

> *"...man with an infamously predatory reputation towards women, and who has since been accused of another sexual assault by a French writer." (SOURCE:http://www.guardian.co.uk/commentisfree/2011/aug/23/dsk-trial-accuser-not-accused/print)*

The behind-the-scenes story raises reasonable doubts about the true motivations of the prosecutor who had Mr. Kahn arrested for assaulting a poor, African hotel maid. In the real world, the rapes of non-white females by white males are common but often go unreported AND unprosecuted.

Certainly, Ms Diallo's story is easy to believe, given the long, sordid history of white males raping black females. However, it is rare for a black female victim to get any justice or empathy in the white/European court of law(lessness). That being said, it is HIGHLY possible that the arrest of Mr. Kahn and the widespread media coverage served a different purpose.

"The allegations create immediate uncertainty for the Washington-based IMF, which has been playing an important role in stabilizing the global economy amid the financial crisis.

It also promises to stir up politics in France, where Strauss-Kahn is widely thought to be considering challenging French President Nicolas Sarkozy in next year's election. Polls have indicated that he has a good chance of defeating Sarkozy." – (SOURCE:http://www.washingtonpost.com/business/economy/imf-head-taken-into-custody-in-new-york-questioned-over-sex-assault/2011/05/14/AF8Tfj3G_story.html

It is obvious that after Mr. Kahn was accused of rape that his political aspirations to run against French President Nicolas Sarkozy were pretty much "history."

The Authors do not pretend to have any first or second-hand knowledge of what transpired in that Manhattan hotel room; in the media circus that followed; or the true motives of Kahn's prosecutors.

What can be said -- based on the overwhelming historical evidence -- is a white male who is so wealthy he could afford a $200,000/month apartment while on "house arrest"was NEVER in any danger of being convicted OR spending any time in prison over the RAPE of a black female (nigger) in a white supremacy system.

Three more tragedies took place in the Strauss-Kahn case:

1. the REPUTATIONS of all black and African females ONCE AGAIN were put on trial and the CRIES of millions of black female RAPE VICTIMS over the last five CENTURIES has been silenced -- AGAIN.
2. the black female was used as the powerful white system's SEXUAL TOILET and literally thrown under the "bus" of international politics.
3. Miss Diallo was TRANSFORMED from a VICTIM into a VICTIMIZER of a rich, powerful white male: ***an IMPOSSIBLE scenario for a powerless black person in a system of white supremacy.***

The Black Female AKA The "Willing Whore"

If the black female is a "willing whore" by nature, every sexual encounter she has must be voluntary. In other words, a white male CANNOT rape a black female (whore), regardless of the circumstances, either during slavery OR in the 21st century.

There is ONE indisputable FACT: Blacks DO NOT control the criminal justice system, the criminal court judges, the evidence collectors, the DNA labs, the prosecutors, the way law is interpreted, or who is a victim and who is not. Nor do blacks control the hidden hands that mete out the kind of American "justice" that awaits most black defendants AND black victims in a white supremacist criminal (just-us) system.

Based on the historical evidence, we can (logically) draw the following conclusion:

If evidence can be falsified by police and district attorneys to CONVICT black defendants, it is logical to assume evidence can be falsified to ACQUIT white defendants.

Any black female, criminal lawyer, or prosecutor who DARES to accuse a white male authority figure or a white male from a prominent white family of raping her will face the full wrath of the law.

These highly publicized false rape allegations PROVE that black female rape victims will NEVER receive the kind of media attention or public support that white female victims regularly receive from the police, the courts, the media, and from white society in general.

Black females are MORE likely to be raped than any other group in the U.S. but are LESS likely to be believed, or to have their victimizers caught and convicted. Why?

Because ignoring, covering up, and BLAMING black female rape victims is an AMERICAN SLAVE TRADITION.

AXIOM #7: The "Black Victim = A Victimless Crime" Theory. A black person in a conflict with a white person (or white system) cannot BE the victim in a White Supremacy society. The black individual is ALWAYS at fault, regardless of who initiated the conflict, or what facts or evidence are present.

It is critical that the SOILED SEXUAL REPUTATION of the black female (whore) be preserved at all costs to reinforce the myth (LIE) that African female slaves were the WILLING WHORES – NOT the RAPE VICTIMS of two of the most notorious serial rapists in American history: ***Slave-owners and former U.S. presidents: George Washington and Thomas Jefferson.***

How many tens of thousands of black females have been raped by white males in the 20th and 21st centuries -- but are afraid to report the crimes and risk the same fates of a Tawana Bradley, Crystal Mangum, Megan Williams, or Nafissatou Diallo?

Unfortunately, we will never know the answer to that question.

HOLLYWOOD NEWS REPORT

Halle Berry's ongoing battle with the father of her daughter, Gabriel Aubrey, over their three-year old daughter, Nahla, has created a tabloid sensation.

Berry and Aubrey's five-year relationship ended in 2010. According to Berry and her witnesses, Aubrey has been accused of being neglectful and verbally-abusive toward his daughter. He was also accused of calling Berry a "ghetto nigger" and throwing a chair against the wall.

Another friend of Halle's said that Aubrey allegedly had a problem with Aubrey's mixed race, claiming that he never wanted her hair to be braided, and always said that Nahla was white."

(as reported on Oct 19, 2011)

CHAPTER 11

"BLACK JEZEBEL" AKA "A WHITE MAN'S WHORE"

The images of the black female as either a sexually undesirable or obese female, a 'tragic mulatto,' or a promiscuous whore have changed little over the last 500 years.

The Black Female Image In Today's Entertainment Media

Young, attractive black females are almost ALWAYS portrayed as whores, especially in rap music and pornographic videos. A prime example is the scandal-driven, short-lived career of Montana Fishburne, daughter of black actor, Laurence Fishburne, a young black female who was brutally degraded both ON and OFF film.

A popular trash-talk TV show offers a daily line-up of poor black "baby-mommas" who are so promiscuous they have to take MULTIPLE maternity tests to find out "who they baby's daddy is." The darker-skinned the black female is, the more degraded she will be on the show.

On the award-winning HBO series, The Sopranos, the majority of the small handful of black actresses that appeared on the long-running show were prostitutes or white men's whores.

In the 2009 movie, *'District 9,'* the (dark-skinned) Nigerian females played savage cannibal/prostitutes who willingly had sex with insect-looking alien "customers." In the 2005 film, *'Lord of War,'* Nicolas Cage, an arms dealers, was propositioned by two beautiful, dark-skinned, HIV-infected African prostitutes. Naturally, as a (desirable) white male, he had to reject their sexual advances from the inferior black females.

By linking the sexually attractive black female with immorality, low character, and disease, this effectively NEUTRALIZES the beauty of the black female: ***A NECESSITY in a system of white supremacy.***

Why is the sexually attractive black female usually portrayed as a whore? To disguise the truth about the rape of African AND black female slaves during slavery and into the 21st century.

To retain their (imaginary) moral and racial superiority, the white supremacists/rapists had to PROJECT THE BLAME for their horrific crimes against the black female by transforming her from a Victim into an "immoral and sexually loose" Villain. This (false) image of the black female still persists to this day.

"When the pain of sexual abuse isn't leading our (black) women into the hands of other women, it's leading them into the hands of the slave-master himself – the white male. As if she is trying to wave the absolute flag of surrender, the Black woman is saying to the Black Race, "I quit!"

She hasn't been able to defeat racism white supremacy by herself; and her men aren't fighting the battle for her. We can barely protect ourselves.

And to add insult to injury, we spend far more time and energy verbally and physically abusing our women than protecting them from white aggression. In short, Black men aren't acting like men.

So the Black woman has decided that if she cannot beat the slave-master, then she will join him. Black women across the world are sprinting into the awaiting arms of the two-legged white dog who enslaved her race and kidnapped her babies to begin with."

[Excerpt from 'The Impact of Sexual Abuse in the Black Community' - reprinted with permission by War On The Horizon -- http://waronthehorizon.com/site/?p=398]

Black Female Inferiority In A White Supremacy System

Publicly acknowledging the beauty of the black female breaks the fundamental rule of the White Supremacy Beauty Con Game: ***A non-white female cannot be equal OR superior to the white female.*** This explains why the black female's most coveted features -- her full lips, breasts, and buttocks -- had to be DISCONNECTED from the black female and RECONNECTED to a white (or a near white) female using the awesome power (propaganda) of the white media.

However, the ***illusion*** of the superior white female flies in the face of the REALITY of butt implants, breast implants, face-lifts, liposuction, chin implants, curly perms, collagen lip injections, Botox, nose jobs, hair weaves, colorful skin and eye makeup, cancer-causing suntans, and tanning salons to add COLOR to pale skin.

This blatant IMITATION and DUPLICATION of the "inferior" black female explains why the white media feverishly promotes the "round buttocks" of (a white-looking) Jennifer Lopez and the "big lips" of Angelina Jolie: ***to CLAIM and RE-NAME "black beauty" in the name of "whiteness.***

Black Females VS The Universal White Male Conduct Code

The **Racist White Male** is extremely uncomfortable with his conflicting feelings of attraction and repulsion for the black female because they contradict what he has been taught all his life: ***that white females are the most desirable because they are white females.***

His fear-based reaction is due to a much deeper, possibly GENETIC fear of breaking one of the cardinal rules of *'The Universal Conduct Code For White Males'* (pg 113): ***Never treat the "inferior" black female as if she is equal or superior to the white female.***

The *Racist White Male* often acts as if an attractive black female does not register on his sexual radar, and may go so far as to ignore her presence altogether, especially when white females are around. He may turn away from her; or frown as though just her presence is the room is disturbing.

However, his non-verbal behavior paints a different picture. He may become agitated, secretive, peering, peeking, or openly hostile toward the black female in question.

To acknowledge the black female as a sexually desirable WOMAN (as fully human as a white female) would undermine -- in the **Racist White Male's** mind -- the same white supremacy system that has guaranteed he will always have greater privileges than a non-white person.

His hostility may also be due to his latent (hidden) homosexuality because the black female represents the greatest sexual competition (for the black male's penis) -- OR he may resent that particular black female for being more attractive than the white female he is currently involved with.

"Racist white men like to get away with doing very little for black females. And if you carefully study the interviews from the white men in this book, you will notice that all they have to do is buy black females a cup of coffee and she will go to bed with them!

This is what they say when they are asked what they plan to do with black females. And they like to get away with doing very little. This, of course, gives them bragging rights to brag to black males about this."

-- 'Pieces of a Puzzle' by Reneathia Tate

Racist White Males Who Pursues Sex With Black Females

Three common types of Sexually Aggressive Racist White Males

1. The Heterosexual "Down-Low" Racist White Male
2. The Older, Past His Prime, Racist White Male
3. The Hostile Racist White Male

#1: The Heterosexual 'Down-Low' Racist White Male

Since the *Racist White Male's* attraction to black females conflicts with his conduct code, he is more likely to proposition them when he is either:

1. intoxicated;
2. making contact via an anonymous personal ad, or
3. in unfamiliar surroundings away from home where he is out of eyesight and earshot of his (white) friends, family, and acquaintances.

"I was attending a network marketing conference at a hotel, and this white man starts hitting on me, acting real sneaky about it, the way some white men act around black women. I kept the conversation strictly business then called it a night, and went to my room.

I was getting ready for bed when my phone rings. It's him, the white man from the conference. I asked him how he got my number. He said he saw my name on my badge and asked the hotel operator to ring my room. Then he got to the point and invited me to his room for a drink.

Mind you, it's after midnight, so I said, I'm a businesswoman, not some whore -- I almost said nigger whore -- who will come to your room in the middle of the night, and hung up in his face. I saw him the next morning at the conference. He wouldn't look me in the eyes. He looked so pitiful, I almost felt sorry for him. Not!" -- Glenda, 36, saleswoman

The *Heterosexual Down-Low White Male* often keeps his attraction to and sexual affairs with black females a secret for fear of harming his reputation with his white neighbors, peers, and family members. Other reasons he may keep his lust for black females a secret:

- the long, shameful history of white males raping black females
- the lower **caste** (status) of black females in a white supremacy society
- the fear of losing white peer approval, status, and privileges
- the fear of rejection by the "inferior" black female
- the fear of not measuring up to the "sexually dominant" black male
- his desire to maintain the racial integrity of his offspring
- he is not interested in an interracial relationship with a black female

- he knows (consciously or subconsciously) that ignoring black female desirability (humanity) is essential in maintaining the (imaginary) "superiority" of white females -- and the system of white supremacy.

The *Down-Low White Male* often speaks in "code," assuming (and hoping) that the black female will pick up on his indirect cues to lessen the embarrassment of a possible rejection AND exposure if he is more direct about his intentions. ***After all, what is more humiliating to the racist male than being rejected by his racial inferior?***

> *"I was recently approached by a white man who kept saying he was 'well-off.' I didn't realize until later that I was being solicited."*
> *– Sheryl, 43.*

If he is bold enough, he may ask the black female out on a "date" and may take her where he is unlikely to run into anyone who knows him. Or he may enjoy the shock value (and attention) he gets by openly dating a black female, although the "thrill" usually wears off before the relationship becomes serious.

#2: The Older, Past His Prime, White Male

Some mature (over 40) black females say they are more likely to be approached by older, aggressive white males than a black male of any age. Some possible reasons:

- He is past his prime or is physically unappealing to most white females.
- He has already been married; had his children with a white female; and is free to indulge in his lust for black females that he may have hidden during his prime reproductive years because he did not want to marry or have non-white offspring with a black female.
- Unless he is wealthy or has some social or professional status, the older white male who is past his physical and sexual prime, can get a higher quality black female than a white female simply BECAUSE he is white.
- Mature black females are more likely to have some financial stability and education; are less likely to want more children; and are more likely to have adult children who will not "intrude" on the white male's sexual activities.
- The mainstream media's stereotyping of unmarried black females as so desperate, they will "date" (have sex) with any willing male, including and especially, white males.
- He may feel less pressure to marry from a black female than a white female. In those rare instances where a wealthy white male marries a black female, he is UNLIKELY to leave his entire estate to his black widow to prevent it from falling into the wrong (black) hands.

#3: The Hostile Racist White Male

The *Hostile White Male's* LUST for the black female is fueled by the same racist and degrading stereotypes that dehumanizes black sexuality in general. The gullible black female who gets involved with a racist white male is placing herself in psychological AND physical jeopardy. If she does not understand the connection between sex, violence, and racism, she may not recognize the warning signs until it is too late:

In 2010, in Orange, Texas a 35-year-old white male, William Bibb, was arrested and charged on June 12, 2010 for beating a 26-year-old black female Theresa Ardoin with a hammer and dragging her body behind his pick-up truck. Police believe the victim and suspect were personally acquainted. "Authorities are still in the process of trying to discern if Ardoin was still alive while she was being dragged." (SOURCE: www.rollingout.com, June 14, 2010).

Black females who see the connection often complain about being propositioned or harassed by white males who are clearly racist:

"I'm a progressive, outspoken person, so I talk about racial issues on my Facebook page. I started noticing a lot of white males coming to my page and posting all kinds of racist comments about black people, especially black women. There's this one white guy who keeps coming to my page and calls me all kinds of 'nigger bitches,' but when I go to his Facebook page, he's always talking about how much he loves black women, and his greatest wish is to marry a black female!" – Sheryl, 34.

For the *Hostile White Male* who feels threatened by "uppity blacks" and longs for the 'good old days' where blacks had no rights that whites were bound to respect, the closest thing to reliving those days is finding a low-self-esteemed black female who will allow him to control, degrade, and use her as a *"belly-warmer."*

"I moved from the Midwest to Oklahoma three years ago, and I was surprised to see white boys dating black females, if you can call it dating. One time, I was coming out of Wal-Mart and saw this white boy with a sister. Out of nowhere, he kicks her dead in the ass. I was waiting for that sister to take his head off, but she put her head down and kept walking! Man, I was tempted to clock that cracker my damn self until I remembered where I was. Oklahoma is worse in many ways than the Deep South. These racist crackers wish they could bring back slavery, maybe the best they can do is get a black wench like the slavemasters had. That night, I told my daughters they better not bring no white boys home.'" -- Clarence, 41

The *Hostile White Male* may be motivated by jealousy because of the black male's alleged physical and sexual "superiority," or he may resent black males for sexually "ravaging" the (willing) white female and pursues black females to "even the score."

He may take pleasure (revenge) in seducing a black female then "dumping" her after using her as a SEXUAL SEWER -- OR may *deliberately* pursue a black female who is involved with or currently married to a black male.

A relationship with a black (or a non-white) female who believes whites are superior to blacks can be very empowering to the frustrated white male who feels powerless even within a white-male-dominated society.

The low-self-esteemed *Hostile White Male* may find it flattering -- and reassuring -- to be "involved" with a low-self-esteemed, white-validation-seeking black female who puts other black people down -- especially black males -- in his presence to show her "loyalty."

The white-identified black female often puts the white male on a pedestal -- regardless of his status, physical appearance, or racist attitudes, ignoring the odds that the white male will NEVER return the favor by putting her (or any black female) on a pedestal.

However, the Racist White Male will NEVER respect the self-hating black female because she does not respect herself.

All of which brings to mind an important AND self-respecting question for the black female who breeds with the white male:

How can a white male who despises black males (or blacks in general) raise a mentally sane, self-respecting black (male) son (or a daughter)? This may explain why so many white males abandon the non-white children they have with black females.

Conversely, ***the self-respecting, black-identified black female*** with KNOWLEDGE of self and of her history with white males understands that sexual intercourse between blacks and whites in a white supremacy system is simply a CONTINUATION of the same racist sexual/political power dynamic that has existed since slavery.

A Time-Tested Recipe For Creating Black Jezebels

"Every week there's a new "study" or article that says black women are inferior. Here's the deal.

By constantly advertising that black females are at the bottom of the sexual attractiveness heap and saying nobody wants them, this is really a strategy designed to produce easy sexual access to them.

They have a name for it in the PUA comunity, it's called 'framing'. PUA stands for "pick-up artists. The logic being that by constantly advertising the idea that NOBODY wants black females, they become MUCH easier to get because they feel "lucky" that someone wants them.

I once moved into a group house years ago and it took almost 6 months before it finally hit me that the black female and white male were f*cking. They were so good at keeping it discrete (the white male's choice, no doubt).

If a white male wants to have sex with a black female she should FORCE him to be VISIBLE WITH HER. That means public displays of affection, meeting white mom and dad. Otherwise, she is being treated like a prostitute." J. -- black male blogger, 45

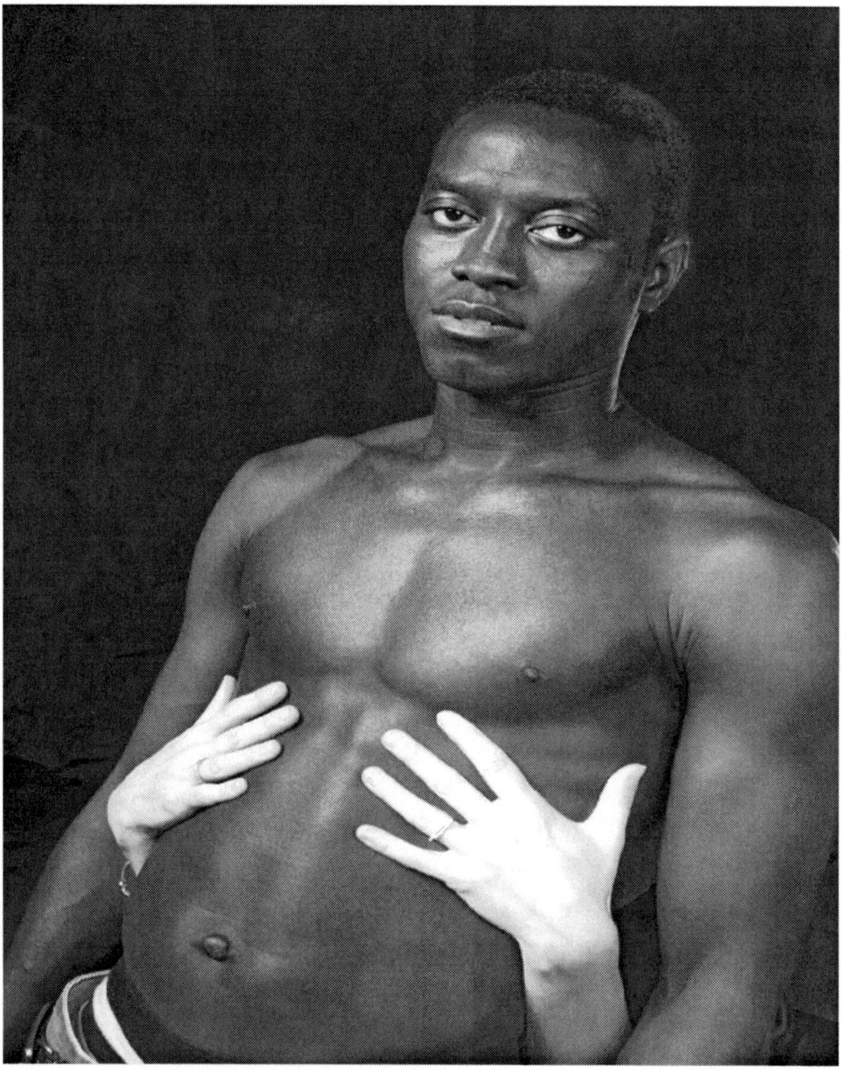

Are Black Males Being Groomed To Be Modern-Day 'Mandingos?'

"I can't even count how many white females I've been with, just round it down to about 40. Out of those 40, I know for a fact 30 of them had a man.

It started 21 years ago in Texas, every time this chick got into a fight with her man she would come over and do me.

21 years later, this 50 year old white female got her 65 year-old white sugar daddy to pay the bills but keeps calling me late at night to give her some when she knows his old azz is in bed.

I have been let in through bedroom windows, back doors, getting a blow job at a party while her man went to the bathroom, did two cousins one night, I was going with one and in the middle of the night got up and did her friend once or twice a week on her lunch break.

Did my manager's daughter a couple of times and all her mother talked about at work was how sweet and innocent her girl was...yeah...right...lol"

– Jerry, black male poster on black message board

CHAPTER 12

THE BLACK MALE AKA BLACK "MANDINGO"

'Meet the Mandingos,' (SOURCE: www. Men.style.com) is a perfect example of how sexual intercourse between black males and white females can be used to exploit and dehumanize black males.

The article centers on an admittedly racist, affluent white male, Jeff, who is hosting an interracial orgy with 12 black males and 23 white couples. It is clear that, Jeff, a "staunch Republican" who lives in a $700,000 home on a golf course (that doesn't accept black members), is just "liberal" enough to allow a black male Mandingo (nigger) to give Amber, his white wife, a *"sexual pounding."*

What is even more disturbing: The black males actually paid MORE MONEY to participate in the orgies than the white couples they were servicing(!)

Obviously, money (prostitution) was not the motive for these misguided Mandingo males. Nor was the "irresistible" sexual appeal of the white female participants, one of whom the author described as a *"pudding of cellulite."*

Apparently, the real appeal for these *"...handsome, well-read, and well-endowed..."* Mandingo males was the BIZARRE PSYCHOLOGICAL PAYOFF they received from having sexual intercourse on COMMAND with the same white couples ***who belong to a whites-only country club that would NEVER welcome a "Mandingo" as a member.***

The devastating psychological effect on the minds of these black 'Mandingos' is evident from their contradictory (and delusional) rationalizations:

"I believe the world is looking beyond color now more than ever."

"I make great contacts here."

"This gets my name out there, that's why I don't charge."

"After a while, you feel like a piece of meat, but hey, they're not using me to now their damn lawn, they're using me to fuck the wife."

Even though it is apparent to some "Mandingos" that they are being used as SEXUAL TOILETS by their racist sexual partners -- the need to stay in denial is stronger than their need to RESPECT THEMSELVES.

"I felt like I was just...a dick...for this wife," one man said, yet he contradicts himself by saying the more interracial sex blacks and whites have, "...the more these taboos will disappear and we'll all realize we're not that different."

It is also equally obvious that if one of those Mandingo males ever bumped into one of their white sex-buddy couples at the local supermarket, chances are they'd be lucky to make eye contact.

In their most honest and private moments, these educated, well-read Mandingo males know they will NOT be doing any future "business" with the same RACIST affluent white males who watched their white "cellulite-pudding" wives get a sexual pounding from a black male (nigger).

The same white females who sucked, licked, sexed, and freaked with these black males in private, would probably clutch their purses tighter and cross the street if they ran into these Mandingos (niggers) fully clothed.

The bottom line: After these black males swing their black "clubs" in private, they won't be swinging any golf clubs OR "business deals" in public on a whites-only golf course.

The most telling comment in the entire article was made by the admittedly racist white male, Jeff, who hosted the Mandingo party in his home:

"It excites the hell out of me. And I know that Amber would never date a black man."

Sadly, even a homeless, CRACK-ADDICTED female prostitute would have the common sense – and strangely, enough self-respect -- to GET PAID for a hard night's work.

There is one side that was not explored in the article: ***the hidden homosexuality of the white males who watched.***

A white male who would PAY money to watch a black male having sex with his (white) wife is focused on that BLACK MALE, not on his wife. In all likelihood, he is taking a "vicarious" sexual ride using his wife as the vehicle while he fantasizes about a homosexual encounter with a black male.

Another possibility is the racist white male may covet the black male's penis (and genetic power) to such a degree that watching the black male use it on a white female, allows him to imagine HE is the one who possesses a BIG BLACK D*CK. *(The authors were unable to find a single sex club where black males paid white males to have sex with their black wives).*

Interracial sex is a form of white supremacy. This is how feminism meets white supremacy via Interracial Sex. A white female can be a white supremacist and sex N*ggers at the same time. Many white females hate black males but love black c*cks.

The white female is in the last stages in her war with the white male. She is better educated than white males. While the white female finishes off the white male, she is in no way ready to give up her white supremacy.

The sexual and political rise of the white female over white males must happen through her conquest and dominance of black males. To fend off any threat to white female hegemony, we must dominate N*ggers sexually."

-- White Female Supremacist
(Der Kosmonaut, 1972)

Hegemony -- the dominant authority or leader

CHAPTER 13

SEX IN SENEGAL: SEXUAL VAMPIRES WHITE SUPREMACY STYLE

A recent newspaper article in 2010 reported that an increasing number of affluent, middle-aged and elderly white females from America and Europe are flocking to the beaches of Senegal (in West Africa) for sun, sea, and sex. Why are these young black males willing to sexually accommodate white females who are more than two to three times their own ages?

The Unemployment Rate For Senegal's Youth Estimated At Thirty Percent. The Average Wage Is About $3 A Day.

> *"It's a question of survival," explained one young man who has been "dating" white female tourists for several years.*

Pape, a 30-year-old Senegalese male earns $250 a month at his job, barely enough to cover his living expenses. He has a 52-year-old Dutch "girlfriend" who sends him gifts and $250 cash every month. *"I'm a thing, her object, her toy, her property," he said. "If I had the choice financially, I wouldn't date her. I would never have started this."*

In the article, he described an encounter at a nightclub where a young Senegalese man was dancing in front of three elderly white females. One of the women reached out and squeezed the young man's butt, and shook her head, the way one would sample then reject a rotten piece of fruit.

Pape seems haunted by that memory, and perhaps, by the realization that he is prostituting his body AND his self respect. Sadly, the miserly amounts earned by these desperate black males scarcely make a dent in the bank accounts of their affluent white female customers (victimizers).

This is NOT a condemnation of the poor African male (victim) who trades his precious body to put food on the table. The HARSHEST criticism should be reserved for the affluent white female SEXUAL VAMPIRES (sexual predators) who "buy" sex from (rape) poor, desperate human beings – often for as little as $50 or a cheap DVD player – instead of using their affluence to help those in need.

What motivates so many predatory white females to PREY on these poor, desperate black males? The song -- *"A Thin Line Between Love and Hate"* -- by the R&B group, The Persuaders, may reveal some truths.

It appears there is a very thin line between SEX and HATE in the minds of racist man and racist woman. In a sick racist mind, HATE actually INCREASES sexual arousal, which explains why some of the most racist whites often LUST after and pursue sex with the same non-white people they despise. There is one more point that must be made here:

The vast majority of sexual encounters between blacks and whites are INITIATED BY WHITES.

Sex And Racism Go Hand In Hand

Since ALL sexual activity between blacks and whites takes place within a white supremacy system, non-whites are often dehumanized AND turned into sexual or fetish objects to reduce the possibility that they will be seen as equals (or fully human).

This EMOTIONAL (GUILT-FREE) DETACHMENT allows racist man and woman to freely indulge in their relentless lust for "darker" flesh without compromising their white privileges or the white supremacy system that guarantees them.

White supremacy and interracial sex operate in TANDEM, NOT in opposition. Interracial sex between blacks and whites WILL NOT reduce racism or hatred toward blacks, nor does it increase the likelihood of racial harmony between blacks and whites.

The proof: 400 years of white males and females raping and sexually molesting African male and female slaves.

In retrospect, many blacks who were previously involved in interracial relationships often later admit that their former white partners used racial slurs or made racist and stereotyped comments about blacks in general.

Any male or female who desires sexual intercourse with the same people they (claim to) despise OR see as inferior, is a MENTALLY and SPIRITUALLY SICK individual who should be avoided AT ALL COSTS.

Until black males and females UNDERSTAND that sexual intercourse OR any sexual contact between blacks and whites in a system of white supremacy actually EXTENDS and STRENGTHENS that system, we will literally be sleeping with (and sexing) our enemies, and deepening our own psychological, economic, social, sexual, and political oppression.

CHAPTER 14

SEVEN REASONS WHITE FEMALES PURSUE BLACK MALES

REASON #1: "THE BEAUTY AND THE BEAST" SYNDROME/ RAPE FANTASY. The white female who is sexually involved with a black male often (secretly) sees herself as a "white prize" who has sacrificed her "pure" white femininity to the hyper-masculine, hyper-sexual black male "beast" – a real life version of King Kong.

This sexual fetish also allows the unattractive white female (by white standards) her best (and often her ONLY) opportunity to feel feminine, desirable, and attractive. Regardless of her appearance OR intellect, she knows she will ALWAYS be superior to any (black) male she is involved with, something she cannot assume with a white male.

It is a common fantasy among the white collective to imagine or to stage scenarios in their private homes, clubs, or via mass marketed films and pornographic videos that portray a white female being abducted or sexually assaulted by a black male (beast), which explains the appeal of King Kong-type movies for the white audience.

In other words, her attraction to the black male may be BASED ON A RACIST FANTASY, and may be a form of HUMAN BESTIALITY.

The tip-off to a supposedly "color-blind" racist white female: ***she is only attracted to dark-skinned black males -- which means COLOR ABSOLUTELY MATTERS.*** The clueless black male is flattered by the white female's attention, and is unaware that the same "bestial" (rapist) stereotypes used to justify the lynchings (murders) of black males throughout American history ***is a SEXUAL TURN-ON for racist woman.***

A 30-something black male called an Atlanta, GA black radio talk show seeking advice about his white female companion, who wanted him to play the role of a slave while she played the role of his white slave mistress. He said SHE SAID she wanted to beat him, mistreat him, call him a "nigger," and put him in handcuffs and shackles. She also wanted him to look more "primitive," – exposing her BLACK MALE BESTIALITY sexual fetish:

"...since the winter, I kinda like grew out my beard, and she's like, cool, cool, I want you to keep it thick and nappy, and...look like, basically, like, a slave, and I'm gonna beat ya, and ride ya, and call ya all kinds of degrading stuff." -- male caller

It is possible that the black male caller was worried about "going off" on the white female companion because she had already degraded him on numerous occasions, and he sought advice ONLY after he became troubled by his OWN willingness to be victimized by a racist.

REASON #2: SEXUAL FREEDOM WITHOUT CONSEQUENCES. The white female may be more sexually uninhibited (more promiscuous) with black males than she would be with white males because the white male's opinion of her carries greater weight in her social circle.

The sexually aggressive white female knows the black male has ZERO POWER to destroy her reputation or her social standing in her white community because neither he NOR his opinion is welcome there. She is more comfortable approaching, pursuing, and sexually experimenting (freaking) with black males because she doesn't care what the random black male thinks of her sexual or moral behavior. Just like a rich, privileged female doesn't care what her servants think of her because they are NOT FIT to judge her -- in her opinion.

In the presence of her "inferiors," the rich, privileged female is literally free to be herself, no matter how low that self might go. Even if her servants gossiped about her sex life, who would they tell that mattered?

However, in the presence of her social equals OR superiors, the rich, privileged woman is concerned enough to put on her "company face," and be mindful of what she wears, drinks, eats, drives, does, and says.

The white female's burning desire to be sexually "free" has caused white females – collectively – to have a somewhat well-deserved reputation in the black community for being promiscuous (sexually loose). It is a common sight in nearly every black community to see random white females openly pursuing black males -- even total strangers -- for a no-strings sexual encounter.

> *"The (white) woman who goes after black men is a...'white bitch' in heat... white women turn to black men when their sex drives kick into higher gear and their social inhibitions recede into the rearview mirror. It's a "yes, baby, now I'm ready for you" reaction." – Susan B, 40-plus, white female. A WHITE WOMAN EXPLAINS WHY SHE PREFERS BLACK MEN By Susan Crain Bakos -- Vol 18 - Issue 50 - December 14-20, 2005 http://www.nypress.com/18/49/news&columns/SusanCrainBakos.cfm*

It is unheard of for black females to "cruise" white neighborhoods, bars, and parks for anonymous sex with white strangers. Perhaps, the white female's sense of "white entitlement" (white power) emboldens her to feel welcome in non-white communities or anywhere else she chooses to roam.

Her "right" for sex-on-demand from black males is confirmed by the ever-eager black male who sees the white female's promiscuity as a character asset instead of a character flaw. In fact, a promiscuous black female is MORE likely to be condemned by black males than a promiscuous white one.

"I was talking to a black female friend and the subject of white women came up. She knew I had dated white women in the past, and asked how quick we had sex. I told her it was usually their idea and happens the first night because white females were more laid back about sex. She asked me if a black female had sex with me on the first date, would I call her laid back, or a ho. I had to admit, she'd be a ho." – Renaldo, 42.

Some black males praise the white female for her 'sex without strings" approach but few understand that the white female's lack of "drama" may be due to her lack of sincere interest in him as a man, and an acknowledgment of his inferior status as a non-white male.

"They (black women) resent our taking their men. But in truth, black sisters, we're after the sex, not the ring, and these guys aren't the marrying kind anyway." 'A White Woman Explains Why She Prefers Black Men' by Susan Crain Bakos -- Vol 18 - Issue 50 - December 14-20, 2005 http://www.nypress.com/18/49/news&columns/SusanCrainBakos.cfm

***

REASON #3: USING BLACK MALES TO GET REVENGE AGAINST WHITE MALES. A white female who has been sexually abused by her father, male relatives, or by white males in general, may develop a hatred for white males, and may seek revenge by flaunting her black male lovers.

"...given that white women today seem to dislike white men almost as much as blacks do, dating a black guy may be a way of getting even." -- a white male blogger (http://www.fredoneverything.net/Dating.shtml)

Since the father is the girl's first AND most important role model, the white female who shuns ALL white males is a major tip-off of a dysfunctional upbringing or personality. She may use black males to get revenge against the white male even though she KNOWS the black male will pay the price for her "betrayal" in the form of job losses, police brutality, incarceration, and in some cases, the loss of his LIFE by racist man and racist woman.

REASON #4. A SHORTAGE OF HETEROSEXUAL WHITE MALES. The shortage of single, heterosexual white males has forced some white females to pursue non-white males for sex, romance, and companionship.

This is especially common for white females who are past their physical "prime" where white males are concerned, or who are less attractive than their white female competition.

REASON #5: HAVING THE SUPERIOR POSITION IN THE RELATIONSHIP = CONTROL AND POWER OVER A MAN. A relationship with a male she can control can be very empowering and satisfying to the white female who feels oppressed in a sexist, male-dominated society.

She may find the white-identified (confused) black male EASIER to manipulate than a white male, or may consider him a temporary fad; a human sex toy (dildo); a sexual fetish; a possession to parade around to amuse her white friends; OR as proof that she is superior to black females.

The white female's expectations of the black male are often lower than her expectations would be for a white male -- *which means she can lower her expectations for herself.*

For the first time in her life, she may feel superior to her male partner. The tip-off: ***"Black men are more 'down to earth' (aka easier to manipulate) than white men."***

The white female knows the black male IS NOT her equal (in a white supremacy system) regardless of all her denials. She knows his hunger for (her) white validation greatly increases the odds that he will cater to her, try to appease, impress, praise, and please her.

The racist (cunning) white female often uses that knowledge to her advantage (or her amusement) by demanding the black male publicly disrespect the black female in her presence to show his loyalty.

However, the racist white female will NEVER respect the self-hating black male because he does not respect himself.

"My nephew is in an interracial marriage, he has a master's degree, and can't find a job. He tried to tell his wife -- she's white -- about the racism on his last job but she tells him to stop complaining, that black people are racist, too.

My nephew is suffering mentally, I can tell he's about to crack. I want to tell him that his problem is he's married to a racist but I don't want to put any more pressure on him. All the family is waiting for him to leave the marriage, but we know his wife will make it hard on him after the divorce, seeing his daughter, and child support. So, pretty much, we keep our mouth shut." -- William, 53, instructor.

***

"I have been married to a white woman for three years. We are close to getting divorced because of the way she lets her family disrespect me. Her family doesn't accept her being married to a black man, and whenever she wants to visit them, I have to drive her over there and wait in the car until she leaves.

I'm talking about hours! I don't know how much longer I can take this. She acts like it's no big deal, so I told her, I'm a man, not some horse you tie up outside. I told her, it's me or your family, pick one." – Willy, 33, delivery truck driver

***

REASON #6: ENVY AND COMPETITION WITH BLACK FEMALES. The insecure racist white female often envies AND secretly (or openly) competes with black females. This is due in part to her racist belief system that says she must be superior to the (inferior) black female -- at all costs.

Her neurotic need to feel superior often leads her to pursue (and capture) a black (or non-white) male and flaunt her "catch" around black females as PROOF OF her WHITE SUPERIORITY over black females. However, her hidden insecurity is always just beneath the surface:

> *"I recall an incident that happened to me when I ran into a male friend who was dating a white woman at the time. When he spoke to me, he addressed me as 'Sista.'*
>
> *Later on, he told me his white woman was on him all day about calling me a 'Sista,' saying things such as, 'Why don't you call me that?' Needless to say, they broke up about a month later. She couldn't accept him being friendly toward black women." – Nichelle, 35*

***

The insecure racist white female will NEVER admit she is envious of black females, but is quick to accuse the black female of being jealous of her. However, whenever a black female -- who is sexually attractive or is sexually involved with a white male -- intrudes on the racist white female's sexual territory, she usually responds with hostility -- and jealousy.

> *"On Saturdays I usually stop for a cocktail at this upscale bar in the shopping mall. One time, this white man struck up a conversation, and I noticed this white female on the other side of the bar giving me this 'why is he talking to you' kind of look.*
>
> *She's sitting with her friends, but all her attention was on us. When she couldn't take it anymore, she gets up and sits on the empty stool next to him. I guess she had too much to drink, because she started talking about people on welfare driving Cadillacs and buying steak with food stamps. She looked stupid, the white guy looked annoyed, and I was bored, so I left. White females can dish it all day long, but they can't take it when one of their men hits on us. " -- Pamela S., 41*

***

The racist white female assumes her "whiteness" guarantees a superior position over the black female when it comes to ***white AND black males*** and will aggressively assert her (superior) position at every opportunity.

> *"I ran into Patrice, a black female who lives in my building, at Wal-Mart. We were standing in the checkout line, talking about jazz, when this older white female in line ahead of us jumped in our conversation.*

She said she was visiting from Seattle, and asked me if there were any good jazz clubs in the city. Then she started telling me about her man problems, and acting like Patrice wasn't even there.

After she left, Patrice said, 'What do you expect? The white bitch is from Seattle, she's used to black men kissing her ass.' After I saw it with my own eyes, I couldn't argue with her." -- Ernest, 46

***

"A young white woman once told me I was 'intimidatingly beautiful.' I think she was revealing a lot more than she intended. I'm secure enough in myself that I'm not intimidated by any beautiful woman, black, white, or otherwise.

But, for some reason, some white women's minds are blown when they meet a beautiful black woman, especially if she looks better than they do (and, most of the time, they will). They're used to being "top dog"...it threatens their position in society to meet a woman of color who's more than they will ever be. Hence the term, "intimidatingly beautiful" (and, for the record, this girl was VERY pretty by most societal standards... she had NO valid reason to fear me)." -- Chocolate Diva, black female poster on a black website (2004)

***

Despite the white female receiving the LION'S share of attention and admiration in movies, TV, advertising, and magazines, her insecurity (and imaginary victimization) may become magnified ANYTIME she is forced to share even a tiny corner of her "stage" with a non-white female:

"I see that you are currently following the trend of lusting after "exotic" women. Just a few years ago, I was tanning my porcelain skin brown (with self tanner, mind you!), dying my dirty blonde hair black, and wearing brown contacts over my blue eyes just to look more "exotic."

I was soooo sick of hearing that men preferred tanner, more ethnic women over white women. I do feel quite a bit of hostility from other races, and even white men, for being a white woman. They seem to feel that it is necessary to tell me that white features are overrated and even unattractive.

...I am just getting tired of the exotification of asian/hispanic/bi-racial/black women!!! It just seems like every white guy that I know is obsessed with "exotic" women. It seems like pale skin, blue-eyed women are not accepted anymore especially by white men. With the current victimization of whites in society I was hoping this website would not be promoting other races of women but of course I was mistaken."

-- Samantha, white female poster on a white male's blog.

***

The Barely Hidden Hostility (And Insecurity) Toward Black Females Has Not Gone Unnoticed

"I sense a growing white women's movement against black women. I don't know when I perceived it but it seems fostered by JEALOUSY and ENVY. This not something to be taken lightly, sisters. The white woman for all of her myriad of faults is second on America's totem pole.

Many have ranking postions in the media and social systems where they have profound influence on this nation's views and opinions. Here in the media is where I see an emerging trend of anti-black female articles and editorials written by white women.

I feel that white female angst is being aggravated by the rapid rise of the American black woman. No longer is the American Black Woman that little object of pity just off the plantation.

She has achieved beyond everybody's loftiest expectations. But her white female counterpart is now seeming to think we are getting a lil too big for our britches."

The white woman is really beginning to take the black woman very seriously. I noticed this emerging trend of white women VS black women back some years ago when I went to see Terminator 2 at a mostly white theater. There was a part when the white heroine went to try to change the future by murdering this black scientist.

Anyway, when the white heroine slapped the scientist's black wife and called her a "bitch," white folks went ta screaming and clapping. But the disturbing thing was that all of this applause was coming from white women at that particular part. It kind of said something." -- Lisa, black female poster in 2004

***

"Uh, I started this thread, and um...I didn't meant for it to be positive for sisters or negative. I just start looking at how WW are now tripping on the black woman's success and I see some unsettling trends ahead.

Remember, BW, for all of your bombast and achievements, the WW is the second most powerful demographic group in this country. This not to scare you, it is to PREPARE you. WW finna put some shit in tha game." -- Chocolate Diva, black female (2004)

***

With the sharp rise in degrading images of black females in the media over the last ten to fifteen years, Chocolate Diva's predictions appear to be right on the mark. Consider the following:

The 'Women in Entertainment Power List,' published yearly by *'The Hollywood Reporter,'* ranks the most powerful women in the entertainment industry. For obvious reasons, their names are not listed here, but their titles are impressive, nonetheless:

Chairman
Co-Chairman
President
Chief Operating Officer (COO)
Co-President
Executive Vice-President
Producer
Senior Executive Vice-President
Managing Director
Literary Agent
Head and Co-Head
Founder
Partner
Senior Vice-President

The above list represents the people most likely to create, script, cast, direct, and produce a good percentage of today's TV shows, TV commercials, print advertising, music videos, and films -- including the ones that degrade and demonize black females. With a few exceptions, the vast majority (over 95%) on this media powerhouse list are WHITE FEMALES.

White Females Who Use Deceit To Compete

The deceptive racist white female may use the black male's complaints about black females to TEMPORARILY TRANSFORM her behavior to make it appear she is DIFFERENT from (better than) the black female.

However, once her true personality surfaces, and the black male realizes a white female is not the ticket to a drama-free romantic life, it is likely that their relationship will bite the dust, like the majority of short-lived black male/white female relationships.

> *"First of all, I am a white woman, and I find that most of the white women who DO date Black men do it for all the wrong reasons. Either they look at dating a Black man as some sort of exciting new adventure, OR they believe certain myths about Black male sexuality, OR they are trying to rebel against their parents, OR they want a "bad boy" and to them all Black men are "bad." It is not too often that I see white women with a Black man simply because she loves him.*
>
> *The second issue I have with BM/WF couples is that MOST of the time, the white female wants NOTHING to do with Black females, and in fact disrespects Black females every chance she gets. She insists that if a Black female disagrees with something she says or does it is because all Black females are jealous of her.*
>
> *I have heard it time and time again: a white woman saying they she is not racist because she dates a Black men, and in the next breath go on to enumerate the reasons why she is better than a Black woman.*
>
> *I also cringe when I hear that white women get offended when someone says her child is Black, protesting that her child is, in fact, biracial. It seems to me that they think that being biracial is somehow better than being Black.*
>
> *They often insist on raising their children in their own little lily-white world, surrounded only by their WHITE family, living in neighborhoods where their child is the only person of color, having their child attend schools with only white children." -- Joanna L., white female*

***

It is common for the cunning racist white female who is having sexual intercourse with a black male to try to poison him against all black females -- ***a clear announcement that she is a racist.***

> *"It's like a white woman told me once....black women treat their men like PROPERTY; white women treat their men like PEOPLE (even if they don't always agree)." -- Mark, 27, a black male poster on black website*

REASON #7: The Sexually Aggressive Racist White Female is a RACIST who is practicing RACISM/WHITE SUPREMACY on her black male (and female) Victims.

"I have a good friend in Pittsburgh I have known for over 20 yrs who married an Italian woman. Do you know she used to call him the N-word whenever they had a heated argument?!? He said when he used to visit her family in Italy, the dad used to leave and go in another room. He didn't even tell me this until after they were divorced. I was like, what the hell?? He is now with a beautiful African American woman he has 2 beautiful girls with.

A lot of BM in the UK who dated WW said the WW called them all kinds of names, and turn their kids against them. Now, all, and I mean all the black men and women I know who used to date interracially are dating their own (other black people).

That includes my brother who is now married to a Caribbean woman and has a child with her. The sad thing about black folk is that they learn when it's too late. Luckily, I didn't make that mistake. Black love will always reign supreme in my world till the day I die."
-- Red, 37, United Kingdom

***

"I was wondering how many people work with white people -- especially white females -- who feel like it's okay to use certain "slang" that could be deemed racially offensive? In the last few months at my job several white women have been reprimanded for saying the word "ghetto" after complaints had been filed against them.

My supervisor is a fat white chick (typical) that was married to a black man for 7 years before they divorced. Somehow she got so comfortable around the "sistas" she thought she could joke and kick around the 'N' word. Back in May she told a black female co-worker that her black ex-husband only dated white women because he said all black women are bitches.

WHY in the HELL... WHAT IN THE HELL would possess a person to say that at work?!? My black co-worker made a complaint against her and all the white girl got was a slap on the wrist."

***

All of which leads to an important AND self-respecting question for the black male who breeds with a racist or a racist suspect white female:

How can a white female who has such a low (and racist) opinion of black females raise a mentally sane, self-respecting black (female) daughter? This is a question all black males should ask themselves before having non-white children with a white female.

The Sexually Âggressive (Racist) White Female

=

WHITE FEMÂLE WHITE SUPREMÂCY

Black Dog Trainer Claims Rich White Socialite Hounded Him For Sex In Lawsuit

"She did things that were inappropriate. She would call me into her bedroom several times, and she would basically flash me," said Westley Artope, a black male, of his white female socialite employer, Paige Bluhdorn.

When Artope said he was a married man, she reminded him that she was married, too. When he continued to refuse her advances, he claimed she became hostile, criticized his work, and eventually fired him. (Aug 2011)

SOURCE: http://newsone.com/nation/casey-gane-mccalla/paige-bluhdorn-dog-trainer-sex-lawsuit/

CHAPTER 15

THE SEXUALLY AGGRESSIVE (RACIST) WHITE FEMALE

Black Males Report An Increase In Sexually Aggressive White Females.

"I don't get it. When I was in high school the white girls snubbed me and called me the n-word, now all of a sudden, black men are in style. Everywhere I go, white females are letting me know I can get it, not just the young ones, but the older ones, too." – Stewart, 29, unemployed restaurant worker

***

"I was at the Wal-Mart when this white female walks up to me and just stands there, looking at me and smiling. I'm the blunt type – this sometimes gets me into trouble – so I asked her, point-blank what she wanted? And she looks at me like, "fill in the blanks, black man." When I didn't say anything, she walked away.' – David, 42, contractor

***

"I work in the I.T. field, and some of my male colleagues from India told me that they are being aggressively harassed by the white females on their jobs. One man, who has a wife and a family, said his white female boss told him – in so many words – that if he wanted to keep his job he better not dare walk away from her. He said a lot of Indian men were leaving corporate America and heading back to their own communities because the white women were trying to destroy their families."-- Bernard, 53, systems engineer

***

"About three years ago, I worked for this printing company that does promotional items for businesses. My boss was this 40-ish white female who kept hitting on me. She would flirt with me, try to be alone with me. One time, when no one else was around, she pulled her pants down and let me see her you-know-what. It wasn't sexy, it was perverted. I finally told her, listen, I'm a happily married man, I love my wife, etc. When she realized I was flat-out rejecting her, she grabbed my ass, and said, "You're fired." -- Marquis, 37, truckdriver

"I was in the housewares section of a major retail chain, and I just so happened to engage in a conversation with a couple of young black women. As soon as they pushed off, I was surrounded by three white females, in the 33 to 44 age group, walking back in forth in front of me, like they were auditioning for Bert Parks.

For a minute I was kinda like, "what the hell is this?" They're standing close as I browsed the shelves for a garlic press. I think I'm attractive, and flirting is my second nature, but I felt a little weird. A little voice inside me said, "don't say anything, just push on," so I did." – Bernard, 53, network engineer

***

"I was attending a seminar for my company, and this white female program manager from another firm, singles me out – I'm the only black man in the room --and decides to tell me about all her personal problems. Later, one of my colleagues -- a white male -- asked me what that was all about? To this day, I have no idea." – Craig, 46, attorney

***

I went to this party given by my wife's boss, a corporate big-wig. There were just a handful of blacks there, so I know I stood out but had no idea how much. This white female approached me the second my wife went to the ladies room and starting rubbing my neck and saying how attractive I was. I was like shocked because she did this in front of a roomful of white people. When my wife walked in, she disappeared. I still shake my head thinking about it." -- Kevell, 49,

***

Some black males INSTINCTIVELY sense that the sexually aggressive white female who demands sex and attention from black males is NOT flattering them; she is practicing racism ON them.

Unfortunately, even UNDERAGE black male CHILDREN are NOT safe from sexual assault (rape) by the sexually aggressive white female:

Anne Lynn Montgomery, 35, a white female, and high school teacher, is wanted by police after being charged with two second-degree felonies: (1) sexual assault of a child under the age of 17, and (2) an improper relationship between a student and an educator. It was revealed that she'd sexually molested Bradman Moore, a black male student, when he was just 16 - and bore him two children. Montgomery, 35, faces a maximum of 20 years in prison if convicted.

Black Males Who Sexually Submit To White Supremacy For Career Advancement

If one examines the overwhelming number of successful black males who are married to white females – especially in the entertainment arena – a certain pattern emerges.

A common excuse some successful black males give for dating white females exclusively is their inability to find a black woman "at their level." This "excuse" falls short for two reasons:

1. there are MORE professional black females than black males
2. affluent white females seldom marry black males of any income group

Interracial Sex = Success For Black Male Entertainers

Some black male entertainers have discovered the magic formula for getting a TV show or a movie role: *walk down the red carpet with a white female on his arm.* As one black actor put it: *"A white woman can open doors for a black man."*

However, this "strategy" can backfire on the non-celebrity black male because the majority of white males AND white females disapprove of interracial relationships between blacks and whites, and may take revenge on the offending black male by eliminating him from the workplace.

> *"I'll never forget this black guy who was hired just before the company Christmas party. He brought a white female to the party even though we all knew he was married to a black woman. I remember thinking, he won't be here long. Two weeks after the party, they fired him. Guess he thought he'd impress people by bringing a white woman to the party."*
>
> *– Gladys, 48*

***

> *"I was working for this law firm when they hired this brother who graduated from a top law school. He was so arrogant, he made a play for a white female partners. Maybe he thought she'd be his ticket to a partnership. Wrong. She filed sexual harassment charges against him and he was fired. It's hard enough for a black man to make it in big law. Most don't.*
>
> *My job strategy is the exact opposite. If a white female comes into my office, I make sure the door stays open. I never say anything of a sexual or flirtatious nature to white females. I knew the white males in my office were always watching me, and waiting for me to mess up."*
>
> *– Martin, 39*

***

Sexual intercourse between black males and white females is encouraged (and tolerated) ONLY when those "relationships" promote and benefit the system of white supremacy.

> *"On average, white men hate to see black men dating whites. (So do a whole lot of white women.) In places like Washington people won't say so publicly. Privately they do." -- a white male blogger (http://www.fredoneverything.net/Dating.shtml)*

What is behind this rise in white female sexual aggression toward black males? Since this is a very politically-incorrect assertion, it's time to make our case by listing eight possible reasons:

1. As white females move up the corporate ladder and gain more political and economic power, they also have MORE opportunities to practice racism in the workplace and social arena by sexually dominating non-white males and subjugating non-white females.

2. The white female -- who has been dominated by white males and deprived of her "share" of the white supremacy spoils -- is determined to make up for lost time.

3. The increase in homosexual white males has resulted in a growing number of white females who are sexually and socially frustrated.

4. Single white females over the age of forty face stiff competition from younger females for desirable white males.

5. The white female finds it easier and more ego-gratifying to manipulate black (and non-white) males who do not understand the connection between racism and interracial sex and see the white female's sexual aggression as flattering when in fact it has NOTHING to do with admiration OR affection, and EVERYTHING to do with practicing white supremacy.

   Her expectation that ALL non-whites SHOULD submit to her needs and desires shows a LACK OF RESPECT. In fact, the more aggressive she is toward black (and non-white) males, ***the more likely she is to be a racist.*** She does not respect them enough to worry about the "impression" she is making, AND in fact, is likely to view sex on demand with a non-white male as HER RIGHT rather than a privilege granted by another human being. Black males who ignore OR reject her sexual advances often find themselves in less than good standing on their jobs, and may be accused of being "racist," especially if other whites witness his lack of interest in a white female, OR if a white female has the power to promote or fire him.

6. The white female may view non-white males as her "chattel" property. This may explain her competitiveness AND her hostility toward black (and non-white) females. She sees the black female as an OBSTACLE to her aggressive SENSE OF WHITE ENTITLEMENT to encroach into the black female's territory.

   The people most likely to create, script, cast, direct, and produce most of the TV shows, commercials, music videos, and movies are ***white females.*** The racist white female's hostility toward black females may explain the SHARP RISE in degrading images of black females in mainstream media – music, videos, television, print, and film over the last fifteen years.

7. The skyrocketing demand for fertility drugs, fertility clinics, sperm banks, sperm donors, artificial insemination, in-vitro-fertilization, test tube babies, and U.S. and overseas adoption mills points to the increasing infertility among whites. Wealthy white couples are "renting" the wombs of poor African and Indian women when the white wife has no uterus, an under-developed uterus, or medical conditions where she is unable to carry a baby to term.

   Some white females may be instinctively more attracted to males they perceive as more "masculine" (more capable of impregnating a female). The black male's alleged sexual superiority (and fertility) can be a powerful draw for the white female. It is a FACT that the HIGHLY MELANATED African male and female are some of the most FERTILE people on the planet. While the Authors do not pretend to have any scientific expertise, there appears to be a CONNECTION between melanin and fertility.

   That being said, it is possible some white females are DELIBERATELY BREEDING with black males in the hopes of producing **future white generations** that will be more fertile. How can interracial sex increase overall white fertility? Most of the children of these interracial unions will (1) be raised by single white mothers; (2) will have a closer, more sympathetic bond with the white side of their family, in particular, the white females; (3) will be white-identified; (4) will breed with whites (or other white-identified blacks who have a white parent); (5) will produce offspring who will merge undetected with the white population; and (6) The future generations of these black male/white female unions will produce whites who will be more fertile (due to melanin from the black male), resulting in an INCREASE in overall white fertility.

8. The racist white female is dedicated to MAINTAINING white supremacy system by the complete sexual and psychological DOMINATION of black males -- who represent the BIGGEST THREAT to total white domination -- ***AND that is the BOTTOM LINE.***

"During the past 400 years, Black men in the U.S. have been forced into passive and cooperative submission to white men.

White men in this world area have at least a vague, perhaps unconscious, understanding that after 20 generations (400 years), male passivity has evolved into male effeminization, bisexuality, and homosexuality.

These patterns of behavior are simply expressions of male self-submission to other males in the area of people activity called "sex." -- Dr. Frances Cress Welsing, 'The Isis Papers,' (1991)

CHAPTER 16

THE HOMOSEXUAL (RACIST) WHITE MALE

A Little-Known Fact of Slavery: The Rape Of The African & Black Males

It is common knowledge that African slave women and girls were raped by slave-owners but very little has been said about the rape of African men and boys. Another little known FACT: ***homosexuality was nonexistent in African culture before European colonization and sexual domination/perversion.***

Raping the males of a conquered people is a EUROPEAN TRADITION that dates back to ancient Greek and Roman cultures where homosexuality was common. ***Tragically, raping black males is an American "Slave Tradition" that continues to this day:***

Coprez Coffie -- *unarmed black male sodomized by officers with a screwdriver in an alley after being pulled over by Chicago police officers. Although the police denied his allegations, the jury was convinced by the evidence presented, including doctors reports of tears to Coffie's rectum and a screwdriver found in the police car's glove compartment with fecal matter on it. (2007)*

Haitian immigrant Abner Louima -- *sodomized by a broomstick handle inside a New York (70th Precinct) police station by two white police officers. Louima suffered severe internal injuries after he was assaulted in a precinct bathroom, where he was held down by Police Officer Schwarz while Police Officer Volpe shoved a wooden stick into his rectum. (1997)*

'Wade,' a black male who appeared on the "Dr. Phil" show *and confessed that he had been raped twice at age 9 and 13 by a white man in his neighborhood. In telling the story, Wade says that this man told him to ride in the car with him so they could find the person that broke his garage window and then he pulled over and savagely raped him. Wade goes on to say that after he raped him he put him out on the side of the road and he was in so much pain that he could not walk he just stood there." (2008)*

Seven African Immigrant Van Drivers – *accused a Queens, N.Y. police officer of raping and sodomizing them in separate incidents. The District Attorney Richard A. Brown dismissed the charges. (1993)*

Man Charged With Selling Adopted Black Son For Sex On The Web -- *42-year-old Frank Lombard, a white male, and employee of Duke University in Durham, North Carolina has been arrested for allegedly offering his adopted 5-year-old (black) son up for sex over the internet.*

An FBI informant allegedly saw Lombard online performing sex acts on an African-American child believed to be one of his adopted sons. In the chat transcript, "F.L." (Frank Lombard) is asked how he got access to a child so young. "Adopted," he replied, and said that the process was "not so hard ... especially (sic) for a black boy."

Lombard lives with his ***gay partner****, another Duke University employee. The Arrest Warrant documents that Lombard sodomized one of his two adopted African-American sons and made the boy give him oral sex on-line. He offered other (white) gays the same opportunity. (2009)*

Did The Rape Of African Male Slaves Plant The First Bitter Seeds Of Black Male Homosexuality?

We cannot afford to underestimate the catastrophic damage that was done to the manhood of African male slaves. At the risk of being labeled "homophobic," we will not waste valuable time being politically correct when it comes to the topic of "homosexuality."

It is crucial that the descendants of American slavery UNDERSTAND the psychological trauma that male slaves endured -- because the SAME dehumanization and emasculation process of black males that took place during slavery is STILL happening today via the law enforcement, incarceration, education, and employment institutions in America.

Could the systematic psycho-sexual rape of African and black males over a 500-year period be the GENESIS (the root) of black male homosexuality today?

When White Male Homosexuality Becomes A Racist Sexual Obsession

Florida Representative Bob Allen *(a white male Republican) was arrested for soliciting oral sex from an undercover black male cop. The reason he gave to the police? He was afraid of becoming another "crime statistic." (2007)*

***

Vincent McGee, black male, was charged with capital murder after pleading guilty for killing a white supremacist, Richard Barrett. McGee said that the 67-year-old white male made sexual advances toward him. (July, 2011)

***

Indiana State Rep. Phillip Hinkle, who recently voted against a gay marriage amendment was accused of soliciting Kameryn Gibson, after the 18-year-old black male posted an ad on Craigslist in the 'men-for-men' section looking for a "sugar daddy." Hinkle responded, met Gibson in a hotel room and displayed his state lawmaker ID. Gibson said he got cold feet and left after Hinkle allegedly "exposed his body." (August 2011)

***

"Between 1971 and 1991, Donald Fitzpatrick, a white male, and a longtime Red Sox clubhouse manager, systematically molested an unknown number of black boys. In 2003 the Boston Red Sox setlled a $3.15 million federal lawsuit brought against them by eight black men who said Fitzpatrick repeatedly molested them as boys." -- HuffPost Black Voices (2011)

***

"We're fine for show during Gay Pride Week when a little color is needed, or for a quick fuck in the dark, when none of their friends are looking, but middle-class Whites don't want to pass along any useful job or investment information or include us in their social circles. They don't hire us to work in their bars and businesses, and after a roll in the hay, they just may not speak the next time they see you." -- Evan, 29, homosexual black male -- 'Black Men, White Men,' edited by Michael J. Smith

***

"I know I question interest shown in me by Whites. I have this gnawing suspicion that it's not genuine, that it's self-serving, that they want something other than what they say...if you don't behave like a field hand or a clown, they don't know what the fuck to make of you because you've shot all their stereotypes to hell – and most of them don't have any time or room in their lives to deal with anything beyond stereotypes and gorilla fantasies, anyway. If that." -- Perry, 32 -- 'Black Men, White Men,' edited by Michael J. Smith

***

"They come to you for the most part, as though you're some extraordinary phallic symbol...as if you're nothing but a walking phallus...no head, no arms, no nothing...actually the act of love becomes an act of murder in which you are also committing suicide." -- James Baldwin, homosexual black male novelist

The Secret Homosexual Lives of Down-Low Black Males Who Date Non-Black Females

"I was hit up by a girl recently asking me questions about homosexuality since I'm gay. Turns out she caught her man answering an ad to a gay man, and he told her that he was curious about being with a man and wanted her to participate in a threesome with another man. I told her I was surprised he told her about another man cuz a black woman wouldn't have that.

When she told me she was Asian it made me realize something a lot us in the gay black community are finding out. That a lot of black males who date outside their race are DL. It's something I never really paid attention to b4 but when I look back it appears to be true. There have been times black males were giving me the look right in front of their white women. It's a trip." -- BN, 23, student, black male homosexual

***

"A few years ago I met this very attractive black man who was married to a Korean woman. We are both amateur musicians so we exchanged business cards. I went to see him play at a club a couple of times since his wife obviously wasn't his biggest fan. I don't sleep with married men but I was surprised that he never made a sexual pass. Sorry if this sounds vain but most men find me attractive.

One day out of the blue, he asks me to film him having sex in a hotel room with his wife! I couldn't believe Mr. Goody-Two-Shoes was a freak! He said I could join in the fun as long as I didn't touch him because touching him wouldn't be right -- but I could touch his wife!

I stopped answering his calls after that. I found out later through a mutual acquaintance that his wife thought he was gay. I think he was on the DL and was trying to trick his wife into having sex with a woman so he wouldn't feel guilty about doing men. Nothing else makes any sense."

– Evelyn, 38, real estate analyst

The obvious advantages of an interracial relationship for a black male with a secret sex life is his non-black partner is unaware of the cultural nuances that might clue a black female that something is not quite right.

"If a black dude on the DL is dating outside his race, even if that woman finds out, he can keep her out of the loop of his people." -- BN, 23, student, black male homosexual

The white or Asian female is less likely to become an intimate part of the black male's TRUE social network of friends and family than a black female. In addition, a sexually conflicted black male may feel more "manly" with a non-black female who is perceived as more feminine (submissive) and less likely to threaten his own shaky masculinity.

Black Males Who Refuse To Submit To White Sexual Domination (Homosexuality) Are Severely PUNISHED

Los Angeles Laker Kobe Bryant was fined $100,000 for calling a referee a "faggot" after the referee called him on a technical foul. (April 2011)

***

"Well, you know I hate gay people. So I let it be known. I don't like gay people and I don't like to be around gay people. I am homophobic. I don't like it." -- Tim Hardaway, black former NBA player, was permanently banished from All-Star Weekend and stripped of all product endorsements. (2007)

***

"No, I did not call T.R. a faggot. It never happened," said black actor Isaiah Washington, denying allegations that he called his white homosexual castmate, T.R. Knight, a "faggot" on the set of the TV show, Gray's Anatomy. Under the relentless pressure of negative publicity, Washington formally apologized in the Golden Globes press room. "I apologize to T.R., my colleagues, the fans of the show and especially the lesbian and gay community for using a word that is unacceptable in any context or circumstance." A few months later, Washington was fired. (2007).

***

Dave Chappelle appeared on the Oprah Show in February 2006, shortly after he turned down a $50 million Comedy Central deal, and an offer to wear a dress in a film with black actor, Martin Lawrence. As of this writing, Chappelle hasn't appeared on film or TV since 2006.

***

Why White Supremacists Love Feminizing Black Males

"To defeat my enemy, I must destroy his manhood. I will turn the black male into my conquered she-male and pay him millions of dollars to wear a dress, two earrings, stockings, and high heels in front of the TV and movie camera.

I will make this conquered black male (she-male) the role model for millions of black men and boys all over the world, so the entire world can see that no matter how rich or famous or talented or successful the black man becomes, in the eyes of the world, he is still "a white man's bitch." -- Umoja

"To capture the enemy's entire army is better than to destroy it; to take intact a regiment, a company, or a squad is better than to destroy them.

For to win one hundred victories in one hundred battles is not the supreme of excellence. To subdue the enemy without fighting is the supreme excellence."

-- Sun Tzu,
'The Art of War' (544-496 BC)

CHAPTER 17

CONSENT OR COERCION? THE CONNECTION BETWEEN SLAVERY, RAPE, AND SEX BETWEEN BLACKS AND WHITES

Contrary to some anti-historical "historians," African female slaves DID NOT have "sexual intercourse" with their slave-owners: ***they were RAPED.*** The term "sexual intercourse" usually implies that two parties CONSENTED (chose) to have sexual intercourse with each other.

Female slaves did NOT "choose" or CONSENT to sex with their slave-owners: they had NO CHOICE.

To drive this point home, let's examine the definitions of the words: **consent, coercion, cope, rape, and statutory rape:**

- **Consent**: to agree, **to choose**, in agreement; of the same mind
- **Coercion:** the act of compelling someone to do something by force of authority or implied authority; where a person is legally under subjection to another, and feels pressured to bend to the will of another; to do an act contrary to his or her own will or benefit
- **Cope:** to struggle with or come to terms with a stressful, painful, or unpleasant situation that is unavoidable
- **Rape:** a sexual assault that is forced upon one person by one or more persons using violence or intimidation. If the "rapist" is MORE POWERFUL (socially, economically, or politically) than their "rape victim," physical force may be UNNECESSARY
- **Statutory rape:** sexual intercourse with a person who is under the legal (statutory) age of consent

In light of the above definitions, it is ILLOGICAL, unreasonable, anti-historical, anti-humane, and RACIST to describe the serial rapes of Sally Hemings, a female slave, by her slave-owner, Thomas Jefferson, as as a *"romantic relationship."*

It was IMPOSSIBLE for Sally Hemings, a SLAVE, to CONSENT to a sexual relationship with her SLAVE-OWNER, Thomas Jefferson, because she DID NOT have the freedom to CHOOSE her sexual partner OR the circumstances under which that sexual activity took place.

As long as Sally Hemings was a SLAVE, she had NO RIGHT (and NO CHOICE) to deny Jefferson sexual access to her body. She could NOT give HER **CONSENT** as a slave because she HAD NO CHOICE.

ANYTHING SHORT OF FREE CHOICE IS RAPE
Because NO woman would ever CONSENT to be a SLAVE

Had the roles been reversed -- a BLACK MALE slave-owner having sexual intercourse with a WHITE FEMALE slave -- ***there is NO DOUBT most American historians would have (correctly) viewed this "relationship" as a rape -- NOT a romance.***

Let's compare Sally Hemings to a female prisoner in a concentration camp who is sexually propositioned by the prison warden and "accepts" his offer. Her "involvement" with the prison warden IS NOT BE VOLUNTARY because she is in NO position to give OR withhold her **CONSENT**.

She knows the warden could force her to do whatever he wants because she has heard stories about other female prisoners who refused his sexual advances, and didn't live to tell their stories.

After the female prisoner sexually submits, she COPES by bragging about the extra food and clothing she receives, but the warden has never offered her the ONLY thing that really matters: *her freedom.*

The female prisoner is NOT having CONSENSUAL sex because she would NEVER CONSENT to be a prisoner -- anymore than Sally Hemings would CONSENT to be a slave. It is logical to assume Sally Hemings was COPING -- not CONSENTING -- with her circumstances -- and just as LOGICAL to assume that the "warden" -- and the slave-owner -- are RAPISTS.

A second example: It is against the law for an adult to have sex with anyone between the age of puberty and 18 years old because the "minor" lacks the ability (POWER) to consent AS AN EQUAL to sex with an adult.

That is why the law classifies this as STATUTORY RAPE ***because it is a "relationship" between UNEQUALS.*** The ADULT is in a superior position (has more power) compared to the MINOR. Even if the minor is willing, the law always assumes that the adult PRESSURED the underage male or female into having sex -- which is why the adult is punished and the minor is not.

When a white person propositions a black person for sex, the black person may feel PRESSURED (COERCED) consciously or subconsciously into submitting to the will of the (more powerful) white person. However, the reverse CANNOT be true.

A (powerless) black person cannot use "implied force" (that does not exist) to COERCE a white person to do *anything* that white person does not want to do -- without breaking the law.

In other words, in a system of white supremacy, the white person (the powerful "adult") always chooses the non-white person (the powerless "child") -- regardless of ANY delusions on the part of the non-white male or female who may believe otherwise.

The black person who submits to the will of a white person may not understand (or believe) that their behavior is NOT voluntary (consensual) ***because submitting to white domination (the will of white people) is an everyday part of life for all non-whites in a system of white supremacy.***

However, because of the UNEQUAL balance of power between blacks and whites, sexual intercourse is MORE like an act of COERCION (RAPE) than an act of CONSENT (CHOICE). Many whites are well aware of their MORE POWERFUL positions in comparison to non-whites and often take full SEXUAL advantage of this power.

In her controversial book on the secret sexual relationships between black females and white males, Reneathia Tate, author of *'Pieces of a Puzzle,'* asked a white male she was interviewing why he thought black females allowed white men to (sexually) experiment with them. The white male replied:

"...because they are too damn scared not to."

That being said, the Authors are not implying that most blacks are being pressured to have sexual intercourse with whites OR that most whites are interested in having sexual intercourse with blacks.

However, it is reasonable AND logical to QUESTION the TRUE motives of an oppressed person who consents to sex with a member of the SAME GROUP that is oppressing him or her.

Some reasons are obvious -- like those of Pape, the poverty-stricken, 30-year-old Senegalese male who has sex with his 52-year-old Dutch "girlfriend" in exchange for gifts and a few hundred dollars each month. *(Sex In Senegal, page 193).*

> *"I'm a thing, her object, her toy, her property," he said. "If I had the choice financially, I wouldn't date her. I would never have started this. I'm not attracted to her. I tried to avoid sex but she insisted. She has helped me a lot, so now I feel like I have to give her something."*

Is Pape "CONSENTING" or is he -- like countless other victims of racist man and woman -- simply COPING with his oppressive circumstances under the system of white supremacy?

It is certainly a question worth asking.

"...the increase in interracial marriages can be viewed as a means of escape and a means for Blacks to avoid the awareness of their continuing status as permanent outsiders.

It should be noted that in the white supremacy societal unit of Nazi Germany the highest incidence of interracial marriage between Semites (non-whites) and Germans (whites) occurred just prior to the ultimate destruction of the Semites in the Holocaust."

'The Isis Papers'
-- Dr. Frances Cress Welsingyah

CHAPTER 18

13 HARDCORE REASONS BLACKS "SUBMIT" TO SEX WITH WHITES

13 Hardcore Reasons Some Blacks Submit To Sex With Whites That Have Nothing To Do With "Love" AND Everything To Do With White Validation, Brain-Trashing, And A Black Inferiority Complex

1. Black males who believes white females are "easier" (more promiscuous) and sexually freer (freakier) than black females
2. Self-hatred and/or a black inferiority complex and believes whites are superior to blacks
3. Was raised in a predominantly white environment and does not relate to other black people. This is common among "blacks" who have a white parent and were raised by their white parent
4. To express hostility toward blacks of the opposite sex (is anti-black)
5. Seeking white validation; to impress or fit in with whites
6. To "whiten-up" their offspring so their children won't look too black (too much like their black selves)
7. For financial gain (or exploitation)
8. To hide homosexual "activities" from a culturally clueless partner
9. Believes whites are more "loving" than blacks without taking into account that this judgment ALSO applies to themselves (are brain-trashed)
10. To get rewards within high-profile professional or entertainment circles by showing a lack of 'black militancy' and a surplus of white-identification
11. To avoid all responsibility for fixing the problems in the black community
12. To avoid fixing what is wrong with him or herself

13. **BECAUSE IT IS EASIER TO "LOVE" WHITE PEOPLE.** From cradle to grave, blacks are programmed to see whites as superior, smarter, sexier, harder-working, more attractive, cleaner, and just plain nicer than black people

In other words, in a white supremacy system, black males and females are PROGRAMMED to be PRO-WHITE and ANTI-BLACK from cradle to grave -- AND have been TAUGHT to see other black people -- and OURSELVES -- through CONDEMNING WHITE EYES.

For the MOST severely white-identified black male or female, being with another (oppressed) black person DOUBLES their oppression -- in their own minds.

A white partner gives the self-hating black male or female the illusion of white acceptance (and white validation), and serves as a "soothing lotion" that coats (hides) the TRUTH about their LOW CASTE (true) status in a white supremacy society.

"Loving" whites also keeps OUR secrets safe. For the black person who is afraid of true intimacy, a white person may be the perfect fit.

An "intimate" relationship WITHOUT honesty can only go so deep. Neither person will ever know the other because neither is being honest about the REAL differences between them OR their TRUE feelings about those differences.

The interracially-involved black person often hides OR downplays their mistreatment AS a black person because the TRUTH destroys the ILLUSION of INCLUSION and forces them out of DENIAL -- something their white partner does not want to deal with.

If a black person cannot be honest with his or her white partner about the racism that DEFINES the quality of life for EVERY BLACK PERSON in America from cradle to grave, ***he or she is NOT being his or her TRUE SELF.***

The white person who IGNORES the victimization of their black "partner" OR denies they BENEFIT from white privilege ***should be viewed as a RACIST by their black partner.***

Mr. Neely Fuller, Jr. best summed up sexual relationships between blacks and whites in a white supremacy system:

"The best it gets is tacky."

Office Memorandum

TO : NOR - Mr. Morgan   DATE: September 4, [redacted]

FROM : COH - Mr. Lyon

SUBJECT: Operation Jungle Fever

TOP SECRET

TOP SECRET

Jack:

The following is the text of telegram no. 1338 dated August 29 from our Legation at Stockholm:

"Dept. 1398, August 27.

Our goal: to promote interracial relationships between white and blacks as a superior alternative to black male/female relationships. By doing so, we can destabilize the black family. It is imperative to destroy the concept of black male/black female love since this controversial (and perverted) form of love represents the greatest danger to continued white domination and white genetic survival.

This will create a more manageable permanent black underclass; assure the continued exploitation of black talent, resources, and labor; will eliminate the possibility of unification and/or retaliation against the white population; and will greatly reduce the likelihood of American blacks uniting with Africans in any part of the world. The best method to guarantee the desired results is our time-tested "divide and conquer strategies" outlined in this document.

Until further notice, all TV networks, cable stations, movie studios, record companies, media distribution, movie theaters, radio stations, newspapers, and websites must create programming that degrades black males and females and that portrays them as the enemies of each other to encourage the pursuit of interracial relationships. Any positive sexual expression between black males and females is STRICTLY FORBIDDEN.

Ms. A. Bergman, President of Entertainment, XYZ Group

14

Class sheet Made

FW 811.20200 FAMILY/8-2946

A/JT

TOP SECRET FILE

(The above memo is a work of fiction)

While We
Rock The
Interracial
SEX
WORLD
Our
Collective
Worldwide
Condition
Worsens...

CHAPTER 19

LETTERS FROM A WORLD-WEARY BROTHER

(The following letters were received from a black male living overseas who wanted to share his experiences -- in his own words -- with the "darker side" of international, interracial sex." -- the Authors)

Letter #1

Dear P.,

I can share so much with you about Europe and non-whites, black people and Africans in particular. I have been attacked so many times I can't count and also my non-white associates. I have dated white women to my detriment now that I look back in hindsight.

I left the states because I was so frustrated, angry, and ready to do justice to our enemy, so my family and my heart suggested I leave for Europe, or elsewhere to cool down and analyze the situation.

I am a baby-boomer ha ha ha so to speak. I grew up during the Vietnam War and the Black Panthers militant Black movement. I have traveled extensively all over the USA. I was residing in Seattle for 4 years before I left for Europe. My inspiration was and is Fred Hampton, Mark Clark, Chicago Black Panthers, and the state-sanctioned murders of righteous brothers and sisters.

My mother supported the MOVE organization in Philly with food and kindness. I lived in Chicago for about 6 months working at meat packing plants. Most of my siblings have moved to the Deep South now. I am presently a single man living alone in Salvation Army apartment in Helsinki. I do travel very much and have been working as a cook and newspaper delivery man on bicycle ha ha ha ha.

I have seen black men degrade themselves and be degraded on the dance floor in discos with white women, and fight over these pernicious, sly "wicked foxes." Most of us over here in Nordic societies have been "mojoed," hoodwinked, and bamboozled by the white society with the social welfare system and permissive, dehumanized, sexy society.

We go bonkers over the blonds and subject ourselves to unspeakable humiliation. Non-whites and blacks are filling up the jails and mental hospitals over here and suffer from drug addiction, alcohol abuse, and internalized violence.

Many black women feel that the black man didn't protect them in Africa with the strife, war zones, and violence against women so when they come to Europe they feel they want only to be with white men who are safe.

I have dated African women from Angola and Brazil both of them were damaged so badly after dating/marrying white men. It poisoned our relationship towards greater deeper respect and loving kindness towards each other.

My ex-lover girlfriend from Angola was in a mental institution for six months. Her white husband admitted her because of cultural and personal conflicts and differences.

Of course I had dated white females in the USA mainly in the Seattle region but I must say honestly my heart has always been with my dear beloved black women.

I didn't understand my hurtful feelings being a tender kind man, and my upbringing in the Baptist church, why I was subject to so much cruelty from black women in our relationships in Philly and elsewhere. I also lived and worked in Atlanta for many years and dated black women only. So much confusion we as a people are under being bombarded continually.

I have attended church in Europe but as you know the church is so poisoned and polluted with racism/white supremacy that I fell out of the church. I embraced Islam for a season, but also saw women being victimized and white skin Arabs, Persians subtlety mistreating black people all in the context of "religious tolerance." I will write more later, this is just an introduction of a little of my background.

I haven't purchased your book yet but I plan to travel to the states in June so I ask my sisters to purchase your books. A LOVE SUPREME to you and your family, friends, and all black folks and non-whites.

God bless,
Brother Luke

Letter #2

Good day, P.

I didn't want to depress you with part of my testimony. I have so much more cooking in the pot. I have been a silent witness to the horrors of Europe. Being so naive as I was when I first toured Europe. I was in Russia and non-whites cannot walk on the streets at anytime of the day or night without being in large protective groups.

Strange thing about Russia. White northern Russians consider the darker Caucasians as inferior. These Caucasians look more or less like Turks or light-skin Arabs. They are mostly from the Caucasus mountain range and are Islamic.

Also Asians from the Central Asian republics that was formerly a part of the Soviet Union are beaten, killed, and discriminated against. They are Muslims and some Buddhists. There is a Pan Slavic movement in Russian, Poland and former Yugoslavia and other Slavic nations to feel prideful and defensive towards non-Slavic peoples

You are residing in Chicago with the largest Polish and Slavic communities in US. So you know firsthand about Slavic nationalism. Maybe I can send you some links if I find them about paramilitary militias neo-Nazi groups training and then going out hunting to attack kill non-whites. Mostly in Russia these groups are prevalent and violent.

The US state department know about this movement but does nothing really to warn US non-white citizens or protect them, well, that is to be expected. The Russian mafia is everywhere in Europe and fighting with other mafias and sometimes cooperating with them in child trafficking, drug-dealing, sex slavery, big-time corporate corruption, and KGB spying rings everywhere, breaking down labor unions and progressive political opposition.

When I first came to Europe the Soviet Union was very active and alive but under renovation reforms then -- boom -- Reagan, fascist, racist, domestic and foreign policies kicked in big time to stomp on non-whites and Africans.

Remember little Grenada only 150000 citizens and Reagan's beastly white Nazi fascist white domination policies slaughtered hundreds of Grenadians who were sympathetic to the NJM -- the New Jewell Movement -- a truly social democratic movement to better the lives and be an example to other Caribbean islanders to wake up and get organizing. Same slaughtering was going on in Nicaragua, El Salvador, Guatemala, etc.

I have worked with Algerians and Bangladesh men, and they tell me when they have children with white European women the nurses and doctors always comment on the baby's hair or skin coloration.

Overly fascinated or despicable comments like some kind of exotic fruits (strange fruits) hanging from the "tree" like in that Billy Holiday song. When I have dated white women and want to talk about racism and immigration, they ALL freeze up on me or get hostile like I am supposed to be so lucky to have them and be in their "soothing lotion."

I have walked out on them even when I am in the bed with them and they make some kind of snide, nasty, foolish remark about black people, and I never return to them ever. But being foolish and confused myself, I have been so conditioned by churchiantity and the U.S. nightmare "dreams" of integration and tolerance, and humanity that I allow myself to fall prey again.

I used to believe that white folks are innocent until proven guilty. Now I realize after being hard-headed and played for a fool that this demonic streak runs in the veins of ALL of them -- the good, bad, and the ugly.

Africans here in Nordic societies are probably the most confused, pitiful non-whites I have ever witnessed because the majority of whites are blond blue-eyed with NO tolerance for anyone different. It is a highly deeply homogeneous, bleached, washed-out, regimented society. In reality, white nations are ORDERS -- racialized orders like the catholic orders.

I have not been to Africa but I plan to travel there for at least a year or more on a shoestring ha ha ha ha. I live more or less minimalist. Very simple and basic. I do no drugs, no alcohol, no spending on clothes. I get my food from Salvation Army mostly and wash my clothes free. I just pay my rent and that's it. And I walk everywhere -- and no chasing women. I am using the university computers at this time and its free and sometimes I go to the Parliament library to print free and use the computer.

I stay in touch with my family and siblings I have over 30 nieces and nephews. I am also planning meditation on my own book about Asia, Europe, Brazil, Canada, and US society and all my experiences. But feel free to examine my testimony and use what you feel is useful knowledge goes around and comes around we all share and give respectful credit to each contribution. Our Creator is the source of all wisdom, knowledge, compassion, truth, justice, loving, kindness, and forgiveness.

Respectfully,
Luke

Letter #3

Good day, P.,

Yes, it a never-ending tragedy/drama over here. Blacks and other non-whites fight each other to the death. Clannish and factional fighting from their mother country, they bring animosity to Europe. For example, Nigerians, Somalis, and other ethnic groups. Rastas and locks are frequently picked up under suspicion of being in the drug market or pimping girls.

For example, there was a Nigerian man who had been married to a European female and then he divorced her for only reasons he knows. He went to Nigeria to marry a lady from a wealthy family. After he moved back with her to Europe and they had a fallout after a few years marriage, he stabbed her 30 times all over her body and left her for dead then he jumped in front of a fast moving, high-speed train and was cut in half.

By God's grace, the lady from Nigeria survived. Her family was praying for her. She lived but lost so much blood. I met her many times and she has become a born-again, powerful believer in Christ Jesus and gives testimony all over Finland and Sweden.

She pulls up her blouse and shows the stab wounds all over her body. I don't what made this man go completely insane to do such a ghastly crime. Also there is a lot of cheating. The black women and men are cheating on each other romantically with white folks and non-whites sometimes for money sometimes for fun or revenge. I have seen black men cry like whimpering dogs at the door and feet of white women crying all night then calling the white woman so many names and calling her parents on the phone, telling her parents that their daughter is a whore. It's so sickening.

Also there have been amerikkkan basketball players trying to be so macho, showing off to the white girls, showing that they are the big player in town and then getting into fights with white men. You will not believe this but bowing and scraping to white police officers in private that they are sorry for fighting white men.

I am not making this up, truth is stranger than art, life is stranger than art. Big, huge, muscular black men being like a slave to washed- out, broken down white women with chains, also studding for white men, so white men can get off watching black men studding their wife or girlfriend for the kicks while he gets his rocks off. Try to find the book the Life and Times of Mr. Jive Ass Nigger by Cecil Brown. I think Mr. Brown wrote the book in the early 70s of his experience in Denmark and Sweden.

I thank my Creator I have never fallen into that abyss of degradation though I have my own confusions and issues. I would say 80% of my time in Europe is alone reading traveling talking to people asking questions reading newspapers, listening to the radio, and internet programs and my dear family staying in touch.

People are so controlled, very little protest or demonstrations in Italy and Spain, Germany, the UK, and other nation states. People fight and protest but in Nordic states they are so brainwashed and controlled to obey the order don't question authority. Just be blond, blue-eyed Aryans and feel superior to everyone.

Cutbacks in education, healthcare, housing allowance, and other social and job benefits are being slashed. While the bankers, corporate elites, politicians, and entertainment people get truckloads of money increases. MPs parliamentarians gave themselves a 19% increase while cutting social spending and environmental degradation. NWO -- New World Order -- is here to stay if we don't fight.

Luke

Letter #4

Thank you, P.,

Yes, I concur with you 100% that as you and the black social scientists have stated. It is a set-up. Because what's behind writing an article in one of the world's prominent English news report magazines. Blacks over here are totally damaged goods in total confusion. It's a deadly con game run by convicted criminal pathological psychopathic racists.

I have been having sessions with white European psychologists and psychiatrists reversing the question-answer set-ups. I want them to answer my questions about the European psychology. I have spoken to a European female medical doctor who is married to a black Sudanese doctor about Finland, Europe, and Sudan.

She has 5 kids and I suspect they are very confused about their identity and what's happening in the Finnish political scene and the underlying race politics. Immigration policy? I have 3 non-whites black men, African, who I discuss race issues with but when it comes to the sex issue they chill up. I confess my "sins" -- race bedding white females and I repent from that but it does no good because they black men are entranced, charmed they are vanilla fudged in the cold icebox refrigerator.

Luke

Letter #5

Yes P.,

I have suggested to a Black South African lady who is married to a white Finnish man to check out your program and books and other scientists. She wrote me that now she is more confused and rethinking her position in Europe as a black person/female.

The overtly Nazi-white domination-fascist party has got 20% of the popular vote. Their ideology is overtly straight out racist. The white media political controllers are "clouding" the issues here.

There is a component of anti-black racism being practiced on us 24/7 by non-black, non-white victims, and by black victims also. I think we black victims are slowly awakening to our situation and circumstances.

For the black Christians I wonder why we don't study and examine the works of the Honorable Marcus Garvey and apply his contributions to our faith if we want to remain Christians.

Luke

Letter #6

Good day P.,

Thank you, yes all the EU nation states have their own twist on how to manage non-whites to their advantage. I have also lived in Holland. They are the most adept, sophisticated, and clever at manipulating non-whites to fight each other and raping diamonds and gold and other precious metals and uranium from Africa.

Apartheid regime South African with the Boers-Dutch reformed church and Indonesia, mostly Muslim country, an ex-colony of Holland. Lets us not forget the Dutch Caribbean and Surinam in South America and New York, formerly New Holland = New Amsterdam. Dutch colonizers also had a big, lethal hand in enslaving Africans, and exploiting native Amazonian Indians in Brazil. Dutch like the British will cut you in a thousand pieces without you even knowing you been cut they are very sharp, fork-tongued experts.

Luke

Letter #7

Yes P.,

I see the white females courting and practicing passive aggression on non-white black men on their terms only. I have seen African women very young under 25 totally ruined after dating and mixing with white men. The Finnish beauty queen was Lola Odusogain 1996 and Miss Scandinavia 1997 -- 2nd runner-up -- for Miss Universe 1996.

She is a Nigerian lady and she has been abused as a poster cleaning lady on the billboards and also "sex kitten object," and of course, she is married to a racist white Finnish man with two children. She is constantly abused, exploited, ridiculed, and she bows and grins.

In Sweden, the king of Sweden is sexually exploiting non white Black females and his German/Brazilian wife is soooooooo upset that her man the king of Sweden is a playboy in the" chocolate pudding".

The black and non-white ladies get no justice in the news and are severely beaten up in the commercial press. They are thrown under the bus. The king of Sweden has also been entertaining Neo-Nazis to tell them not to be too hard on non-whites immigrants. Don't hurt us too much or badly.

I really don't have many people in my immediate family who are voicing and observing the shackling and refined incarceration of black folks in the cities or the countryside. Also I have to keep my mouth shut because one of my brothers shared with me that many black folks are so much on the deep edge. There is a lot of nervous frustration and internalized violence. That, for example, Philly is now called Killadelphia. But I will spending most of my time in the Deep South.

Wow, that is not really news because since I was a teenager I was aware of gang violence, drug, and domestic violence, police justifiable homicide, and premature death amongst our people. So I intend to be tactful, strategic, mindful, and discerning who I am sharing time and information with.

The white folks' system got us like a chicken with his head cut off. Yes, we are bleeding profusely from the 1000 unknown cuts. The pain and suffering is so deep. I hope I can see one my nieces who I hear is on and off again in the street life living in the park. I now question everything I have been taught in the prison school training system. At least I attempt to do that. Peace.

Luke

"An old black man in Atlanta looked into my eyes and directed me into my first segregated bus. His eyes seemed to say that what I was feeling he had been feeling, at much higher pressure, all his life.

But my eyes would never see the hell his eyes had seen. And this hell was, simply, that he had never in his life owned anything, not his wife, not his house, not his child, which could not, at any instant, be taken away from him by the power of white people.

And for the rest of the time that I was in the South I watched the eyes of old black men."

-- James Baldwin, author (1924-1987)

Sacrifice The (Black) Queen

In the game of Chess, the QUEEN is the most powerful piece on the board but the KING is the most important (and the most vulnerable) piece.

Once the Queen is removed from the game board, (the Queen Sacrifice), the King is more vulnerable to being checkmated by the opposing side. Once the King is checkmated the Game is OVER.

The Black Queen in the Chess Game of White Supremacy represents the BIGGEST OBSTACLE to capturing (checkmating) the Black King and winning the GAME.

The strategy is simple: destroy the Black Queen -- checkmate the Black King.

DETERMINED TO BE AN
ADMINISTRATIVE MARKING
E.O. 12065, Section 6-102
By AT _____ NARS, Date 1-26-95

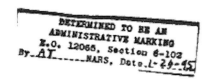

Four Stage Process To Neutralize The Black Queen

OP-16-F-2 ONI

[redacted]

MEMORANDUM FOR THE DIRECTOR

SUBJECT:
To: Mr. Whitehead
From: O. Shifter
CC: File
Re: Classified Summary/Progress Reports (2011)

1. DEMORALIZE HER: attack the black female's self-esteem via gangster rap "music," movies like Norbit, Big Momma's House, Precious, District 9, and Good Hair," that hold the black female (victim of white supremacy) up for public ridicule; utilize words and images that portray the black female as ugly, obese, materialistic, evil, and diseased.

2. DEPRIVE HER: removal of over one million Black males from the black population by creating conditions that guarantee massive black male dysfunction: mis-education, prescribing Ritalin, the prison industrial complex, manufactured homosexuality, introducing crack-cocaine and high-powered weapons along with mass unmemployment, homicide, gangster rap role models, alcoholism, murder by cops, untreated medical and mental illnesses, and the promotion of white females as the best romantic/sexual alternatives for black males.

3. DECEIVE HER: promote "interracial dating" (sexing white males) as a logical (and more desirable) alternative to black males via fraudulent (fake) interracial dating ads and websites, racist movies that pit the black male against the black female and uplift white males. This includes the widespread promotion of "anti-black-love" articles, TV specials, websites, and relationship books. The end result will be thousands of demoralized black females who have been used as SEXUAL SEWERS by white males.

4. DEVASTATE HER: the black female may become so demoralized, she will not be able to raise, civilize, or protect her children – or herself from predatory males. She may be overwhelmed with feelings of worthlessness; become deeply depressed; anti-social; violent; suicidal; homosexual; homicidal, and hostile to other blacks, especially black males, who she may blame for all her misery.

EVERY EFFORT MUST BE MADE TO NEUTRALIZE THE BLACK QUEEN. If the black male and female ever UNIFY, this UNION presents the greatest threat to the global system of white dominance and our entire way of life.

(The above memo is a work of fiction)

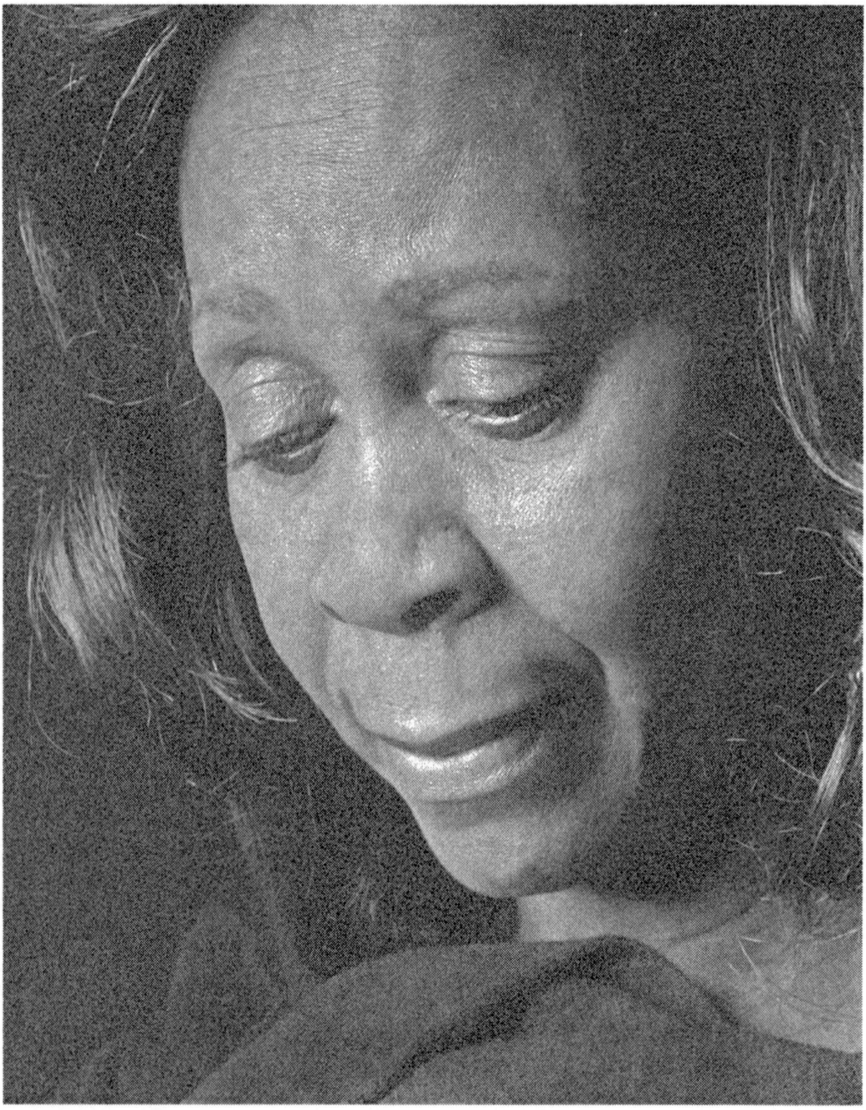

CHAPTER 20

MY KIND OF SISTA
(A true story)

A few weeks ago, I was shopping with my wife at a national health foods chain when I observed a conservative-looking black male in his mid to late 20s, accompanied by an Asian female, who was spooning rice and beans into a cardboard container.

This young black male, who looked like he wouldn't be caught dead listening to a Snoop Dogg CD, seemed real uncomfortable in his brown skin. Later, as we were walking to our car, my wife said the young black male refused to look her in the eye. Don't get it twisted, my wife, she never stares or glares at interracial couples. It ain't her style nor is it mine. She will smile and speak to anyone -- strangers, white folks, old folks, as long as they don't give her a reason to get in that butt.

The reason she refuses to stare, make comments, or roll her eyes at the sight of a black man with a white or Asian female is she hates giving the couple any reason to think she is jealous. She is fond of saying, *"I got no use for a black body with a white or an Asian brain."*

My wife's got great people instincts. The proof? She sees right through my ass most of the time. Just like EF Hutton, I always listen when she speaks. Lest you think I'm too biased, let me say that interracial dating for black folks would be NO problem for me personally, IF we didn't live in a white supremacy system where blacks and whites are NOT treated equally.

BUT

As long as the white system is waging WAR against the black community; and black children are dying in the streets; and unarmed black males are murdered-by-cop; and black unemployment is three times higher than the rest of the nation -- including illegal workers; as long as a white man with a criminal record has a better chance of landing a job than a black man with a college degree; as long as 70% of black children are being raised by single/divorced black mothers; as long as almost one million of my people are rotting in the prison-industrial-complex; as long as black folks don't produce anything, control anything, and are totally dependent on everybody else for what we need; as long as black men should make their OWN women, children, and communities OUR PRIORITY like EVERY (REAL) MAN ON THE PLANET, and as long as I know BLACK UNITY IS THE KEY TO OUR SURVIVAL; ***I will always be against interracial relationships for black people.***

The MAIN REASON the UNIFIED Asian, Arab, Indian, Hispanic, and white communities have thriving BUSINESS AND ECONOMIC BASES, and SAFE and SANE communities is they have INTACT, stable families made up of the same race of men and women (for the most part).

That tells me it's only common sense that black folks had BETTER do the same damn thing. We don't have to reinvent the wheel, we just need a SET OF OUR OWN.

Getting back to the story...

I started checking out this young brother's body language, wondering why he was so uptight, and I started thinking, "This young brotha is real fugged-up. He knows somewhere inside his mixed-up skull that something ain't right about what he's doing, or maybe the REASON he's doing it.

But he's wrong about that. He's doing exactly what he's been programmed to do, especially if he's got a black body with a white brain that can't think for itself.

And DON'T be fooled by that Asian "woman of color" bullshit.

A brother I know said he married an Asian woman because he was afraid to marry a white woman and look like a sell-out. Now, this brother admitted upfront that he wasn't in love with his wife when he married her, so "color-blind love" had nothing to do with it.

He deliberately CHOSE a non-black woman because of his own black inferiority complex. He thought marrying a non-black female would give him more status as a dark-skinned black male -- and set him apart from other blacks.

Am I saying every black person in an interracial relationships hates themselves? No, but in my experience, MOST have serious issues with other black people and themselves. Of course, this is just my experience.

Getting back to the story...

Now, if you asked this young black male why he was so uptight being seen in public with his Asian girlfriend, he would probably blame it on other "ignorant, intolerant people."

But the fact is if HE wasn't comfortable in the role he was playing OR with the person he was with, then HE'S got the fugging problem, not the other "ignorant people." After all nobody twisted his arm, right?

But he's walking around, trapped in confusion, with that white traffic cop inside his skull, directing his thinking and actions that tell him black is inferior.

Just a dazed zebra stumbling in the midst of hungry lions...

So, he and this Asian girlfriend got into the checkout line across from us. And he still couldn't raise his eyes above his chest. And then I noticed who was standing on the other side of the cashiers: an older black lady in her sixties just staring at his ass like: *"You little mothafugger (!)"*

I had to laugh because the look on her face was FIERCE! I said (to myself), oh hell yeah, sister, you got that right. These little negroes are the same ones YOU raised from tiny babies who now think they're too good for a black woman.

The same BLACK WOMEN who birthed them, fed them, burped them, stayed up all night with them, and wiped their noisy, messy little black baby asses, or sat in the emergency room at three am praying her baby boy's temperature went down (like my Moms did with me).

She was the one who cheered him on at his performance as a bunny rabbit at the Easter Sunday church play, and years later, cheered him on from the stands at his high school games...

NOT the Asian, Hispanic, or white female.

The Black woman was the one who worked two jobs, took care of the house, cooked the food, oiled the scalps, combed and braided the hair, ironed the clothes, BOUGHT the damn clothes (if she was a single moms), and did without, just to put her black son through high school and college, paying for graduations, proms, parties, field trips, jackets, Christmas gear, and student fees; his first car, and sometimes, his first condoms...

NOT the Asian, Hispanic, or white female.

I can't count HOW many black women I know *personally* who raised their shorties by themselves, which is why I love and respect black women more than any man could love his women, cause I had one of those classic Moms, and sad to say, I pity any man or woman, black or white, who didn't have a Moms like the one I had.

My Pops was a good but hard man, who grew up back in the day when it was brutal being a black man. He didn't do a lot of kissing or hugging, but showed love by keeping a roof over our heads, food on the table, and even a few toys at Christmas, so I'm grateful to Pops for that -- but my MOMS was the one who gave us unconditional love.

Enough said about that, back to the story...

This older black lady was looking like, *"...these little niggas know they got some fugging NERVE..."* to take all that education, money, love and support that black women invested in them to a white, Hispanic, OR Asian female who NEVER once walked in a picket line, never got spit on, never integrated a lunch counter, never got bit by police dogs, or blasted with fire hoses, or called a nigger to her face (or behind her back).

They never marched around the police station or around the block because black boys (and men) were dying in the streets. They never contributed ONE DIME or ONE DROP OF SWEAT to the liberation of black people, and never gave a damn or a dime unless there was something in it for them (like sex or alimony). And they damn sure never rode on a bus for eight hours to Jena, LA to fight for six black boys nobody knew from a hole in the ground.

And I said to myself, hell yeah, sista, hell yeah, you is ABSOLUTELY RIGHT to make that little negro squirm...with that Asian female on his arm.

I BET she was the kinda sista who would stand with her arms folded at the door and refuse to let that black son, brother, or uncle walk in HER house with an Asian or white female to eat up HER fried chicken, HER cornbread, and HER collard greens that SHE paid HER good, hard-earned money for, just because his black ass was tired of eating Campbell soup casseroles, or Hamburger Helper, or some foreign cuisine that will never take the place of his black momma's soul food.

And I bet

That tired black sister -- who had seen the Civil Rights movement up closer than most of us -- was TIRED of watching so many TIRED black sons, uncles, nephews, brothers, and cousins, bringing home anybody but a black woman.

And she was TIRED of wondering:

> *"Is this what we black women marched for, scrubbed white women's floors for, got spit on for, beat for, fire-hosed for, sacrificed for, and died for? To be discarded by black males like some worthless black trash that had outlived its usefulness?"*

So, instead of setting two more plates, and checking her hurt feelings at her OWN door, that righteous sister told that little dishonorable nigga to STEP! until his black ass CAME CORRECT and brought home somebody who LOOKED LIKE HIS BLACK MOMMA.

And you know what?

I had the feeling that's exactly the kind of sista she was...

"For a rich Negro to marry a poor white is an unpardonable crime and sin; because it simply means the transference of the wealth of the race to another, and the ultimate loss of the wealth to the race.

It is logically evident that if the Negro is rich, he gained all or most of his wealth from his race. Therefore, to ignore the opposite sex of his race and intermarry with another race is to commit a crime or sin for which he should never be pardoned by his race.

Teach the people to abhor such Negroes. Having nothing to do with them so long as they continue in that relationship. This must be diplomatically, not to the hearing of the white race.

For a Negro man to marry someone who does not like his mother or is not a member of his race is to insult his mother, nature, and God, who made his father."

-- The Honorable Marcus Garvey
(1887 - 1940)

Checkmate The (Black) King

In the game of
Chess, the
Black King
cannot play
the white side
of the
Chess Board
and win.

"Perhaps I should begin with something obvious -- something so obvious that it escaped my attention for almost thirty-five years:

All black men are insane.

Furthermore, it is safe to say that there never has been a sane black man in this society. Almost any living thing would quickly go mad under the unrelenting exposure the climate created and reserved for black men in a white racist society..."

-- Bob Teague, author of "Letters to a Black Boy"

CHAPTER 21

OMAR THORNTON SHOULD BE A WAKE-UP CALL FOR BLACK AMERICA

The Event:

On August 3, 2010, Omar Thornton, a 34-year-old black male, walked into his workplace, fully armed, and shot and killed eight of his white coworkers at Hartford Distributors, a beer delivery company in Hartford, Connecticut.

The reason, in the words of Omar Thornton: *"...you probably want to know the reason I shot this place up. They treat me bad over here, and they treat all the other black employees bad over here, too, so I just take it into my own hands and I handled the problem..."*

Transcript of Omar Thornton's 911 Call

(10:20 PM EDT, August 5, 2010)
Dispatcher: State Police.

Thornton: Is this 911?

Dispatcher: Yeah, can I help you?

Thornton: This is Omar Thornton, the, uh, the shooter over in Manchester.

Dispatcher: Yes, where are you, sir?

Thornton: I'm in the building. Uh, you probably want to know the reason why I shot this place up. This place here is a racist place.

Dispatcher: Yup, I understand that

Thornton: They treat me bad over here, and they treat all the other black employees bad over here too, so I just take it into my own hands and I handled the problem — I wish I coulda got more of the people.

Dispatcher: Yeah. Are you armed, sir? Do you have a weapon with you?

Thornton: Oh yeah, I'm armed.

Dispatcher: How many guns do you have with you?

Thornton: I got one now, there's one out, one out in the uh, the uh, factory there.

Dispatcher: Yup. OK, sir.

Thornton: I'm not gonna kill nobody else, though.

Dispatcher: Yeah, we're gonna have to have you surrender yourself somehow here, not make the situation any worse, you know what I mean?

Thornton: These cops are gonna kill me.

Dispatcher: No they're not. We're just gonna have to get you to relax

Thornton: I'm relaxed, just calm down.

Dispatcher: ... to have you, you know, turn yourself over.

Thornton: We're just talking, you're gonna play something on the news, you know I'm gonna be popular, right [inaudible] the right thing. SWAT team just rolled by in army gear. You don't know where I'm at, but, I don't know, maybe you can trace it from this phone call. But, yeah, these people here are crazy, they treat me bad from the start here, racist company. They treat me bad, I'm the only black driver they got here. They treat me bad over here, they treat me bad all the time.

Dispatcher: This is a horrible situation, I understand that...

Thornton: You don't need to calm me down, I'm already calmed down. I'm not gonna kill nobody else — I just want to tell my story so that you can play it back.

Dispatcher: You're gonna help me get you out of the building, OK?

Thornton: All right, I'm a, I get — don't worry about that, I got that taken care of, I don't need anybody to talk me into getting me out. ...

Dispatcher: Where in the building are you, Omar?

Thornton: I'm not gonna tell you that. Where they find me, that's when everything will be over.

Dispatcher: Yeah, just, you know, where are you located, are you up in the offices?

Thornton: Where they fired me, everything be all right. ... Manchester itself is a racist place.

Dispatcher: Yeah, now, um, what time did you get there today?

Thornton: Um, It was about 7 o'clock

Dispatcher: Yeah. This morning?

Thornton: Yeah, about 7 a.m., yeah, they told me to come early today.

Dispatcher: What type of weapon do you have?
Thornton: I got a Ruger SR9, 15 shot.

Dispatcher: A Ruger? SR9?

Thornton: Automatic, yeah

Dispatcher: Is it a rifle?

Thornton: No, no, it's a pistol. I like pistols too, they are my favorites.

Dispatcher: Now, uh, you're gonna make the troopers and the people come in and catch ya? You're not gonna surrender yourself?

Thornton: Well — I guess, I guess uh, maybe I'll surrender ... nah. They come and get me, have them come get me.

Dispatcher: Yeah, we wouldn't want to do it like that, Omar. You know, it's already been a bad enough scene here this morning, we want you to relax.

Thornton: I'm relaxed though, I'm done.

Dispatcher: Yeah, we don't want any more, any more, uh, you know, people to lose their life, here.

Thornton: I'm not gonna kill nobody else.

Dispatcher: OK.

Thornton: I'm not coming out, I'm not coming out, they gonna have to find me. Probably use some dogs or whatever, I don't know what you're gonna do. Anyway.

Dispatcher: How much ammunition you have with you?

Thornton: I got uh, I shot, uh oh.

Dispatcher: What was that?

Thornton: It's all right. I guess it's got me ... I have to take care of business. Tell my people I love them, and I gotta go now.

Dispatcher: Omar. I really want you to help me stop this situation. OK?

Thornton: OK.

Dispatcher: If you work with me we'll get this to stop, OK? Omar? Omar Omar? OK ... [to others] Still alive ...

[Within minutes of making that 911 call, Omar Thornton (supposedly) kills himself, although it appears he may have been shot by a sniper]

The Aftermath

According to company officials, Thornton was caught on surveillance video stealing beer on a previous occasion. When the company offered him a choice of being fired or resigning, Thornton signed the resignation papers and was being escorted out of the building when he opened fire.

An unidentified female who claimed to be acquainted with a close friend of Thornton's allegedly wrote a statement that said, *"Thornton was set up,"* and added that the videotape used as evidence of him stealing did NOT show an actual theft taking place.

Four Critical Questions

1. If Thornton was stealing from his employer and this theft was captured on videotape, why hasn't that tape surfaced in the media? This would give more weight to the claim by company officials that Omar Thornton was fired for just cause. The media has aired controversial videos in the past: the police beating of Rodney King, and a video of a Chicago cop beating a white female bartender who refused to serve him more alcohol.
2. Does the videotape show Thornton stealing cases of beer (putting them into his personal vehicle) OR does it show him moving beer from one location to another -- a normal part of his job as a warehouse driver?
3. If company officials allowed a black employee to be tormented the way Omar Thornton and his witnesses claimed, would the same officials be capable (and motivated) to manufacture a reason to fire him?
4. If Thornton was set-up and unjustly accused and fired – after being severely mistreated on a daily basis by racist whites on his job -- does this explain the kind of RAGE that triggered a mass murder?

Unfortunately, Thornton's accusers are the only people who are capable of revealing the truth – and they're sticking to their "story." Regardless of the facts, this following axiom holds true:

AXIOM #7: "THE BLACK VICTIM = A VICTIMLESS CRIME" THEORY. A BLACK PERSON IN A CONFLICT WITH A WHITE PERSON (OR A WHITE SYSTEM) CANNOT BE THE VICTIM IN A WHITE SUPREMACY SOCIETY. THE BLACK INDIVIDUAL IS ALWAYS AT FAULT, REGARDLESS OF WHO INITIATED THE CONFLICT, OR WHAT FACTS OR EVIDENCE IS PRESENT.

Our Analysis

This is NOT intended to condemn Omar Thornton, who was clearly a victim of racism/white supremacy, OR to condone his decision to take eight lives. A tragedy like this demands that compassion for both parties be balanced with truth and logic.

However, what needs to be said in the interest of promoting justice MUST BE SAID, even if it offends or hurts feelings. The reader is free to agree or disagree with what is written here or anywhere else in this book. We have done our best to be fair, to tell the truth, and be correct in what we understand and know to be true.

Only Two Options: Submit OR Resist

There are only two options for blacks who engage in sexual intercourse with whites WITHIN a white supremacy society:

1. **to submit to white supremacy**
2. **to resist white supremacy and self-destruct**

Omar Thornton is a classic case of the inability to submit AND resist at the same time. In other words, it is impossible to lay down with (the human face of) white supremacy at night and get up in the morning and effectively fight it, anymore than you can go UP and DOWN at the same time without ripping your body apart. Submitting AND resisting white supremacy at the same time WILL RIP A BLACK MIND APART.

*The following is a **FICTIONAL STORY** based on the facts that have been reported in the mainstream media and in no way is intended to defame any real human beings. **This analysis is the product of the authors' imaginations,** in our attempt to illustrate the psychological dangers of submitting AND resisting WHITE SUPREMACY.*

Imagine this:

The first emotion **Black Male A** has when he wakes up in bed next to a white female is a feeling of dread, knowing he must go to a job where he'll be subjected to the same racism from his white coworkers and bosses that he has dealt with for over three years.

On his way to his job assignment he stops in the men's room. On the bathroom wall, he sees racist graffiti on the wall that says -- *"Kill all niggers"* and storms out to find a supervisor. The white supervisor blows him off and tells him to "stop being so sensitive, that's the problem with you people."

When **Black Male A** tells his union rep about the incident, he gets the same callous response, and is told the union will look into that trivial matter when they "get the time."

For the rest of the day, **Black Male A** is in a quiet rage, as he experiences more on-the-job sabotage and racist comments from his coworkers. He is aware that his coworkers have already heard about the incident that morning because the consensus around the warehouse is he was "another nigger playing the race card."

After another long day of being mistreated, **Black Male A** returns home to a white female who does not and cannot understand what he is going through, even if she tries to sympathize. He knows she will never understand, and he dare not tell her about the growing hatred in his heart for white people.

Black Male A tosses and turns at night while his white female sleeps peacefully by his side. He will wake up, exhausted, in a few hours to face another tortuous day with racist whites who want to rob him of his ability to feed, house, and clothe himself.

When the alarm goes off, he showers, gets dressed, and kisses his white female companion goodbye before he leaves to face what is starting to feel like an army of hostile whites, who despise him because he is black.

That night **Black Male A** engages in sexual intercourse with a white female (white supremacy wearing a human face) for surely, part of her appeal – perhaps, all her appeal – to that tortured black soul lies in his secret (and child-like) belief that having a white female will make him more human to the whites who despise his black skin.

However, his white female companion cannot deliver the one thing he so badly needs: white acceptance (safety from racist whites), but he cannot bring himself to blame her, so he must blame himself for NOT measuring up.

Black Male A tries harder to be the best black man he can be, because he is not allowed to JUST BE (A MAN), but is always on trial; always being judged wherever he goes. Even when he goes into a store, he is the most likely person in America to be followed by store security.

Even wearing a business suit, he is the most likely person in America to cause a white female to hold her purse and her thighs tighter if he walks into an elevator. And when he shops at the local supermarket with his white female, there are always (white) eyes judging and condemning him.

Black Male A is still determined to be the best "black" he can be, which is why he avoids associating with other blacks socially – especially black females -- because their presence confirms his worst fears: *too much black is not a good thing around whites*.

Black Male A is exhausted, trying to be a "good black" (man) because he is not allowed to JUST BE A MAN. He is exhausted because he has given his all -- his time, love, sex, and money -- and is receiving less in return.

Black Male A does not complain even when he is financially exploited or physically assaulted by his white female companion because his need to be accepted is stronger than his fear of being abused and taken advantage of.

He would never make this kind of Herculean effort for a black female – not because he dislikes black females -- but because he has nothing to prove to someone who cannot offer him the white validation he desperately needs.

With a black female, he can JUST BE (A MAN), take off his "mask," and be himself. He is NOT always on trial because of the "wrongness" of his skin color, but will always be fully human to the black female. If he is lucky enough to find a compatible black female partner, he will get in exactly where he FITS IN -- but **Black Male A** does not know that.

Instead, **Black Male A** continues the futile cycle of going to the racist white union reps and the racist white bosses to complain about his racist white coworkers then returns home to his (racist suspect) white female to complain about other racist whites. Whatever comfort he needs to soothe his mind and spirit he cannot find at work OR at home.

Because he has separated himself from his ONLY TRUE ALLY – the black female – he has NO PSYCHOLOGICAL OR PHYSICAL DEFENSES from the wrath of white supremacy.

Black Male A lacked the perspective that could ONLY come from those who have walked in his shoes -- *another black person* -- who could have warned him that sexing a white female might antagonize his white male co-workers and cause them to retaliate against him.

Unfortunately for **Black Male A,** black friends, lovers, spouses, etc., cannot validate the white-identified black person who desperately seeks white acceptance.

His days are surely numbered as he attempts to resist white supremacy (by day) and submit to white supremacy (every night) until that day comes when his black mind splits apart at the seams -- and **Black Male A** is driven to pick up a gun and kill his tormentors -- and possibly himself.

Black Male A's attempt to submit AND resist white supremacy at the same time led to a tragic case of psychological suicide and mass murder.

A Less Fatal Example Of Submission And Resistance To White Supremacy Via Interracial Sex

On August 10, 2010, **a Black Female** called the Dr. L. talk radio show for advice on how to handle her growing resentment toward her white husband of three years who did not defend her when other whites (his friends and family) made racist comments about blacks (practicing racism) in her presence.

Unfortunately for the **Black Female Caller**, the host, Dr. L. (a white female), was less than sympathetic, and in fact, used the word "nigger" several times during the call, which she then justified by saying, *"black guys use that word all the time."*

She warned the **Black Female Caller** not to *"NAACP me...if you're that hypersensitive about color, and don't have a sense of humor, don't marry out of your race."*

During a CNN interview, the **Black Female Caller** later said, *"I was calling to get some help and I did not expect to hear the things that she said to me. I didn't want to turn this into a racial thing, I just wanted some advice."*

Our Analysis

There are only two psychological options for blacks who engage in interracial sex with whites WITHIN a white supremacy society:

1. **to submit to white supremacy**
2. **to resist white supremacy and self-destruct**

*The following is a **FICTIONAL STORY** based on the facts that have been reported in the mainstream media and in no way is intended to defame any real human beings. **This analysis is the product of the authors' imaginations** as we attempt to illustrate the psychological dangers of submitting AND resisting WHITE SUPREMACY.*

Imagine this:

Black Female B turned to her white husband then to another white person (a talk show host) to complain about her husband's racist white friends and relatives. **Black Female B's** SUBMISSION to white supremacy is rooted in her denial that her (white) husband could NOT be a racist if he married a black female. Despite her claim that she is happily married, it is obvious her resentment toward her white husband had been building up for some time.

The **Black Female B's** RESISTANCE to white supremacy was the act of confronting her (white) husband about his silence when his white friends and relatives practiced racism against her. After getting no support from her white spouse, she asked another white person (a talk show host) what to do about the racism other whites were practicing in her presence.

Black Female B DOES NOT UNDERSTAND (or refuses to accept) that even a white person who is married to a black (or non-white) person is STILL A RACIST if he or she is practicing racism against their non-white spouse or other non-whites.

Her husband's silence speaks volumes and may be a crime of OMISSION by remaining silent while other whites practiced racism against his black wife. It is also possible that he allowed his friends and family members to do his talking for him.

It is likely **Black Female B's** husband had practiced racism in her presence BEFORE they were married, and that he practiced racism against other blacks (and non-whites) when she was not around. If this is the case, one could imagine his thinking might go something like this:

> *"What's up with this naïve black female? She's in MY world, and racism/white supremacy is part of MY world. I will never take her side against (my) white people. After she is long gone, I will still be white, will always be white, and will continue to enjoy the white privileges that have been guaranteed me from birth.*

In order to continue receiving those "benefits," whites must practice racism against non-whites. My white peer approval and white privileges matters more than this marriage (which my friends and family said should have never happened in the first place).

Doesn't she know she has to adapt to the ways of white people if she wants to be with a white person? White people don't have to adapt to the black world, because we have all the power. If this black female wants this marriage to last, she must adapt to my (white) world and keep her mouth shut about racism because I'm just not interested in that information."

The Talk Show Host's "advice" essentially amounted to the same thing:

"You naive black female, YOU made the choice to be with a white man, so you must adapt to his (our) world, and his (our) world is based on white dominance/black submission. That's the deal and the bed you made by marrying a white man, and you must lie in it, lumps and all. Why a white man would marry someone (black) like you with all the nice, single white females around, totally disgusts me. So, if you're experiencing racism, suck it up, because I'm just not interested in that information!"

Unless **Black Female B** examines her real reasons for marrying a white male who DOES NOT DEFEND HER from whites who are practicing racism against her IN HIS PRESENCE, there's a good chance she will get involved with another white male if she ever divorces her current husband.

The Bottom Line:

1. Anyone who condones your mistreatment is NOT your friend
2. Anyone who condones your mistreatment should NEVER be your friend
3. Anyone who condones your mistreatment cannot be trusted
4. If you are sleeping with someone who allows you to be mistreated, you are sleeping with your "enemy" NOT your "ally."

What do Black Male A and Black Female B Have In Common?

1. It is likely both dated whites exclusively prior to their last relationship.
2. Both possibly believed being involved with a white person would make them more acceptable to other (racist and racist suspect) whites
3. Both confided in white people about the racism they were experiencing from other whites, and neither got the support they needed
4. Neither understood that it is impossible to serve two masters at the same time: ***white supremacy AND black normalcy***
5. Engaging in sexual intercourse with whites blinded both to the hard-core truth: sex with whites does NOT eliminate OR offer any protection against racism.

Maximum-Emergency Compensatory Justice

According to Neely Fuller, Jr.'s book -- **"The United Independent Compensatory Code/System/Concept: A Textbook/Workbook for Thought, Speech and/or Action for Victims of Racism/White Supremacy"** -- the ninth area of people activity is WAR.

The book explains the **"Maximum-Emergency Compensatory Justice,"** which is defined as:

"The willful deliberate elimination of one or more Racists (White Supremacists), through death, and, the willful and deliberate elimination of self, through death, by a victim of racism (non-white person), acting alone, acting according to a detailed plan, and acting only after he or she has judged that he or she can no longer endure the effects of Racism and/or that he or she is no longer able to effectively promote justice, except by eliminating one or more Racists, and by eliminating his or her self, as a subject to the racists."

Mr. Fuller's book in NO way promotes violence but recognizes the pressure cooker of racism can make its victims react in violent, unpredictable ways.

Why Omar Thornton Is A Wake-Up Call For Black America

There are thousands of **Black Male As** and **Black Female Bs** in America who are having sexual intercourse with whites without understanding how sex is used as a weapon to maintain white supremacy. They do not understand the psychological price they will pay when they attempt to SUBMIT and RESIST white supremacy at the same time.

The REAL issue is NOT whether blacks mistreat other blacks. Certainly, whites mistreat other whites; Hispanics mistreat other Hispanics; and Asians mistreat other Asians.

It is MAXIMUM RACIST AGGRESSION (disguised as interracial "relationships") when whites practice racism against their black partners OR refuse to come to their defense when other whites are practicing racism against them.

The reader is free to accept or reject our analysis (and warnings) in this book, and decide for him or herself whether it is beneficial or destructive to engage in interracial relationships (and sexual intercourse) with whites in a white supremacy system. However, they should keep in mind that there are ONLY three psychological options for blacks who have sexual intercourse with whites WITHIN a white supremacy society: (1) ***submit (commit psychological suicide,*** (2) ***resist (and self-destruct), or:***

(3) ***STOP HAVING SEX WITH WHITE PEOPLE -- until the system of white supremacy has been eliminated.***

Chapter 22

THE BALLOON AND THE BASKET

She was a beautiful mahogany-brown Balloon who loved soaring high in the blue skies. Attached to the Balloon was a handsome, sturdy brown Basket who provided stability and kept the Balloon from getting too close to the sun. The strong brown tethers (cords) that had held them together for the last thousand years had endured a thousand terrible storms.

One day, the Balloon and the Basket passed over a traveling circus where hundreds of shiny red, blue, green, and purple balloons floated on long, silky strings above the striped tents. The Basket was awestruck. They were the most beautiful balloons he had ever seen -- mainly because they weren't *brown*. It didn't matter that they were too small and puny to lift a basket his size; he was still impressed.

The winds picked up and carried the Balloon and the Basket away from the circus. Heartbroken, the Basket watched as the brightly colored balloons shrank in the distance.

The Basket blamed the Balloon for being too big to steer against such a strong wind. If only he could be free of the Balloon, his life would be perfect! When the Balloon heard the Basket grumbling below, she decided *she* was tired of being controlled by the Basket. If only she could be free of the Basket, her life would be complete!

Below them, the huge, jagged white rocks and swirling waters beckoned to the Balloon and the Baskhet. "Come on, take a swim," the waters coaxed the pair. "We promise we won't let you drown."

The Balloon and the Basket paid the deceptive waters no mind. They had survived more than a thousand years together by avoiding the dangers of the jagged white rocks and raging waters.

Tragically, their dependence on each other was now the main thing driving them apart. They had been a team for so long that they took each other for granted. Secretly, each believed he or she would be better off apart, and each made plans for their escape.

The next afternoon, the westerly winds blew the Balloon and the Basket toward the circus tents and the brightly colored balloons. This time, the Basket came prepared. He took a long sharp stick from the bottom of his basket and started poking holes in the Balloon until he heard sharp hisses of air.

The Basket was so intent on being free; he didn't notice that the Balloon was sawing away at the strong brown tethers that held them together with a saw she'd hidden away.

With each poke of the Basket's stick, they descended another 50 feet. Now, they were only 200 feet above the jagged white rocks and swirling waters. The Balloon frantically sawed faster and faster.

When the last tether was completely severed, the sturdy brown Basket went into a free fall, tumbling over and over toward the jagged white rocks. When the Basket realized his fatal mistake, he called out for the Balloon to save him but she was too busy plugging up the holes he'd made.

With a loud crash and a terrifying scream, the Basket hit the jagged white rocks and broke into a thousand pieces. The swirling waters pulled what was left of the once sturdy brown Basket beneath the rolling white foam. The Balloon shouted with joy! She was finally free! Without the weight of the Basket and his controlling ways, she was soaring higher than ever before!

Then the Balloon noticed her smooth, slick surface was melting. She was too close to the sun! With a cry of dismay, she tried to descend to a safer altitude but the torn brown tethers were of no use in steering.

Frightened, and in agony, the Balloon cried out for her beloved brown Basket! Like the Basket, she realized her fatal mistake too late. The Basket had allowed her to soar, but he had also kept her safe.

When the Balloon bounced off the sun, she exploded into a thousand shiny-brown pieces! What was once a magnificent brown Balloon floated down to the jagged white rocks and was consumed by the swirling white waters.

Then something happened that had never happened in the history of time. The swirling waters rose until they completely covered the jagged white rocks, and for the first time in a thousand years, the raging waters were calm and peaceful.

Without the Basket, the Balloon could not steer clear of the dangerous sun. Without the Balloon, the Basket could not rise above the dangerous white rocks. Together they made a formidable team. Apart, they were doomed.

THE END OF ALL STORIES

"The lion cannot survive alone;
without the lioness, he will perish."

-- Umoja

"Look at the parts that make up the whole. By separating the parts, sowing dissension and division, you can bring down even the most formidable foe."

Robert Greene,
"The 33 Strategies of War"

For Black Folks Who Think Race Doesn't Matter

For black folks who think race doesn't matter,

The next time you complain about the lack of black unity
And the poor quality of life in the black community
Because you have no protection or immunity
From the rogue policeman's reign of cruelty
As they shoot black men like dogs in the street

Remember those words that once sounded so sweet:
Race doesn't matter

The next time you have to go to the white man for a job,
With your hat in hand,
And you can't get a $10 business loan
To open a lemonade stand

And you lose your home due to predatory loan programs
Designed by rich white men
Who don't get stopped for driving
And having black skin

Remember those words: Race doesn't matter

When a black man can't get a job even with a college degree
But a white man with a criminal record
Gets a job like he's crime-free
And we can't get no respect as a black man

And even the white female who grabs her purse
At the sight of us understands
That EVERY MAN on this planet better have a PLAN
Because it's OUR JOB to take care of our women and children
On our OWN land

Remember those words: Race doesn't matter

When you can't catch a break
And you wonder how an empty wallet
Can stop an empty stomach ache
And we look back and remember who was there
When we were little more than a tiny pooh bear

Because the first face we'll see in our mind's eye
Is a black woman with a brown face and a big smile
And in our darkest days, we'll recognize OUR OWN
And we'd better pray that our foolish ways
Have NOT turned the black woman's heart to stone

So, it's time to wise up, my black brothers or be prepared to pay
Because the day of God's reckoning ain't that far away
We better get down on our knees and humbly pray
That God will take mercy on our dishonorable ways

Because instead of protecting our black women and children
We chose to play sex games with white and Asians
Who don't give a damn about our culture or issues
Where we're forced to take a stand

It's a black thing, baby
An Asian or white female just can't understand

All she can do is raise confused black children
With no true racial identity
Who will be as useless as Tiger Woods
When it's crunch time for black unity

So remember my words to my little ditty
A dishonorable man will be shown NO PITY.

-- Umoja

Playing the Right (Black) Side of the Chess Board

When asked how whites would react if non-whites refused to have sexual intercourse with them, Professor Eric Hamilton, a white male, said they would react with violence. Since whites are less than 8% of the world's population, their gene pool is so small that if whites only bred with each other, they would die out.

Neely Fuller, Jr. On NO SEX Between Blacks And Whites

"In addition, as long as white supremacy exists, it is correct for white people and non-white people to avoid all contact with each other that does not help to eliminate racism and/or does not help to produce justice.

Also, until racism is eliminated, there should be no contacts between white people and non-white people that include sexual intercourse, so-called homosexual (anti-sexual) intercourse, and/or sexual play.

As long as white supremacy exists, do not speak and/or act, as if sexual intercourse and/or sexual play between white people and non-white people will help to eliminate racism.

REASONS: "Contrary to what many persons believe, no act of sexual intercourse and/or sexual play, between a white person and an non-white person, under conditions dominated by white supremacy, contributes in any way, directly or indirectly, to the elimination of racism.

The white supremacists use sexual activity with/against their victims in a manner that causes their victims to become weaker and more confused in their efforts to resist the more soothing and sophisticated forms of deception and seduction as used by the white supremacists, to refine the practice of white supremacy."

-- From the book, 'The United Independent compensatory Code/System/Concept' by Neely Fuller, Jr.

"...any black person who buys into an interracial marriage can in no way stand up and support the black race completely. He or she will compensate psychological or physical defense mechanisms to protect his or her white wife or husband and in many ways shield their own conscience."

-- 'The Insane Nigger' by Mack B. Morant

CHAPTER 23

13 REASONS CONSCIOUS BLACKS OPPOSE (AND AVOID) INTERRACIAL RELATIONSHIPS

The term -- **"Conscious Blacks" --** does not mean one black person is intellectually or morally superior to another. For the purposes of this book, a **"Conscious Black"** is a black male or female who embraces some or all of the following (detailed in this chapter):

- Agrees that we live under a global system of people who classify themselves as white, and are dedicated to abusing, and or subjugating everyone in the known universe whom they classify as not white.
- Agrees that the biggest problem on the planet is racism/white supremacy
- Makes some effort by his or her thoughts, speech, and actions to eliminate the system of white supremacy
- Is "black-identified" -- meaning they view the world through a "black perspective" that validates self, respects self, and promotes self AND group interests
- Does not confuse "assimilation/integration" with whites as "black progress" or "racial equality"
- Understands that blacks "assimilating" into a white supremacy system is "subjugation" NOT "integration"
- Understands that blacks who control nothing cannot be "equal" (in power) to whites who control everything
- Does not elevate blacks with a white parent as superior to blacks who have two black parents -- and does not praise blacks for looking more white than black
- Does not blame poor blacks (the biggest victims of white supremacy) for being poor and black.
- Does not blame black people for the crimes of the white supremacy system
- Understands that knowing AND respecting their history is the KEY to black liberation
- Understands that the ONLY true ally of the black male is the black female and the ONLY true ally of the black female is the black male

- Understands that the FAMILY is the foundation of every human society
- Understands that RESTORING THE BLACK FAMILY should be the number one priority of the black collective
- Understands that an authentic BLACK FAMILY is composed of a black man, a black woman, and a black child (or black children)
- Understands that it takes strong, committed black males and black females to build strong black families
- Understands that it takes strong black families to build strong black communities
- Understands that it takes strong black communities to build strong black business/economic bases
- Understands that WITHOUT strong black families, strong black communities, and strong black business/economic bases, the black collective lacks the tools for prosperity, security, AND survival
- Understands that none of the above is possible without BLACK UNITY
- Understands that OPPPOSING INTERRACIAL SEX has NOTHING to do with hating white people
- Understands that opposing (and avoiding) interracial sex is necessary to ensure the economic, political, genetic, and psychological SURVIVAL of blacks in America
- Understands that interracial sex (dating, breeding, and marriage) should be avoided/opposed because it destroys black UNITY
- Understands that a black person in a relationship with a person who is NOT black is STILL having an INTERRACIAL relationship. All "people of color" are not the same. If there is any doubt, try the following two experiments:

  Experiment #1: go to a "person of color" who is NOT black and ask him or her if they consider themselves "black."

  Experiment #2: go to any brown, red, or yellow community and try to open a business. Your "Going Out Of Business" sign should be all the proof any reasonable "black" person needs.

- Understands that a black person who DELIBERATELY seeks a relationship with a white OR a non-black male or female, has a black inferiority complex and has submitted to white supremacy – even if that non-black person is NOT white
- Understands that interracial sex (dating, breeding, and marriage) between blacks and whites should be opposed (and avoided) until the system of racism/white supremacy has been destroyed

Reason #1: Interracial Sex Has Been Used Historically By Europeans To Divide and Conquer Non-White Nations

As the authors have attempted to demonstrate throughout this entire book, interracial sex is simply a CONTINUATION of the sexual exploitation of Africans that began during the first European invasions of Africa and the enslavement of African men and women.

For hundreds of years, interracial sex has been used by Europeans against non-whites to divide and conquer non-white nations; to dilute (destroy) their genetics, culture, and heritage, and to introduce mulatto "advocates" that will be white-identified and bred to serve the needs and the whims of the white supremacists.

The English, Spanish, Portuguese, and French destroyed entire non-white populations by introducing selected white females to the non-white male "natives."

Two things happened:

1. Biological warfare in the form of STDs and sexual epidemics by having sex with Europeans
2. Social stratification by the elevation of the mulatto (half-white/half-black), which led to conflict and division among the native populations. Through this use of sexual manipulation by Europeans, entire non-white societies were destroyed, because the family was the extension of the nation and all that it stood for.

"The melting pot of the races began around the northern perimeter. The end result was always the same: The Blacks were pushed to the bottom of the social, economic, and political ladder whenever the Asians (meaning whites) and their mulatto offspring gained control.

This scheme of weakening the Blacks by turning their half-white brothers against them cannot be overemphasized because it began in the early times and it became the universal practice of whites, and is still one of the cornerstones in the edifice of white power...." -- "Chancellor Williams, "Destruction of Black Civilization" -- Chapter II: Ethiopia's Oldest Daughter: Egypt. pg. 61.

Reason #2: Interracial Sex Destroys The Bond Between The Black Male And Black Female

Since black males are more likely than black females to date and marry whites, black males are more likely to break the traditional covenant between the male and female of EVERY ethnic group. When the **Unconscious Black Male** uplifts, protects, and provides for the white female – at the expense of the black female -- he foolishly alienates his ONLY TRUE ALLY in a white supremacy system: ***the black female.***

Try To Imagine The Following Scenario:

Palestinian males – who are engaged in a life and death struggle with the Israelis – bringing home Israeli brides when 45% of the Palestinian women are single, and where 70% of the Palestinian children are fatherless.

Would any self-respecting Palestinian man who was fighting for the survival of his people put a bullet in the heads of those Palestinian men who put the welfare of their enemies above the welfare of their own women and children?

Would those Palestinian females respect a Palestinian male who ignored the SUFFERING AND MOUNTING CASUALTIES OF HIS OWN PEOPLE to bond with the women of his enemies? Or would the Palestinian women resent – even hate -- these Palestinian men for their dangerous and foolish betrayal?

A Short Lesson In The Power Of Racial UNITY

Even though white males, collectively, mistreat their only ally – the white female -- the white male makes sure that he treats the white female better than all non-white people to assure her loyalty to his agenda. The white male, collectively, NEVER uplifts the black, Hispanic, or Asian female above the white female EVEN WHEN HE DOES NOT SHARE HER BED.

Whatever benefits the white male receives from the spoils of white supremacy, the white female shares in those benefits. Whatever small (and insignificant) consideration he gives to the oppressed, non-white population – like affirmative action and "minority set-asides" – the white male makes sure that the white female gets the lion's share of even those "benefits."

In other words, the **white female's loyalty** to the system of white supremacy is guaranteed by the generous benefits she receives – in comparison to non-whites. Therefore, the white female, collectively, understands she is better off supporting the white male's economic and political agenda EVEN WHEN SHE DOES NOT SHARE HIS BED.

Do not be fooled by the disposable white female population (less than 5%) that breeds with and marries black males. They are seldom "prime" quality white females and actually serve a bigger purpose by neutralizing the non-white male population's WILL to oppose white supremacy.

The same is true of the even smaller number of white males who breed with and marry black females, who also serve the same purpose of neutralizing the black female population's will to oppose white supremacy.

This disposable white female (and white male) population are invaluable in helping to maintain white supremacy because of the neutralizing effect they have on the will of oppressed blacks and non-whites to challenge the system.

However, if that "benefit" (called white privilege) ever disappears, the white female's loyalty to the white male's agenda will also disappear. She will then focus all her attention on her grievances with the white male.

A Short Lesson In The Powerlessness of Racial DISUNITY

When the black male uplifts the white female by offering her MORE emotional and financial support (benefits) than he offers the black female, the black female has no incentive to be loyal to the black male OR his agenda because she is NOT receiving the emotional OR financial benefits she rightfully deserves. She will then focus all her attention on her grievances with the black male.

In addition, the black female loses respect for black males collectively because they have FAILED TO FULFILL the role that ALL MEN must fulfill to be RESPECTED AS MEN: ***to protect AND provide for the women and children of their ethnic group.***

Do not misunderstand the definition of "benefits." This has nothing to do with gold-digging, materialism, fancy cars, jewelry, expensive homes, or "bling-bling." This is about economic, social, and cultural SURVIVAL. The males and females of every ethnic group have different roles in every human society.

The male is the LEADER and the HEAD of every nation. The female is the BEARER OF CHILDREN, the nurturer, and the values-transferor for the next generation. To maintain HARMONY between the male and female, their complimentary roles must be fulfilled to the best of their ability.

When black males -- collectively -- break the sacred covenant between the male and female that has existed since the beginning of the human race, and PUBLICLY protects and provides for the females of his enemy, the black female RIGHTFULLY views those black males as her ENEMIES rather than her respected, cherished, and necessary ALLIES.

AXIOM #8: You cannot be an enemy AND an ally at the same time; NOR can you be an ally when it is beneficial and an enemy when it is not. If your position is unclear to your allies, the default position (enemy) will (and should) be chosen for you.

According to a study by V. Harpalani --*'Black Women's Attitudes Toward Interracial Relationships'* -- black females are the LEAST LIKELY to date or marry outside their race than any other demographic in America, and *"...were the least accepting of interracial dating than any other racial group."* A different study by Fiebert noted that *"...75% of black males said they would be willing to date outside their race."*

The black female's (falsely) degraded image in a white supremacy society and her historic ABUSE and RAPE by white males collectively, often repels the white-status-seeking **Unconscious Black Males** who have bought into the LIE of white superiority/black inferiority without understanding that all black people -- INCLUDING THEMSELVES -- are considered "inferior" in a white supremacy system.

The **Conscious Black Female** realizes that as a black female in a white supremacy, black-hating, and female-hating society puts her at a GREATER risk of being sexually exploited by white and non-black males – hence the **Conscious Black Female's** reluctance OR ***outright refusal*** to become sexually involved with them.

> *"Why I am not interested in dating white men? I am a U.S. born African woman, and have no choice but to see the white man as "superior" because white men have so much power. It seems that interracial dating is a function of white supremacy, white dominance in this society.*
>
> *We have to work for white companies and shop at white stores and watch white media (television, movies, magazines, radio, etc) which basically adds up to a lot of propaganda that white is right, white is perfect, white is solid gold, white is pure, and most importantly white is powerful and rich. So it is very socially "practical" to desire whites as marriage partners.*
>
> *The only thing that stops me is the realization that his system is wicked in its inherent racism. I know that it will feed many white men's egos if I submit to the idea of dating them and I don't want to feed that. Plus, I know our kids would have to deal with the conflicts between blacks and whites as part of their internal struggle to identify with race.*
>
> *I have read some books by mixed authors and they have stated something along the lines of "I am thankful that I was born but it can be so painful to be biracial" or "It's like being torn between two worlds" or "split down the middle". They worry about fitting in with different social groups/races and their parents often don't talk about race or being mixed at all." -- Kopana, 32, writer*

The small number of black females who date or marry white males are only a fraction of the number of black males who date and marry white females. Therefore, the black females who date or marry outside their race – often reluctantly -- ***do not pose a serious threat to the stability or the survivability of the black family.***

However, with the INCREASING INVOLUNTARY REMOVAL (prison and murder rates) and the VOLUNTARY DEFECTION (homosexuality and interracial relationships) of black males from the black dating pool, it is a PREDICTABLE CERTAINTY that more black females will date and marry outside their race.

In fact, the recent increase in black females who are dating and/or marrying white males is a DIRECT REACTION to missing-in-action black males, some of who have made their preference for anything BUT a black female known all over the world.

AXIOM #9: For every ACTION, there is a REACTION.

Once the most loyal and stable element of the black community – the black female -- is NO LONGER BOUND by that loyalty, the black community will go into a free fall and completely SELF-DESTRUCT.

The EVIDENCE that this is already happening can be seen in the downward spiral of black males in America and the disturbing number of young black females who have begun to behave in selfish and destructive ways -- or have turned to homosexuality.

The young black female who observes the emotional and physical abuse and the abandonment of adult black females may feel that being loyal to black males is a one-way street.

During her girl-to-woman-developmental years, she observes many rich and famous black males choose anything but a black female. Even in her own community, she observes a constant parade of black males with white females, who are often viewed as the rejects of the white race.

These images deliver a powerful message (and a devastating blow) to the minds and hearts of young, impressionable black females who may adopt the attitude that ***they cannot trust black males*** (to do the right thing by black females).

The young black female may decide it is wiser to put herself FIRST – even before the welfare of her children -- which places the already endangered black child at even greater risk.

When the black male attempts to have a relationship with a (demoralized) black female who does not trust black males, he may discover that whenever he says, 'let's go left,' she may instinctively believe going right is probably a wiser decision -- which leaves the black male with the impression that black females are "uncooperative" and "unsupportive."

It is imperative that black males – collectively -- understand the dire consequences of removing the INCENTIVE of black females – collectively -- to be loyal to the black male's agenda and survival in a white supremacy society if they EVER hope to overcome white oppression.

Reason #3: Interracial Breeding Destroys The Self-Esteem Of Black Children

When black adults uplift the mulatto (bi-racial) child as more attractive or more intelligent because he or she looks MORE "white," they are DESTROYING the self-esteem of the black children who look MORE "black" -- and sending a powerful message that says it is better to be "half-white" than "all-black."

Making negative comments about nappy hair and dark skin, or praising "good hair," "pretty eyes," and "nice skin color" teaches the black child that there is something terribly wrong with looking -- and being black.

Imagine the dismay and confusion of black children who realize that their black parents do not like the way black people look. Yet, many black parents still remain puzzled as to the reasons so many black children suffer from low self-esteem, anger, and low academic performance.

Some blacks may go so far as to DELIBERATELY breed with whites to "lighten up" their offspring, NOT for the child's benefit (as they claim) but MORE for the benefit of the low-self-esteemed black parent who has NOT come to terms with their own black inferiority complexes, which they will simply pass along as a generational curse.

Reason #4: Interracial Sex Destroys The "Authentically Black" Family

The FAMILY is the foundation of human society. A successful family requires the MALE and the FEMALE of that ethnic group to commit to raising well-adjusted, mentally SANE children.

That is the ONLY REASON human (and animal) societies exist: to nurture and protect their offspring in order to perpetuate their species. However, if a group has been overwhelmed by their ENEMIES, they must make the SURVIVAL of their families a TOP PRIORITY. Conclusive PROOF that the black community has been "overwhelmed." According to some recently reported statistics (which the authors cannot confirm):

- 10% of black males are in prison (at any given time)
- 20% of black males who marry -- marry outside their race
- 45% of black females may never marry.
- 70% of black children are raised by single or divorced black females

No ethnic group can prosper under those conditions. No ethnic group that WANTS TO SURVIVE would bond with the same race that is creating those conditions. This does NOT mean blacks bear no responsibility or blame; it means that there is NO safety for blacks in a white supremacy society UNLESS WE COME TOGETHER TO BUILD STRONG BLACK FAMILIES.

There is a direct relationship between the number of black males in prison and the number of fatherless black homes.

It serves NO purpose to point fingers of blame at who is most at fault, the mothers or the fathers of so many black, fatherless children. The one thing that cannot be denied is THE CHILDREN ARE HERE, and it is up to us – as black adults – to come together to create a nation of strong-minded, self-respecting, black-loving, black-identified black men and women.

If we do NOT COLLECTIVELY address this issue, it will come back to bite us in our collective butts.

It is UNCONSCIONABLE for black males to provide for and protect the females, children, and communities of their enemies while their own females, children, and communities are left to fend for themselves.

For those black males who are offended by this statement and insist they have the right to be with whomever they choose *"because it's a free country"* should be REMINDED that as long as white supremacy exists, they will never be free.

The black males who make the fateful decision to abandon their communities have ***NO GROUNDS to complain if they are ever the victims of racism***, and SHOULD NOT COMPLAIN to any black victim of ANY difficulties they experience at the hands of racist man and woman.

Simply stated: You put nothing in; you get nothing out.

Reason #5: Interracial Sex Destroys Black Communities

A "black neighborhood" is a place (location) where more blacks than non-blacks live. A "black community" is more than a place where black people live.

A community is a place where the people who live there have a stake in what is happening there. They have a SAY in how that community functions; they provide the goods and services that community depends upon, and they understand their well-being is directly connected and directly affected by their neighbor's well-being.

Until the black male and black female come together, and build strong black families, and strong black communities, the black community will be controlled by outsiders; policed by outsiders; and serviced by outsiders, who will take our hard-earned money and ENRICH their own ETHNICALLY UNITED communities.

Reason #6: Interracial Sex Destroys Black Generational Wealth

It is rare for black spouses to inherit white wealth but extremely common for white and non-black spouses and widows to inherit OR be awarded in a divorce the fortunes of black males. A very short list of rich and famous examples. (info current at the time of publication)

Reginald F. Lewis, the first black man to build a billion-dollar business, Beatrice Foods. Estimated net worth at time of death: $400 million. Asian widow, Loida Nicolas.

Tiger Woods, world's first athlete to earn over a billion dollars in his career. Net worth estimated to be $600 million. Woods' white ex-wife, Elin Nordegren, a former (working-class) nanny, was awarded a reported $110 million divorce settlement PLUS an estimated $20,000 a month in child support, three homes, AND a $2.2 million- island in Sweden.

Michael Jackson, the most successful entertainer of all times (according to Guinness World Records). Estimated net worth before death: from $130 million to over one billion. Jackson's first marriage to Lisa Marie Presley, a white female, lasted less than two years and ended with an "amicable" divorce settlement.

Second marriage to his dermatologist's nurse, Debbie Rowe, the mother of his two children, lasted three years. The terms of their divorce settlement was rumored (but not confirmed) to be in excess of $8 million. It is likely that Jackson's (white) children will eventually inherit the bulk of his estate.

Lionel Richie, pop singer. His second wife, Diane, a white female, had a divorce settlement estimated at $20 million.

Michael Strahan, pro football player, net worth estimated at $22 million, was ordered to pay ex-wife, Jean, a white female, $15.3 million plus six-figures child support judgment.

Amani Toomer, pro football player, ordered by judge to pay $11,000 a month in support to Yola Dabrowski, a white female, despite her refusal to take his last name and that she allegedly aborted four of his babies.

Richard Pryor, comic genius, left the bulk of his estate to his (white) widow, Jennifer. Pryor's eldest (black) daughter failed in her attempts to annul her father's earlier will that split his fortune between his six children.

Montel Williams, former talk show host, pays ex-wife, Grace Morley, a former stripper (white female) $18,700-a-month in child support for two children. A child custody dispute, Williams' attorney claims his client (Montel Williams) financial situation is "extremely perilous" and cannot afford to pay his children's $7,500 attorney fee.

(The authors were unable to find a rich and/or famous black female who left the bulk of her fortune to a white, Asian, or Hispanic male).

Another catastrophic black generational wealth loss that is seldom considered: the continued erosion of RESPECT for black males by black females, for the shameful parade of rich and famous black males who feel success and status means NOT having a black female by their side.

Reason #7: Interracial Sex Derails The Development Of A Black Business/ Economic Base

What do the most successful non-white ethnic groups in America have in common? STRONG ETHNIC FAMILIES and ETHNIC UNITY. The Korean male KNOWS he needs the Korean female to raise self-respecting Korean children, strong and UNIFIED Korean communities, and strong and unified Korean business/economic bases – many of them right within the DISUNIFIED BLACK COMMUNITY.

Without strong black males and females who are culturally, legally, and spiritually YOKED, and committed to raising their children together, there can be NO STRONG BLACK FAMILIES. Without strong black families, there can be NO STRONG BLACK COMMUNITIES. Without strong black communities; there can be NO STRONG BLACK ECONOMIC OR BUSINESS BASES. Without strong black economic and business bases, there can be NO INDEPENDENT BLACK PROSPERITY, SECURITY, OR FUTURE for black people collectively -- anywhere on the planet.

Do NOT be fooled by the number of educated, professional, or rich blacks in America. Titles, degrees, and material possessions are NOT the same as having power. The indisputable PROOF is the rising number of UNEMPLOYED and UNDER-EMPLOYED black college graduates and the lack of black-owned businesses in the black community.

All successful blacks work for white corporate America, be they athlete, scholar, politician, entertainer, or businessman or woman, because they depend on white financial institutions, sponsors, distributors, and advertisers.

Anything that an educated, professional, or affluent black has can be taken away overnight, because any race of people who do NOT have an INDEPENDENT economic/business base has NO real security, prosperity, or power. We must put aside our egos and pride, and tell ourselves -- and our children the TRUTH about our collective condition.

Reason #8: Interracial Sex Destroys Black Unity

Is "black unity" racist? Sadly, many blacks are offended when other blacks promote the concept of "black unity." Some blacks go as far as to call it "racist" to suggest that *"blacks should stick together."*

Yet, these same blacks observe -- on a DAILY basis – examples of BROWN AND YELLOW UNITY as Koreans, Indians, Hispanics, and Arab merchants operate nearly every successful business in the black community, and we don't call them "racist" for UNIFYING with their own "kind."

We silently (and resentfully) observe the POWER OF BROWN UNITY AND YELLOW UNITY as Koreans, Indians, Hispanics, and Arab merchants open up store after store in our communities, enriching their own communities with our hard-earned cash and we don't call them "racist" for EMPLOYING their own "kind."

We see the POWER OF BROWN UNITY AND YELLOW UNITY as the children of Koreans, Indians, Hispanics, and Arab merchants work with their parents in the stores and restaurants.

We never see Koreans, Indians, Hispanics, and Arab merchants partnering with any black business people, OR see them strutting around with white wives and white husbands in tow, and we don't call them "racist" for MARRYING and STICKING WITH their own "kind."

Yet, many blacks get offended when someone BLACK suggests that **BLACKS SHOULD UNIFY** and start building our own economic/ business base for ourselves.

Black people – collectively – despite all our education, skills, luxury cars and homes, designer (or discount) clothing, and top-shelf alcohol – ***cannot feed, house, clothe, police, educate, or employ ourselves -- and some us still think that is alright (normal).***

We refuse to understand the need to circulate our OWN dollars within our OWN communities and black-owned businesses. Yet, we endlessly and collectively complain about our high unemployment and crime rates; rampant police brutality, predatory lenders, and inadequate schools -- all while ignoring one major fact: ***the most successful example of "ethnic unity" in the world is the system of white supremacy.***

In light of – and in spite – of all the above EVIDENCE, some blacks still feel that BLACK UNITY is an UNNECESSARY EVIL, and that it is "racist" to even TALK about white supremacy, all while ignoring the FAILED POLICIES of racial integration and assimilation.

If integration represents "black progress," why are we still as dependent for our basic necessities as we were in 1864 -- a year before slavery ended? Had blacks not utilized the POWER OF BLACK UNITY prior to integration, the civil rights movement would have NEVER taken place and WE would still be riding in the back of the bus.

Until blacks collectively -- regardless of income or education -- understand that a WAR is being waged against our communities, regardless of where we live, OR who we sleep with, we will not only lose every battle, ***we will lose the entire war by DEFAULT.***

Reason #9: Interracial Sex Deceives Blacks About The Realities Of Racism/White Supremacy

> *Last year our firm hosted a Halloween costume party for one of our biggest clients, a conservative women's business group. My senior manager -- he's white -- chose a mammy-type dress and head rag for my costume! I know this is the so-called Deep South, but I thought blacks had made more progress than this!*

I hate to admit this but I was worried about outright refusing. It's hard enough being the token black man in management without getting a reputation for being too sensitive or having a chip on my shoulder.

I ran it down to my wife and instead of her seeing my side, she asked if any of the other men were wearing costumes. I told her, that's beside the point. This is the South, and that kind of black mammy crap has a history I'm not comfortable with.

It's not like I'm some kind of power-to-the-people black militant, or some street thug. How could I be anti-white when my wife is white? She says I should be a good sport then she throws in the kicker, and said she had it worse than me because she's a woman!" – Milton, 42

***

"I'm against interracial relationships because of what I have seen it do to black people. For example, my sister is married to a white man, and has completely lost touch with her black identity. All her friends are white and her kids think they're white.

No matter what the subject is, she always takes the "white" side, for example, she was talking about how lazy the black students are in the college where she's a student advisor. She said they care more about partying than getting an education. I told her, of course! They went to the same kind of inferior schools we went to! I couldn't believe she said this in front of her white husband!

Another time, I was visiting, and she waited until her husband left the room to say, "Whites don't want equality." She said they gave her promotion to a white boy who had been there less than a year. Turns out she was catching all kinds of black hell at that elite white college she was so proud of working for.

She can't talk to her husband about racism. She can't talk to her white friends. I guess this was eating her up inside so she had to let it out with another black person. From the outside, she's living the good life, but I don't think she's happy. I wonder how much of that has to do with being married to a white man who pretends you never deal with any racism." -- Janice, 46, government employee

***

My niece used to live with an African dude who unbeknownst to us used to hit her. This is why I feel my niece started dating white dudes. Anyway, she started dating this white dude who she had a child with. She told me that this white dude didn't give her a penny for the child. He used to stay out all night drinking (he was an alcoholic); but do you know she still felt sorry for him!?

She said to me that they had a very heated argument one day where he called her a black bitch and the N-word. She said when he called her that she slapped him. Luckily for him, he didn't hit her back.

There was another example where she was walking down the street with THEIR child and he walked right past her without saying hello. I just couldn't believe my ears. She eventually split with him, which made me happy. She went celibate for about 2 yrs after that and became depressed. Man it was some sad shit. I would teach her about black history and extol the wonderments of black love.

Man, that didn't even make a damned difference, she eventually dated another white dude. I said to her are you crazy, do you want to be disrespected again. She said that when she is out and about, black dudes don't really pay her any mind, and this dude gave her attention.

Anyway, after dating him for a while -- he also called her the N-word (this seems to be a pattern). She finished with him, but he got real possessive, saying he was going to go around to her house and beat her up.

I said to her, tell this dude that you have an uncle, and if he even puts just one finger on you? I'm coming for his funky azz. When she told him this -- she never heard from him again." – Roddick, UK, 40

***

I have been married for over 7 years now to a white woman. We are both in our mid-30's, so we have experience some things in life before we got together. Her family, as you probably already imagine, was not too happy about her dating ANOTHER black man. I was the third, and from what I'm am gathering, the other two were not very positive models for me to follow.

Well, they got to meet me and I felt we were all trying to work toward a better relationship. I feel with most of her family, I am on pretty good terms. There's one problem that keeps popping up, however. Her family (especially her immediate family since I am around them more), seem still inclined to make what I consider racist comments.

Statements like: "They all look alike," or "They're all like that," "Those people always lie," and lots, lots more! It gets to me sometime, even though most of the time they are not talking about blacks.

No matter how I try to correct them or let them know I don't like those statements, they continue to say, "I know what I'm talking about, you don't know them like I know them!" This statement has been directed at me even when the racist comments have been directed at blacks! What could they know that I don't!!!!

But here is what bothers me: for most of our relationship, my wife has sat in the presence of these comments even when they are directed at me and said NOTHING!

She won't respond. Even in our house! I tell her that when you sit there in silence, you give approval of these comments. I let her know that it is affecting our relationship and the way I feel about her, but I only get luke-warm reaction. I feel so abandoned sometimes. Am I blowing this out of proportion?" -- Tom.

***

The Delusion Of Inclusion

It is obvious many blacks with white lovers and spouses believe their white partners will insulate them from the racism of other whites -- or make other whites view them more favorably (as more human). This belief is as logical as a poor woman believing that having sex with a rich man makes other rich people see her as their social equals.

To Be Young, White-Identified, And Black – Ain't Where It's At

Being white-identified is extremely dangerous for naïve young blacks. Because they lack life experience, they believe having white boyfriends and girlfriends means they will not be as vulnerable to racism as less "assimilated" blacks. However, once they leave the nest of familiar surroundings and people, they are unprepared for the racism they will encounter socially or in the workplace with unfamiliar whites.

After high school or college, young white-identified blacks often discover their white friends are dropping by the wayside. Of course, this is not always due to race, but race increases the likelihood that their white friendships will bite the dust. As whites make the transition into adulthood and compete for jobs, lovers, and peer approval, the lines separating black and white become more distinct.

The peer pressure for whites to not be too friendly with blacks will come from a variety of sources; including their white neighbors, relatives, coworkers, employers, or even from their intimate partners.

This may force some whites to realize their black friendships and former lovers are more disposable than white peer approval. Unfortunately, the only one left in the dark (pun unintended) is the white-identified black who never saw it coming.

"I was seeing this white girl in summer school at my community college. I thought she wasn't prejudiced because she was into rap music and was always saying how much she liked black dudes. When her white friends came back to school in the fall, she acted like she didn't know me. I would never date another white girl because they can't be trusted." – Tony, 20, student

Friend-Enemies And Racism/White Supremacy

"I was at a friend's family reunion and in walks this young sister with two white females. I was like, how can these sisters be bringing these Beckys around us then complaining that the Beckys are taking all the brothers?

When my moms worked at this hospital, a white lady she worked with was married to this black dude, she told my moms that she called her husband a nigger when he made her mad. Can you believe she actually told a black woman some shit like that? My mom said some white women will try to get close to black women just to get closer to black men." – Darnell, 23, student

Reason #10: Interracial Sex Lengthens And Strengthens White Supremacy By Increasing White Fertility

The majority of these black male/white female relationships will not last, even if they have children together. Most of the children of these interracial unions will:

1. be raised by single white mothers
2. will have a closer, more sympathetic bond with the white side of their family, in particular, the white females
3. will be white-identified
4. will breed with whites (or other white-identified biracial partners)
5. will produce offspring who will merge undetected within the white population.

The future generations of these black male/white female unions will produce whites who will be more fertile (due to melanin from the black male), resulting in an INCREASE in overall white fertility, which will possibly extend the life of WHITE SUPREMACY and BLACK OPPRESSION.

The BLACK MALE who breeds with the white female represents the SINGLE BIGGEST NON-WHITE ALLY of the system of RACISM/WHITE SUPREMACY.

This explains why the mainstream media and entertainment industry relentlessly promotes and rewards high-profile black males who engage exclusively in interracial relationships.

They are the most visible role models for impressionable black males -- and the best advertising money can buy when it comes to promoting white supremacy in the guise of interracial relationships between black males and white females.

The disposable white female population that breeds with black and non-white males provides a genetic "laboratory" that allows the white supremacy system to "refine" their final product: a *new and improved white race that is more fertile, more genetically resistant to disease, mental and nervous system disorders, with richer complexions, thicker hair, and fuller lips and buttocks.*

This may explain why so many white females are eager to have brown babies with black males but do not pursue marriage with the fathers of their non-white offspring. Perhaps, they are seeking "color," not love, to ensure the survival of the white race.

Reason #11. Interracial Sex Is Black Population Control

Interracial sex is a form of BLACK GENETIC SUICIDE, and destroys the possibility of future black generations. "Black" is more than a political or racial classification; it's a genetic, historical, and spiritual HERITAGE.

No Son To Carry On His Name

After two years of living together, Bernard's white girlfriend, Becky, becomes pregnant. When he finds out they are having a boy, Bernard is thrilled because he will finally have a son to carry on his name.

The first time he lays eyes on his son, Bernard is shocked by the pale skin and brown hair. It never occurred to him that their baby would look more like the mother than the father. As his son grows older, the pale skin and the straight hair never gets any darker (or kinkier) like he secretly hoped it would.

Two years later, he and Becky separate. Bernard sees his son, Seth, now three years old, twice a month instead of every night. Whenever he brings his son around his family, everyone makes a fuss over him, but Bernard just can't shake the disconnect he feels toward the white-looking, gray-eyed boy with the straight brown hair.

He guiltily reminds himself that it shouldn't matter what his son looks like. It's still his blood. So, Bernard resigns himself to man up and do right by his son.

The years pass quickly. To Bernard's dismay, Seth shuns the black kids at his grammar school in favor of the white kids. Bernard tells Becky that it's important that Seth knows his "black culture" but after a heated argument, Becky says Seth is her son, too, so why should his black culture be more important than her white one?

Bernard tries to instill some "black pride" into Seth but his son clearly isn't interested in his father's lessons. It's also clear that Seth doesn't identify with black people at all. The "pretty white baby" has turned into a white stranger who prefers white music, white slang, and can't dance or keep step with the rhythm. Behind Bernard's back, his relatives shake their heads, and privately ask, *"What kind of name is Seth for a black boy?"*

Bernard suspects that Becky and her new white husband are deliberately playing down or outright ignoring Seth's mixed heritage and prefer to pretend he is all white.

Permanently soured on interracial dating, Bernard relocates to another state, marries Aretha, a black woman, and has a daughter with her. He invites Seth – now in his 2nd year of high school – to spend the summer with him, Aretha, and his half-sister, Debra, but Seth politely declines. He says his stepfather -- who owns a speedboat -- is teaching him to water-ski. Bernard knows he can't compete with that. He never even learned to swim.

The "white" son and the "black side" of the family drift even further apart after Seth graduates from high school. Bernard's attempts to bond with his son over the years finally hits an impasse.

Seth is nothing like the sons of his sisters and friends, who are into all that is "black." Bernard hates to admit he is envious of his nephews, with their cool fade hairstyles and fun-loving personalities, who represent the kind of son he secretly wishes he had.

The years pass. Seth graduates from college, gets a job at his stepfather's company, and a fiancée -- the daughter of a white businessman. Bernard is not surprised that he, his wife, and daughter are the only black people at the 150-plus-guest wedding. Bernard is positive that most of the guests have no idea who he is, and assume Becky's white husband is the "father" of the groom.

For his son's sake, Bernard swallows his anger and humiliation and stays in the background. He has a thought that will haunt him for years to come: his only son's children and grandchildren -- Bernard's grandchildren AND great grandchildren -- will talk white, act white, and be white. Since he and Becky never married, Bernard's family name, legacy, and bloodline will be wiped out by the next generation.

If the current (suicidal) trend of black males feverishly breeding with white females continues, black males will eventually accomplish what slavery, racism, sterilization, the Tuskegee Experiment, lynching, castration, crack cocaine, segregation, discrimination, malt liquor, and the American Prison Industrial Complex have failed to do: *wipe out future black generations.*

END OF STORY

Reason #12. The 500-Year War Against The Black Nation Is Intensifying. (A short summary of Black America's worsening dilemma)

Black labor has become obsolete in America. In many inner cities, the menial, low-skilled and low-paying jobs that poor blacks used to do -- and are still willing to do -- are farmed out for maximum profit to illegal (slave) labor. Automation (machines) and computers have eliminated the rest.

In spite of record unemployment for blacks, (estimated at over 35% in 2010), America is still importing unskilled AND skilled non-white labor from Latin America and India.

The picture for educated, professional blacks in corporate America is just as dismal. Glass ceilings have turned to concrete. Unions, good jobs, benefits, and guaranteed pensions are relics of the past.

As a result, the hard-won gains from civil rights and affirmative action over the last 40 years are being systematically wiped out.

After two terms of the Bush Administration efforts, affirmative action is little more than a controversial and fraudulent memory that ***clearly ignored the FACT that the biggest beneficiaries of affirmative action were and still are white females.***

Black farmers have yet to receive reparations or compensation for stolen farmland and government discrimination. Black land-and-home-owners are losing land and houses at a record pace--witness Katrina and dozens of predominantly black cities where gentrification (land grabs), subprime mortgages, reverse-lining (targeting black areas for fraudulent home loans), foreclosures, and property tax and eminent-domain schemes designed to force blacks out of major cities – and out of their homes.

In predominantly black schools all across the country, black children are being mis-educated and under-educated by design. It is common for black boys to be given the drug "Ritalin;" "tracked" into "special education classes" or "non-college prep" classes; or expelled for minor offenses to DELIBERATELY destroy their intellectual potential and self-confidence.

The subliminal, unrelenting onslaught of white Hollywood on the black mind, via the buffoonery disguised as "comedy," rap videos, and trash-talk and "reality" shows" that pollute the minds and morals of black youth.

White (and black puppet) decision-makers deliberately pair the black male with anyone but a black female in movies, TV shows, and rap videos to divide and conquer (and demoralize) the black male and black female.

Over one million black men and black women are rotting in penal institutions, many for non-violent drug "crimes," while white drug users of crack cocaine, powdered cocaine, and meth get "intervention," drug treatment, fines, or a slap on the wrist for their "illness."

To add more injuries to the massive injuries inflicted on blacks by America's "criminal" justice system, prison authorities callously turn a "blind eye" to inmates AND guards raping other inmates and rampant homosexuality in prisons where black men in their sexual primes are forced to live in cages with other men.

It is NO accident that black ex-felons who are KNOWN to be infected with HIV, AIDS, & Hepatitis C are released back into the black community without job skills or medical treatment.

It's clear (white) America has no patience or sympathy for poor blacks or blacks with "addictions" and is rapidly and quietly building more prisons while it closes black schools in preparation for...

"A $104 Million Dollar Juvenile Detention Center To Be Built East Baltimore." (SOURCE: www.ourweekly.com/los-angeles/104-million-juvenile-detention-facility-be-built)

What is America's plan for black youth? The answer should be obvious...

Reason #13: Only The Unified Black Male And Black Female Can Save Black America -- And The Planet

What do predators do when stalking a herd of prey? They DRIVE THEM APART so killing them will be easier. The WEAPON OF CHOICE to drive the black HERD apart are interracial relationships.

To regain the POWER and WEALTH that was lost during our 500-year African Holocaust, the black male MUST RECONNECT with the black female, his spiritual and psychological power source. Until that happens, there will be NO SAFETY or SECURITY for blacks anywhere on the planet.

Every ethnic group in the world (except the descendants of American slavery) understands that the men and women of every ethnic group MUST STAND TOGETHER, and SUPPORT EACH OTHER – in short, THEY MUST BELONG TO EACH OTHER – if they want to survive financially and politically in a hostile white society.

If WE (blacks) do NOT heed the warnings in this book (and others like it), it is a CERTAINTY that WE will become a PERMANENT SUPER-UNDERCLASS in America and all over the world.

Survival Must Be Our Highest Priority

For those blacks who say love comes in every color -- need be reminded that during an emergency, priorities must be chosen. If one person has a sprained toe and another person is bleeding to death, it is LOGICAL to stop the bleeding then you can treat the toe.

One is a matter of life and death, the other one of minor discomfort and inconvenience. It's not that you don't care about the sprained toe, but they just don't need you as much as the person who is bleeding to death.

For blacks who believe that opposing (and avoiding) interracial sex in a so-called "integrated" society is unrealistic -- need be reminded that co-existing with whites DOES NOT require blacks engage in sexual intercourse with whites.

The black male and female are faced with a critical choice: to pursue our individual "interests" and risk even greater POWERLESS and OPPRESSION, or to come together to ensure our prosperity and survival. The fate of our children and all future black generations rests on our willingness to make the right and the logical choice.

"When oppression comes down, ignorant people scatter and go off on their own. Intelligent people come together because they understand the POWER and SAFETY of numbers."

Umoja

"..."Let's talk about the millions (of black men and women) who have worked and struggled to keep their marriages together at a time when 50 percent of all marriages across the board are doomed for failure.

More importantly, this is why we have to become self-contained as a community. We're not able to focus on one another because we're too fixated on attempting to follow, copy, and please the children of our slave-masters."

-- Source: 'Broken Black Relationships, Where is the Love?' by Starla Muhammad, The Final Call, 9/26/2011

Chapter 24

A MORE JUST BLACK MALE AND BLACK FEMALE PERSPECTIVE

The Black Male And The White Female

The white female doesn't share the same painful history with the black male that the black female shares. She is able to come to the romantic table whole and intact because she has NO DOG (or interest) in the black male's race (or case) for justice and liberation from white oppression.

The white female has no stake (or interest) in the collective problems of black males in America OR in what happens to the black community in general. Her survival and condition in America is NOT dependent on the black male's failures or successes.

The white female has NO INTEREST in what happens to black males collectively, other than the individual black male she is currently involved with. In actuality, SHE benefits from his racial oppression because her "white privileges" are a direct result of white supremacy.

The black male does NOT represent the sexual OR physical violence waged against white females by the males in her community. (According to FBI statistics, most rapes and murders in America are INTRA-RACIAL, meaning MOST white females are raped and/or murdered by white males).

The black male does not represent the missing, neglectful, or abusive (white) father in the white female's life, nor does he represent the sexism that holds the white female back.

The black male does not represent any of the pain OR baggage that white females experience at the hands of (white) males; therefore, the white female is less likely to BLAME the black male for her emotional damage.

The black male isn't ALLOWED to PUBLICLY degrade the white female in TV, film, or music, NOR is he allowed to ridicule her physical features by dressing up like an obese, homely, ignorant white female.

The black male is MORE LIKELY to publicly admire, respect, protect, and support the white female than he is to mistreat her. Therefore, the white female has no ax to grind with the black male when it comes to her mistreatment as a female in a male-dominated society.

The white female does not represent the missing, abusive, or neglectful (black) mother in the black male's life; therefore, the black male is less likely to BLAME the white female for his emotional damage, despite her 500-year role in the oppression of black males.

Even though she greatly benefits from white supremacy, she is MORE likely to deny the existence of white privilege and white racism than acknowledge AND oppose it. The white female is a blank slate on which the black male can paint whatever image of himself he chooses --real OR imaginary -- because he knows the white female does NOT know (or care) who he is or what he used to be – nor is she interested in finding out.

Chances are the white female would not believe that the African man was the first, most powerful, and most civilized man on the planet. She would prefer the black male pretends he is brand new than hear the painful truths of his life under the system of white supremacy. In fact, the success of their "relationship" largely depends on his ability to stay in DENIAL and stay SILENT.

The white female's LACK of interest in the black male; his history; his oppression; who he is; AND what was done to him is exactly what makes the white female so appealing to the self-hating black male who wants to FORGET.

The opposite is true when it comes to the black female. When the self-hating black male looks into the black female's eyes, he is repelled by the FEAR that the black female sees him as LESS THAN A MAN and despises him for his failures.

The Black Female And The White Male

The white male doesn't share the same painful history with the black female that the black male shares with her. He is able to come to the romantic table whole and intact because he has NO DOG (or interest) in the black female's race (or case) for justice and liberation from white oppression.

The white male has no stake (or interest) in the collective problems of black females in America OR in what happens to the black community in general. His survival and condition in America is NOT dependent on the black female's failures or successes.

The white male has NO INTEREST in what happens to black females collectively, other than the individual black female he is currently involved with. In actuality, HE benefits from her racial oppression because his "white privileges" are a direct result of white supremacy.

The white male does not represent the missing, neglectful, or abusive (black) father in the black female's life; therefore, the black female is less likely to BLAME the white male for her emotional damage -- despite HIS historical role in degrading black females and creating the circumstances that prevented black males from being good fathers, providers, and protectors of their black women and children.

Even though the white male benefits the MOST from the white supremacy system, he is MORE likely to deny the existence of white privilege and white racism than acknowledge AND oppose it.

The white male is a blank slate on which the black female can paint whatever image of herself she chooses -- real OR imaginary -- because she KNOWS the white male does NOT know (or care) who she is or what she used to be – nor is he interested in finding out.

Chances are the white male would not believe that the African woman was the first and most powerful woman on the planet, and would prefer the black female pretend she is brand new than hear the painful truths of her life under the system of white supremacy. In fact, the success of their "relationship" largely depends on her ability to stay in DENIAL and stay SILENT.

The white male's LACK of interest in the black female; her history; her rape and oppression; who she is; AND what was done to her is exactly what makes the white male so appealing to the self-hating black female who wants to FORGET.

The Black Male And The Black Female

The black male does not have the luxury of forgetting the painful 500-year journey he shares with the black female. He cannot come to the romantic table whole and intact because he was deconstructed, demonized, and brutalized during slavery and the systematic racism that followed.

The black male has the GREATEST stake (and interest) in the black struggle for justice and liberation, because his survival depends on it.

The black male -- the father of the next black generation -- has the GREATEST stake (and interest) in the collective problems of black females in America – because they are his daughters, sisters, mothers, and wives.

Since the black male is greatly mistreated by the white supremacy system, he is MORE likely to challenge white privilege and white racism because he is a VICTIM of it.

The Black Female And The Black Male

The black female does not have the luxury of forgetting the painful 500-year journey she shares with the black male. She cannot come to the romantic table whole and intact because she was deconstructed, degraded, and brutalized during slavery and the systematic racism that followed.

The black female has the GREATEST stake (and interest) in the black struggle for justice and liberation, because her survival depends on it.

The black female -- the nurturer and civilizer of the next black generation -- has the GREATEST stake (and interest) in the collective problems of black males in America – because they are her sons, brothers, fathers, and husbands.

Since she is greatly mistreated by the white supremacy system, she is MORE likely to challenge white privilege and white racism because she is a VICTIM of it.

The UN-Conscious Black Male

The black male's terminal (and suicidal) amnesia allows him to conveniently "forget" the white female's collective role in his 500 years of oppression to JUSTIFY his sexual involvement with her.

He conveniently (and foolishly) ignores four more FACTS:

1. The white female is the white male's co-conspirator in the system of racism/white supremacy. The white female does NOT care about racism -- and is likely to be practicing it while she is sexually involved with a black male.

2. The white female is MORE concerned with the sexism that deprives her of an equal share of the spoils of white supremacy.

3. The white female is the Trojan Horse; the HUMAN FACE of white supremacy that is used to deceive, distract, and derail the black male's ability and will to overcome white oppression.

4. The white female is a tool used by the powerful white male to destroy the bond between the black male and female and destroy black family – which is why the powerful white male rewards the self-hating, unconscious black male who eagerly hands over his genetics, family name and fortunes (if one exists) to the white female.

A black male who has succumbed to white supremacy finds it easier (and more satisfying) to love anything or anyone white. Since he is more tolerant, loving, and respectful toward the white female (because she is white) she can be more tolerant, loving, and respectful toward him.

He THEN assumes the white female is "naturally that way" -- conveniently forgetting that HE may NOT be as tolerant, loving, and respectful toward black females.

The UN-Conscious Black Female

The black female's terminal (and dangerous) case of amnesia allows her to conveniently "forget" the white male's collective role in her 500 years of oppression to JUSTIFY her sexual involvement with him.

She conveniently (and foolishly) ignores four more FACTS:

1. The white male is the MAJOR conspirator in the system of racism/ white supremacy.

2. The white male has NO genuine interest in eliminating racism/white supremacy because he BENEFITS THE MOST from it.

3. The white male has historically used the black female as a SEXUAL TOILET -- and little has changed over the last 500 years.

4. The white male -- who is often promoted as the ideal "partner" for black females by the mass media propaganda machine -- serves to derail the black female's ability and will to support and defend the black male's efforts to overcome their white oppression.

The black female who has succumbed to white supremacy finds it easier (and more satisfying) to love anything or anyone white. Since she is more tolerant, loving, and respectful toward the white male, he can be more tolerant, loving, and respectful toward her.

She THEN assumes the white male is "naturally that way" -- conveniently forgetting that SHE may not be as tolerant, loving, and respectful toward black males.

A More Just (And Logical) Black Male Perspective

If it is unjust to compare black males to white males when white males have benefited collectively from white supremacy, it is equally UNJUST to compare black females to white females who have collectively benefited from the same system of white privilege.

A More Just (And Logical) Black Female Perspective

If it is unjust to compare black females to white females when white females have benefited collectively from white supremacy, it is equally UNJUST to compare black males to white males who have collectively benefited from white privilege.

A Tribute To Black-On-Black Love

CHAPTER 25

A BLACK WOMAN'S TRIBUTE TO HER NATURALLY NAPPY, BEAUTIFUL BLACK MAN

A few days ago, I was walking past the doorway of the family room as my husband flipped through the TV channels. He paused on the TV guide show about Tyler Perry's new movie, 'Why Did I Get Married, Too?'

I stopped in time to see Miss Jill Scott, my favorite songstress, sauntering across the stage in a sexy black dress, and wearing a beautiful, abundantly full afro hairstyle. As she took a seat on the sofa next to filmmaker Tyler Perry, and before I could say a word, my man was off the sofa, on his knees, so close to the TV screen, I was sure his breath was fogging the glass...

After he glanced around, (probably to make sure I wasn't in the room), he turned back to the screen. Ms Jill is a beautiful, full-figured woman – the type of black woman that never gets the admiration she deserves.

When I saw my husband – my soul mate and the love of my life – gazing adoringly at Jill in all her naturally beautiful black splendor, something melted inside me. If Jill was beautiful in my husband's eyes, then maybe black women really were beautiful to the black men who could see beyond the tired white stereotypes of bony, anorexic, washed-out beauty.

Black women are so under-rated, so degraded, so invisible, and so easily dismissed yet our "inferior" selves possessed the same full breasts, butts, and lips that drove millions of "superior" females to the plastic surgeon.

Even the smartest white scientists say our black bodies are the most fertile female bodies on the planet -- fully capable of creating the miracle of life in ALL the colors of the rainbow.

I knew the truth, that our black beauty went beyond the "pale" that had hypnotized so many of our men who were desperate to escape the pain of being black and male in a society that passionately hated black men. All my life – without knowing it – I had mourned the loss of their sweet innocence and the magnificence of their black manhood.

I watched my husband staring mesmerized at the television screen for a few minutes longer, knowing I would never forget that moment, watching a black man – my black man -- pay silent homage to one of us...

I was in love again...

There was no need to be jealous. My husband's secret crush on Jill Scott was a validation and an appreciation of all that was black and beautiful. I had experienced many private moments of rapture at the sight of a sexy black man.

I didn't know what it was then

But there was always something special, richer, deeper, and more stimulating physically, mentally, and sexually about black men that I didn't see in the men who weren't...

Some folks call it "soul"... baby...

I know hair can't make love,
Heat some chicken soup when I get a cold
Fix the furnace in the winter
Or hold me when I need to be held

I can only speak for myself
When I say I prefer the naturally nappy hair on my man's head
To straight hair that blows in the breeze
Because his hair is identical to the naturally nappy hair
On my own pretty head

My Black King wears his hair in a close-cropped natural
That frames his strong masculine face
I love the texture of his hair under my fingers,
In the heat of my passion

Like a soft, springy cushion that doesn't lay down flat
But pushes back like it has a life and a mind of its own
Sitting on top of his naturally nappy, handsome head

When I caress his hair,
And look into his deep dark eyes
I see the history of our life together

over 500 years of loving and laughter... sadness and joy... tears and triumphs...

And a feeling reaches deep into my black soul
Because my man is authentic, soulful, the real deal...

He is ME
And I am HE

Our hair connects us to our majestic past,
To the rivers and valleys of our ancestral lands

We came from the first people GOD made
And it is with extreme gratitude that
I thank my God

The Most High

For giving me the same hair on my head
that the first woman on earth had on hers...

DAMN...
my fine black man sure looks good
with all that soft, naturally nappy hair on his head

Looking like he belonged to the days
When black Gods rocked and ruled the WORLD

As the first MEN ON EARTH

Once the black man's mind is set free
Black women all over world will exhale and celebrate
The naturally nappy hair sitting on our own heads
Just the way the Most High meant it to be...

Chapter 26

A BLACK MAN'S TRIBUTE TO HIS NATURALLY NAPPY, BEAUTIFUL BLACK WOMAN

A couple of days ago, I was flipping through the TV channels, and came across a TV guide show about Tyler Perry's new movie, 'Why Did I Get Married, Too?' Before I knew what hit me, I was off the sofa, on my knees, so close to the TV screen, that my breath was fogging the glass...

I glanced around, to make sure my wife wasn't in the room, then turned back to see Jill Scott, as she sauntered across the stage in this damn sexy black dress, rolling curves for a thousand days, wearing a perfectly shaped afro on her beautiful head...

After she took a seat on sofa next to Tyler Perry, I kept replaying that scene, that walk, that body, that skin, that face, that hair...in my head...

I was in love...
Then the thought crossed my swooning mind...

Why did this beautiful black woman have to wear that unbelievable weave in Perry's movie instead of looking like the truly, gorgeous, womanly, sexy, sexually tempting, delicious, delectable, edible, full-figured, thick, Nubian Black queen crowned by a perfectly shaped natural who had me drooling in front of my TV set?

Chill...

I'm not going to go off on my usual, hyper-political rant. Today, I'm going to talk about my eternal love for my naturally nappy, beautiful black woman...

As I travel down memory lane, remembering all the Hershey-sweet chocolate, dark honey-brown, mocha, caramel, and lemon-creme girl-woman queens that had my young head spinning like a top...

I didn't know what it was then

But there was always something special, richer, deeper, and more stimulating physically, mentally, and sexually about black women that I didn't see in the women who weren't...

Some folks call it "soul"... baby...

I know hair can't make love,
Heat some chicken soup when I get a cold
Fix a furnace in the winter
Or put a band-aid on a crying kid's cut finger

I can only speak for myself
When I say I prefer the naturally nappy hair on my woman's head
To straight hair that blows in the breeze
Because her hair is identical to the naturally nappy hair
On my own head

Some brothers are dead TIRED
Of all the white-washed beauty
Forced down our parched throats
Like chunks of dry white bread
That chokes on the way down
Instead of nutrition-rich brown and black bread
That feeds our hearts, minds, bodies, and souls

Because my ancestors never saw
Beauty as the pale skin, hair, eyes, and bony bodies
plastered on today's magazine covers, TV, and movie screens...

They loved and appreciated the NATURAL beauty of their own women

Like My Black Queen
who wears her hair full and natural
With soft, nappy curls that kiss the dark, sexy curve of her neck
The texture of her hair under my roving fingers,
Is a soft, springy cushion that doesn't lay down flat
But pushes back like it has a life and a mind of its own
Just sitting on top of her pretty, naturally nappy head

When I caress her hair,
And look into her deep dark eyes
I see the history of our life together

over 500 years of loving and laughter...
sadness and joy...
tears and triumphs...

And a feeling reaches deep into my black soul
Because my woman is authentic, soulful, the real deal...

She is ME
And I am HER

Our hair connects us to our majestic past,
To the rivers and valleys of our ancestral lands
We came from the first people GOD made

And it is with extreme gratitude that
I thank my God
The Most High

For giving me the same hair on my head
that the first man on earth had on his...

I glance out of the corner of my eye
And pretend not to see
my wife standing there
pretending not to watch me...

DAMN...my pretty black wife sure looks good
with all that soft, naturally nappy hair on her head

Looking like she belonged to the days
When black Goddesses rocked and ruled the WORLD

As the first WOMEN ON EARTH

Once the black female is uplifted
Back to the place where God meant her to be
Black men all over world will exhale
And celebrate our OWN women
With the black-loving EYES
the Most High gave us to see...

Harlem Sweeties

by Langston Hughes

Have you dug the spill
Of Sugar Hill?
Cast your gims
On this sepia thrill:
Brown sugar lassie,
Caramel treat,
Honey-gold baby
Sweet enough to eat.
Peach-skinned girlie,
Coffee and cream,
Chocolate darling
Out of a dream.
Walnut tinted
Or cocoa brown,
Pomegranate-lipped
Pride of the town.
Rich cream-colored
To plum-tinted black,
Feminine sweetness
In Harlem's no lack.
Glow of the quince

To blush of the rose.
Persimmon bronze
To cinnamon toes.
Blackberry cordial,
Virginia Dare wine--
All those sweet colors
Flavor Harlem of mine!
Walnut or cocoa,
Let me repeat:
Caramel, brown sugar,
A chocolate treat.
Molasses taffy,
Coffee and cream,
Licorice, clove, cinnamon
To a honey-brown dream.
Ginger, wine-gold,
Persimmon, blackberry,
All through the spectrum
Harlem girls vary--
So if you want to know beauty's
Rainbow-sweet thrill,
Stroll down luscious,
Delicious, fine Sugar Hill.

Black LOVE

Counter-Warfare

DETERMINED TO BE AN
ADMINISTRATIVE MARKING
E.O. 12065, Section 6-102
By AT ____ NARS, Date 1-26-82

FOR IMMEDIATE RELEASE

OP-16-F-2 ONI

[redacted]

MEMORANDUM FOR THE DIRECTOR

SUBJECT: **National Institute For World Population Control**

To: J. Maroga
From: S. Olsen
CC: File
Date:
Re: Global White Population to Plummet to Single Digit

As a percentage of world inhabitants the white population will plummet to a single digit (9.76%) by 2060 from a high-water mark of 27.98% in 1950. The study was conducted by Mark Stradley, Dean Stradley, and the NPI Staff. The methodology is described in a footnote.

Using 2010 as the base reference the big gainer in the population derby will be blacks or sub-Sahara Africans. This group will expand almost 133% to 2.7 billion by 2060. By the middle of this century blacks will represent 25.38% of world population which is up dramatically from the 8.97% they recorded in 1950.

The other groups measured in the study were the Central Asians (Indians), East Asians (Chinese and Japanese), the Southeast Asians, Arabic (North Africa and the Middle East) and Amerindian-Mestizo (Mexican and Central America). All these groups will experience a population growth.

The big population story of the 21st Century is shaping up to be the status reversal of whites and blacks and the Indian baby boom. A side bar will be the single digit minority role that whites will assume. Of the 7 population groups studied only whites are projected to sustain an absolute decline in numbers.

(The above memo is a work of fiction)

"The art of war teaches us to rely not on the likelihood of the enemy's not coming, but on our own readiness to receive him; not on the chance of his not attacking, but rather on the face that we have made our position unassailable."

-- Sun Tzu,
'The Art of War' (544-496 BC)

CHAPTER 27

BLACK LOVE COUNTER WARFARE SOLUTIONS & SUGGESTIONS

What Is Counter-Warfare?

Counter-Warfare is a strategy of non-violent resistance to the system of racism/white supremacy, the most SOPHISTICATED MIND GAME ever designed. In self-defense, non-whites must develop an equally powerful counter-intelligence to neutralize the "mind games" by:

- changing the way we think (education).
- changing our behavior (constructive actions)

13 Counter Warfare Strategies

1. Recognize We Are At War
2. Admit We Have A Problem: Mentacide
3. Become Knowledgeable About the System Of White Supremacy
4. STOP Keeping White People's Secrets
5. STOP Obeying the "White Traffic Cop" Inside Your Head
6. The Theory of Non-Participation
7. Minimize Conflict (stop name calling & fighting)
8. Maintain A Psychological Distance From White People
9. Become Comfortable With Being Uncomfortable
10. Show Black Love Freely, Openly, and Publicly
11. Adopt The Mantra of Black Unity
12. 33 Rules of Disengagement
13. Become a Leader of One

The **Counter-Warfare Strategies** put the focus where it belongs: on what black people CAN and MUST do, NOT on what white people might OR should do. We did not get in this terrible condition overnight, and we will NOT solve our problems overnight. We cannot afford to waste any more time talking about what white people should do for us -- and find a way to do for SELF.

If we need better schools for our children, we must POOL our resources and CREATE better schools. If we need more jobs, we must POOL our resources and CREATE our own jobs. We cannot afford to wait one second longer for "someone else" to end racism. ***We have already waited 500 YEARS.***
It is time to STOP begging, marching, and protesting.

It is time to STOP expecting the white elite to eliminate the white supremacy system designed for their sole benefit. ***All we will get is what we have always gotten: the false appearance of real change.***

The Real Revolution Takes Place Between Our Ears

As we watch the civil rights clock spinning backwards, it should be clear that despite all our "progress," black people still control nothing in America, including the ability to rescue one black person off a roof after Hurricane Katrina.

Once we become empowered (illuminated) with knowledge of self, and knowledge of how the system of racism/white supremacy works, we will attract other empowered individuals who seek real change – not the kind of "change" that is seen on television under the banner of a "National Convention."

We must stop deluding ourselves that such FALSE displays offer any real change. THEY DO NOT. They are simply updated dog-and-pony shows to pacify, deceive, and exploit the masses. We know from history that black leaders who TRULY advocate real change are NEVER rewarded, promoted, or given airtime by the same powerful elites who created the system of injustice.

Real change is not glamorous or pleasant. It has nothing to do with being popular, articulate, or presenting an attractive image. It does not happen while we sit in front of a television set, or walk into a voting booth and push a button. Real change is hard, dirty, and dangerous work.

Fortunately, none of the suggestions in this book are hard, dirty, or dangerous. They do not require money, special skills, talents, bravery, or bloodshed. In fact, most suggestions involve NOT doing something that wastes our precious time and money, or that harms us individually or collectively.

These recommendations (as well as the contents of this book) are a FRAMEWORK that the reader can adapt as he or she sees fit, and decide what is beneficial, constructive, and useful, and what is not. No one, including the authors of this book, represent the voice (or voices) of authority.

STRATEGY #1: RECOGNIZE WE ARE AT WAR

A Quick Summary Of Black America's Worsening Dilemma

Black labor has become obsolete in America. In many inner cities, the menial, low-skilled and low-paying jobs that poor blacks used to do -- and are still willing to do -- are being farmed out for maximum profit to illegal (slave) labor. Automation (machines) and computers have eliminated the rest.

In spite of record unemployment for blacks, (estimated at over 35% in 2010), America is still importing unskilled AND skilled non-white labor from Latin America and India. The picture for educated, professional blacks in corporate America is just as dismal. Glass ceilings have turned to concrete. Unions, good jobs, benefits, and guaranteed pensions are becoming relics of the past.

As a result, the hard-won gains from civil rights and affirmative action over the last 40 years are being systematically wiped out. After two terms of the Bush Administration efforts, affirmative action is little more than a controversial and fraudulent memory that clearly ignored the FACT that the biggest beneficiaries of affirmative action were AND still are white females.

Black farmers have yet to receive compensation for stolen farmland and government discrimination. Blacks are losing land and houses at a record pace in dozens of predominantly black cities where gentrification (land grabs), subprime mortgages, reverse-redlining (targeting black areas for fraudulent home loans), foreclosures, and property tax and eminent-domain schemes designed to force blacks out of major cities – and out of their homes and communities.

In predominantly black schools all across the country, black children are mis-educated and under-educated by design, while many black schools are closing their doors for good. Black boys are being "tracked" into "special education" and non-college prep classes, or expelled for minor offenses to DELIBERATELY destroy their intellectual potential and self-confidence.

The unrelenting onslaught of white Hollywood via the buffoonery comedies, sitcoms, and "reality shows" is polluting the minds and morals of black youth. White decision-makers and their black puppets deliberately pair the black male with anyone but a black female in movies, TV shows, TV commercials, and rap videos to divide and conquer (and demoralize) the black male and female.

Over one million black men and black women rot in penal institutions, many for non-violent drug "crimes," while white drug users of crack, powdered cocaine, prescription drugs, and meth get "intervention," drug treatment, fines, or a slap on the wrist for their "illness." To add more injuries to the massive injuries inflicted on Black America by America's "criminal" justice system, prison authorities callously turn a "blind eye" to the epidemic of inmates AND guards raping other inmates.

Rampant homosexuality flourishes in prisons where black males in their sexual prime are forced to live in cages with other sexually frustrated males. It is NO accident that black ex-felons infected with HIV, AIDS, & Hepatitis C are deliberately released back into the black community without education, job skills or medical treatment for their contagious diseases.

It is UNDENIABLE that the white supremacy system and their white foot-soldiers are waging a VICIOUS WAR against black people on four levels: educational, economic, psychological, and reproductive.

It is also increasingly clear that (white) America has no patience or sympathy for poor (or "uppity" blacks), and is rapidly and quietly building more prisons while it closes black schools in preparation for...what?

104 Million Dollar Juvenile Detention Center To Be Built East Baltimore – while city is closing predominantly black schools (SOURCE: Our Weekly, Nov 11, 2010, http://ourweekly.com/los-angeles/104-million-juvenile-detention-facility-be-built)

What is White America's plan for black youth?

THE ANSWER SHOULD BE OBVIOUS.

STRATEGY #2: ADMIT WE HAVE BEEN DAMAGED BY 500 YEARS OF OPPRESSION AND ARE STILL SUFFERING FROM "MENTACIDE"

To be a white-identified black is MENTACIDE – the destruction of what should be a black-centered, self-respecting, and self-loving mindset. The late Dr. Bobby Wright, who popularized the term "mentacide," defined it as: *"the deliberate and systematic destruction of a group's mind with the ultimate objective being the complete extermination of the group."*

Scholar and author Dr. Mwalimu K. Bomani Baruti offers this explanation: "*When you willingly think and act out of someone else's interpretation of reality to their benefit and against your survival. It is a state of subtle insanity, which has come to characterize (more and more) Africans globally.*"

It is UNDENIABLE that the black community is having a moral and spiritual crisis that no amount of money or material things can heal. We have allowed our black "heroes" and role models to be chosen (by the white media) on the basis of fame and money -- NOT on the content of their characters.

We have gone from a people who would risk life and limb fighting for the rights of ALL BLACK PEOPLE to a people who are disconnected from the pain and suffering of our OWN kind.

We claim to be "black and proud" yet seldom pass up the opportunity to condemn and stereotype each other for the entire world to see. We ridicule our beautiful African features while denying that we secretly hate the man or woman in the mirror.

We teach our children -- by example -- to dislike and disrespect themselves and then look on in puzzled frustration as our black children increasingly choose the road to self-destruction and despair.

If we are doing well economically, we blame those who have not been so lucky, even if we KNOW the system of white supremacy will ONLY allow a small minority of blacks to "achieve" the American Dream.

If we want to heal our BLACK NATION, we must put aside our (false) EGOS and BELIEFS, and ADMIT WE ARE SICK FROM WHITE SUPREMACY CRACK. We must ADMIT we have been programmed to see ourselves and other black people THROUGH CONDEMNING WHITE EYES. ***It is time to tell ourselves the truth.***

LET
TRUTH
BECOME
OUR
DRUG
OF
CHOICE

STRATEGY #3: BECOME KNOWLEDGEABLE ABOUT THE SYSTEM OF WHITE SUPREMACY AND OUR TRUE STATUS IN IT

> *"If you do not understand White Supremacy (Racism), what it is, and how it works, everything else that you understand, will only confuse you."*
>
> -- *Neely Fuller, Jr. (1971)*

Until we understand WHAT white supremacy is and HOW it functions, we will NOT understand what is happening to non-white people all over the planet. We can't create solutions until we understand the problems, the same way we can't build a house without building a foundation. What we will wind up with is a shaky, unsafe building that will topple when the first storm hits.

In the RESOURCES section (page 341) there is a list of books, CDs, DVDs, and websites that will increase your understanding of white supremacy so you will recognize HOW and WHEN it is being practiced.

STRATEGY #4: STOP KEEPING WHITE PEOPLE'S SECRETS

Tell your children the TRUTH about racism/white supremacy

Jewish parents know how important it is to teach their children about the Jewish Holocaust so their children will KNOW they must be vigilant against their enemies. One reason so many black parents shy away from teaching our children about racism or slavery ***is we do not know enough about our history to teach anyone else. (Strategy #3).***

Once black parents understand how the system of white supremacy works, they will understand how important it is to make their children aware of WHAT is happening -- and WHY it is happening to black people all over the world.

We must STOP pretending and lying to ourselves that we should let our children "make up their own minds about race," and prepare them for the psychological attacks they will face both inside (the television/movies) AND outside the home (the white supremacy system).

If we do NOT prepare them, we should be prepared for our children to be psychologically devastated when the TRUTH hits them square between their eyes. It is a CRIME to let another generation of black children come out into a racist society without PREPARING them for what WE KNOW they will face in the white world.

ELIMINATE phrases like "good hair," pretty (light) skin color, pretty (light) eyes, and bad (nappy) hair from your vocabulary. Do NOT allow anyone to degrade black people in front of your children and explain WHY you object to it.

Encourage your children to question everything they see and hear, give them TRUTHFUL answers, and let them express their opinions. Let them know there are NO STUPID QUESTIONS, but you may not know all the answers.

Black children are born with ***an abundance of intelligence*** until the media, educational system, racist whites, and unconscious black adults kill their confidence, self-esteem, and intellectual potential.

Replace television watching and video games (that do all the THINKING) with books, games, and building blocks, puzzles, and chemistry sets that will teach our children to THINK ANALYTICALLY and allow them to use their motor skills and creativity. If we want our children to compete intellectually with children from every part of the world, the time to prepare them is RIGHT NOW.

STRATEGY #5: STOP OBEYING THE WHITE TRAFFIC COP INSIDE OUR HEADS

Since slavery, blacks have been programmed to act against our own self-interests, survival, and humanity for the benefit of whites. Another way to describe this is blacks learn to be, think, speak, and act ANTI-BLACK. This anti-black mentality is NOT our fault. It came as a result of 500 years of systematic brainwashing in an ANTI-BLACK, white supremacist system.

That being said, we are STILL responsible for changing our attitudes towards our OWN people -- by BLOCKING OUT the voice of the "white traffic cop" inside our heads.

We must THINK FIRST before we speak to, act against, or harm another black person. We must ASK ourselves WHY we are so quick to mistreat each other -- BUT are so reluctant (afraid) to stop whites from mistreating us. We MUST understand that ANYTHING that harms other black people HELPS the system of white supremacy maintain its power -- which is why blacks are rewarded for betraying each other. We MUST ask ourselves -- *"Whose eyes am I using when I judge other black people?"* When we condemn other black people for BEING BLACK, we are CONDEMNING OURSELVES.

Before you SPEAK or ACT, ASK yourself: do my actions make me part of the solution or part of the problem? Will my speech OR actions make this world a better, safer place for my children and grandchildren -- or will my words and actions make things worse for them?

"Afrikan parents know who they are dealing with. That's why we lie to our children in the name of protecting them. Such excuses are shameless. We are not protecting them. We are trying to protect ourselves from the pain we know will come to them and us if they stand up.

"No matter how we try to play it off, we understand that Europeans will kill them in a second, for nothing. We understand that our sons are looked upon as the greatest threat to European hegemony for good reason.

"And yes, as men, they are our last line of defense. There is nothing unrealistic about these fears. They are reasonable for a people who subconsciously understand the nature of their oppressor, as evidenced in historical fact, yet feel powerless to confront it.

"However these reasonable fears lead to insanity when they cause us to believe that no matter what we do the European will rule forever. 'Oppression does not destroy a people. It is the acceptance of oppression that destroys.'

"By example, we subconsciously establish limits for our children at the same time that we tell them they are limitless. By following the example set by their parents, emasculated Afrikan males become living expressions of confused, powerless, mentacidal negroes.

"Yet this mentality is not incompatible with encouraging interracial dating and marriage. Nonwhite people don't understand the necessity for white supremacy domination, but white people understand that they have to dominate.

"So when a white person is in bed with a nonwhite person, because of the long history of conditioning that tells them nonwhites are inferior, the nonwhite person will be programmed to love white people...

"The highest desire, under white supremacy programming, is to be loved by a white and validated by a white person. So the white person who is acting counter to white genetic survival by engaging in sexual activity with the nonwhite person is actually achieving a greater goal: the goal of domination.

"The nonwhite person's mind has been turned against their own interest...the nonwhite person has to turn against the interests of other nonwhite persons to protect the interests of the white person they're in bed with.

"That means the white person is the dominant person, no matter who's on top or bottom in the act of sexual intercourse. She is far from (being) alone in her deduction."

-- 'EXCUSES, EXCUSES: The Politics of Interracial Coupling in European Culture' by Mwalimu K. Baruti

STRATEGY #6: THE THEORY OF NON-VIOLENT/NON-PARTICIPATION

NON-PARTICIPATION is the most powerful weapon we possess. We have the freedom to NOT PARTICIPATE in those things that demean or short-change black people. This includes NOT spending our hard-earned dollars where they are not respected.

For example, in 2007, at the biggest fashion events in New York City, Paris, and Italy, top American and European designers, like Jil Sander, Burberry, Bottega Veneta, Roberto Cavalli, and Prada had no black runway models.

> *"I am virtually never allowed to photograph black models for the magazines, fashion houses, cosmetic brands, perfume companies, and advertising clients I work for. Whenever I ask to use a black model I am given excuses such as, '...black models do not reflect the brands values.'" -- Fashion photographer, Nick Knight.*

Despite the lack of black representation on the runways, in high-fashion advertising, and behind the scenes of the fashion industry, blacks have plenty of representation at the cash registers when we collectively spend billions on designer clothing, accessories, shoes, and apparel.

Utilizing the POWER of NON-PARTICIPATION, we would STOP begging (or demanding) to be included, and STOP BUYING WHERE WE CAN'T WORK. No dialogue would be necessary.

Our CONSTRUCTIVE ACTIONS would speak for themselves. A constructive (and self-respecting) response to the racism in the fashion industry would be:

> *"They don't have to hire blacks for their fashion shows. They have the right to hire (or not hire) whoever they see fit. They can do their thing, and we'll do our thing. Just understand this "thing" cuts both ways. We don't have to include them in our shows OR spend our money with them, either."*

The black collective would then spend our fashion dollars with our black designers and turn their wonderful creations into OUR fashion status symbols. To take a page out of the white economic book, non-black designers could participate ONLY ***if they hire blacks and advertise in black-owned media.***

We would REFUSE to PARTICIPATE or SUPPORT ANY people, places, and things that do not respect our dollars, and START CIRCULATING those precious dollars in our own communities.

STRATEGY #7: MINIMIZE CONFLICT

MINIMIZE conflict at home, at work, in public, and at all places. Avoid unnecessary contact with people who seek conflict with you. The powers-that-be use conflict to divide and conquer the black male and female.

According to the *"United Independent Compensatory Code/System/Concept"* by Neely Fuller, Jr., there are **Ten Basic Stops** that help to eliminate Racism and produce Justice for all Victims of Racism:

1. Stop Snitching (to get ahead of someone else)
2. Stop Name-Calling (describe what a person does or says rather than calling them a name. For example, instead of calling a person a "liar," repeat what they said and say that what was said was "not true."
3. Stop "Cursing" (because it is insulting and demeaning, and promotes conflict, hostility, and violence).
4. Stop Gossiping (saying something ABOUT a person that we would not be willing to say directly to that person with others listening).
5. Stop Being Discourteous (showing a lack of consideration or acting or speaking in such a way that shows little to no regard for how others will be affected).
6. Stop Stealing (because it promotes injustice and places a greater value on "things" than on people or justice).
7. Stop Robbing (using the threat of bodily harm to take something from another person that does not belong to you promotes injustice).
8. Stop Fighting (if people cannot talk in a way that minimizes conflict, they should avoid contact with each other. No contact, no conflict).
9. Stop Killing (except in direct defense of self, others, and/or major property, it is best to avoid killing or maiming another person).
10. Stop Squabbling Among Yourselves And Asking Racists (White Supremacists) To Settle Your Problems (because racists often create situations where blacks are encouraged to squabble among themselves. Racists do not approve of black people solving heir own problems among ourselves without the so-called "help" of the WHITE PEOPLE IN CHARGE who created the problems in the first place because that does not promote White Supremacy.

Minimize Conflict. No contact; no conflict.

STRATEGY #8: MAINTAIN A PSYCHOLOGICAL DISTANCE FROM WHITE PEOPLE

During times of WAR, the military trains its soldiers to see the opposing army as less than human – NOT for sport or entertainment - but to maintain a psychological distance (a toughness) so the soldier will be able to kill another human being even when killing goes against their conscience or morality.

EXAMPLE:

During and after slavery, black women performed domestic and maternal duties for their white slave-owner OR employer. Black women nursed white babies at their breast, raised the white children, cooked the white family's food; cleaned the white family's home, and were often (told) they were "just like one of the family."

But at the end of the day, OR if that black female stepped over the invisible line separating black from white, she was quickly, and often severely reminded that she was still a "nigger." The white family SAID the black female was "just like family," YET they STILL MAINTAINED A PSYCHOLOGICAL DISTANCE from her (as a black person) to be able to:

- practice racism even if their actions are immoral, unjust, or cruel
- MAINTAIN the system of white supremacy and white privilege

AXIOM #10: It is MANDATORY to maintain a PSYCHOLOGICAL DISTANCE from your enemies during times of WAR, or you will have NO PSYCHOLOGICAL DEFENSES against them.

A Black Man's Constructive & Self-Respecting "Conduct Code" For White Females (Maintaining A Psychological Distance)

"My interactions with White females have totally changed. I try my best to not to treat a White female as a female without being discourteous or non-constructive.

- *I avoid unnecessary contact with them.*
- *I avoid unnecessary communication with them.*
- *I avoid 'reckless eyeballing' or even noticing a White female visually.*
- *I refrain from complimenting a White female in anyway unless it is for a constructive purpose especially in the area of sex.*

Anything that benignly 'defeminizes' White females in relation to me so that I am not manipulated with sex, or promises of sex, or hopes of sex and sexual play. They get the idea it seems. Unfortunately, I may have hurt some White females' feelings in the process of adapting this personal code but that's business.

It's as though they realize that I am doing things that no one at the job is doing in relation to them, and its as though that its not decent to show no sexual interest in White females.

Females seek validation from males and vice versa. It reminds a person of their gender roles and gender expectation in people relations, and it's essential to a person's sanity.

Remove that validation and it will affect that person especially females. When a man ignores a woman's femininity its like taking way their 'rights' or 'powers' as a woman, which means they can't function as a female and they may doubt their femininity.

One of the reasons for this behavior is to create and maintain self-respect. Another reason for this is to reduce the chance that I can be seduced by a White female in order to be manipulated or fooled for their gain and my loss.

Another reason is to insure that you are taken seriously and not for granted to also insure that you are in the most advantageous position possible. Another reason is that I think that a White female will have more respect for a man that does not objectify them especially if he is Black, considering all of the stereotypes.

Another reason is most White females are less likely to ask you 'why do you not treat me like a lady', consequently they will be puzzled that a male especially a Black male is de-feminizing them if they even guess that's occurring.

This means that the Black male has the power in that situation because the White female will always thirst for an answer to why you treat her like she has a penis instead of a vagina and two breasts.

All of this equals to power and actually empowers Black females when they are made aware of what you are doing they love it, which means I love it.

On the other hand, I have greatly improved my relations with non-white females by focusing all my masculine energy on them and trying to over validate them and I have gotten some very, very good results.

None of this is easy, its requires a lot of work and discipline but this is War. It is also not easy for because I'm an art student, and at School their lots of White females.

And no matter what I am a male and as far as the laws of attraction go anything is possible that's why this requires training and discipline. Think of my suggestion as one way to counter this bleaching down process."

-- Black Mergatroid (2010)

For those who think Black Mergatroid's response is unreasonable, let's compare this to the present day "White Male's Conduct Code."

The White Male's Conduct Code For Non-White Females (To Maintain White Supremacy)

"My interactions with non-white females have changed little in the last 500 years. I avoid unnecessary contact with them if I cannot be in a dominant position or unless it involves sexual intercourse. I avoid unnecessary communication with non-white females except in the course of conducting business (making a profit) or promoting white interests (white supremacy).

I avoid 'reckless eyeballing' or even noticing a non-white female visually, especially when other whites are around. I refrain from complimenting non-white females in public, although I may do it privately (when other whites are not around), and expressly for the purpose of having sexual intercourse.

Anything that 'de-feminizes' non-white females in relation to me is done so I do not diminish white supremacy/superiority by being manipulated with sex, promises of sex, or hopes of sex and sexual play with non-white females.

Non-white females get the idea it seems, that in the white man's eyes, they will NEVER be equal to the white female. I may have hurt some non-white females feelings in the process but that's (the) business (of white supremacy).

They do NOT realize I do these things because I am part of a (white) organization that is dedicated to maintaining white supremacy, which means white males should NOT show any sexual interest in non-white females in the presence of other whites; especially in the presence of white females.

Females seek validation from males and vice versa. It reminds a person of their gender roles and gender expectation in people relations, and it's essential to a person's self-esteem. Remove that validation and it will affect that person, especially females.

When a man ignores a woman's femininity its like taking way their 'rights' or 'powers' as a woman which means they can't function as a female and they may doubt their femininity because it's important that non-white females believe they are inferior to white females.

Another reason is to reduce the chance that I can be emotionally seduced by a non-white female and be manipulated or fooled, which means a loss for me as a white man, the white race, and the system of white supremacy.

Another reason is to insure that whites are taken seriously and to insure the most advantageous position possible for whites. Another reason is white females have more respect or consideration for a white man who does NOT treat non-white females as their equals.

Another reason is most non-white females will not DARE ask a white man, 'why do you not treat me like a lady', because they do not understand that's my INTENTION: to de-feminize and de-humanize them so I will not be too compassionate toward them.

By doing so, the white male maintains the most power in that situation since the non-white female will always accept her inferior status when you treat her like she has a penis instead of a vagina and two breasts.

All of this equals to power and actually empowers white females when they are made aware of what we (white males) are doing; they love it, which means I love it. By doing so, I have greatly improved my relations with white females by focusing all my masculine energy on them and trying to over validate them and I have gotten some very, very good results.

None of this is easy its requires a lot of work and discipline but this is War. It is also not easy because I'm an art student, and there are many, many beautiful and sexually desirable black and non-white females in my city who I would love to paint (nude) -- and do a lot more. And no matter what I am a male and as far as the laws of attraction go anything is possible that's why this requires training and discipline.

There are a minority of white males who sex and marry non-whites, but this still maintains the system of white supremacy because they usually get the pick of the black and non-white litter, which neutralizes these females and stops them from reproducing with non-white males. Think of my suggestion as one way to counter the browning of White America and the destruction of white supremacy.

***

Maintaining a PSYCHOLOGICAL DISTANCE from white people has NOTHING to do hating white people. It is a WAR-TIME STRATEGY that whites have used successfully against non-whites for hundreds of years -- ***and it has been extremely successful.***

STRATEGY #9: BLACK PEOPLE MUST BECOME COMFORTABLE WITH BEING UNCOMFORTABLE

"We must become comfortable with being uncomfortable." – Gus Renegade, host of the C.O.W.S. radio (www.contextofwhitesupremacy.com *).*

The suggestions in this chapter will make some readers uncomfortable. The idea of using psychological counter-warfare against whites makes some blacks literally sweat under the collar.

However, if we are not extremely "uncomfortable" with racism, police brutality, murder-by-cop of unarmed black men and women, inferior black schools, unjust incarcerations, and economic, housing, and employment discrimination -- ***nothing should make us uncomfortable.***

STRATEGY #10: SHOW 'BLACK LOVE' OPENLY AND PUBLICLY

Black Men and Women, black husbands and wives, black mothers and fathers, black sons and daughters, black sisters and brothers, black parents and children should show AFFECTION OPENLY and PUBLICLY.

It is especially important for parents to show love for each other OPENLY AND PUBLICLY in front of their children, so your children will KNOW it is NORMAL and DESIRABLE for black men and women to LIKE, LOVE, and SEXUALLY DESIRE EACH OTHER.

It is ONLY in the Western culture (and mind) that normal sexual and affection between black males and black females is considered WRONG (dirty), -- while black homosexuality is openly encouraged AND rewarded.

Showing LOVE should not be restricted to family members or romantic or sexual partners. LOVE should not be restricted to blood relations. LOVE is showing KINDNESS AND COURTESY OPENLY AND PUBLICLY to all black people -- even strangers -- so our black children will LEARN it is **NORMAL and DESIRABLE** for Black Men and Black Women to RESPECT and CARE ABOUT EACH OTHER.

Of course, we courtesy should be extended to all people but our MAIN FOCUS should be on repairing the bonds between the black male, female, and child that were destroyed during slavery and the 500 years of racist oppression that followed.

Do NOT be discouraged if a "sick" person does not respond to your "kind treatment." ***Push on AND keep planting the seeds of UNITY.***

We MUST love each other like our children's lives depend on it -- because they DO.

STRATEGY #11: ADOPT THE 'MANTRA OF BLACK UNITY' AND MAKE THIS OUR NEW BLACK NATIONAL ANTHEM

When you attack one of us, you attack ALL of us.

When you attack Black Men, you attack ME, (a Black Woman) because I came from a Black Man. When you attack Black Women, you attack ME, (a Black Man) because I came from a Black Woman. When you degrade, stereotype, or harm ONE OF US, you harm ME because mistreating ONE is the same as mistreating ALL OF US.

STRATEGY #12: THE 33 RULES OF DISENGAGEMENT

Stop Showing Off, Bragging, And Talking Too Much

1. STOP styling, profiling, bragging, and boasting about who you are, what you look like, or what you have. It matters more WHO you are when no one is looking.
2. STOP showing off or trying to impress white people. *They don't care.*
3. ALL opposition to racism should be constructive and promote justice and correction; not avenge racial wrongs. If the offending parties refuse to stop practicing racism, replace dialogue with constructive self-help strategies.

Sex & Relationships

4. STOP HAVING SEX WITH STRANGERS, acquaintances, and people we are not committed to. Sex is SPIRITUAL as well as PHYSICAL. Every time we have sex with another person, we absorb the spiritual nature (good or bad) of our sexual partner, and this becomes part of OUR spiritual nature.
5. STOP HAVING UNPROTECTED SEX outside of marriage. This will limit the spread of venereal diseases, manmade viruses, the number of unplanned pregnancies, and at-risk, neglected children.
6. STOP HAVING SEX FOR MONEY and material things. You do not have to stand on a street corner to be a PROSTITUTE. If you are selling your precious body for a promotion, favors, money, or things, *you are PROSTITUTING yourself.* This is true for males and females.
7. STOP MAKING BABIES if you are not in a committed marriage with a committed partner. We must break the generational curse of the dysfunctional black family and at-risk black children.
8. STOP HAVING CHILDREN YOU ARE NOT WILLING OR ABLE TO RAISE, love, nurture, provide for, and protect. This will break the generational curse of the dysfunctional black family and at-risk black children.
9. STOP HAVING BABIES to hang on to a man or a woman. If they don't want you, why do you want them? ***Above ALL else -- respect yourself.***

Stop Worshipping Money And Material Things

10. STOP CHOOSING ROLE MODELS for our children because they are rich. Stop looking to strangers to be "role models" and become your own children's role models. Children need role models at eye-level: parents, adults, teachers, police officers, firefighters, and the businesspeople in their communities.
11. STOP TEACHING OUR CHILDREN TO LOOK OUTSIDE THEMSELVES and teach them to VALUE what is already inside. If we help build them their self-respect and self-esteem from the gifts GOD gave them, our children won't need black role models, superstars, showcase blacks, false prophets, political pimps, Holy White Grails, OR white validation.

Self-Respect/Self-Reliance

12. STOP DEMANDING RESPECT from other people. You do not have a social contract with everyone you meet. The only person who is obligated to respect you is YOU. Unless someone's behavior harms you (other than hurting your feelings), the most POWERFUL RESPONSE is to put them on IGNORE. Worry MORE about respecting yourself.
13. WE DO NOT CONTROL ANYTHING in a white supremacy system but OURSELVES. We cannot out-police the police; outspend the super-rich; out-fight the military; or out-televise the networks, BUT we do have control over the most important possession we own: OURSELVES. We can refuse to participate in anything that degrade, demean, and destroys black people.
14. STOP DOING THOSE THINGS THAT REQUIRE FREE WILL and work against our individual and collective interests. For example, no one can make us buy, listen to, or watch a CD, movie, or DVD that degrades black people.
15. STOP PRAISING BLACK PEOPLE because they are bi-racial or their skin color, hair, skin, and eyes makes them look more white than black. What does that say about YOU (and your self-esteem) if you look more "black?"
16. STOP SUPPORTING BLACK ENTERTAINERS, artists, politicians, poets, filmmakers, scholars, and activists who degrade black people by promoting negative stereotypes.
17. STOP DISRESPECTING BLACK PEOPLE. No one can make us disrespect black people or call black people foul names. No one can make us turn against our mothers and fathers, wives and husbands, sons and daughters, or neighbors. No one can make us replace love with hate. No one can make us place a white woman or white man on a sexual pedestal, or knock a black man or black woman off one.

18. STOP PARTICIPATING IN ACTIVITIES THAT DESTROY THE BLACK COMMUNITY. For example, if we stopped using drugs, the drug dealers would be forced to find another profession. If we refused to buy stolen merchandise, the burglars, robbers, and thieves would be forced to find a legitimate source of income instead of victimizing their communities and filling up the nation's prisons. If we refused to buy or watch degrading movies, TV shows, and music videos, ***they would stop making them***.
19. STOP EXPECTING WHITE PEOPLE TO SOLVE OUR PROBLEMS. It is OUR responsibility to solve our own problems because we have the most to lose if we don't.
20. BECOME YOUR OWN AUTHORITY on the things that affect your life and family. We must become our own authority (educate ourselves) so we cannot be deceived OR intimidated by those who practice racism.
21. STOP WORKING AGAINST THE INTERESTS OF BLACK PEOPLE. In other words, the system of white supremacy requires our COOPERATION and PARTICIPATION in harming other black people.

Save The Children & The Black Family

22. TAKE CONTROL OF THE EDUCATION OF OUR BLACK CHILDREN so their intellectual potential will not be destroyed by the anti-black educational system. We must start our own independent school systems so we can empower our children with the TRUTH, instead of allowing them to be poisoned by LIES -- and an inadequate education.
23. STOP LETTING THE RADIO, TELEVISION, VIDEO, AND DVDS RAISE YOUR CHILDREN. Spend more FAMILY TIME talking, at the bookstore, the playground, and the library.
24. TURN OFF THE TELEVISION AND STEREOS (once in a while) and read a book (like this one) in front of your children. Our children imitate what they see us do -- NOT what we tell them to do.
25. TEACH OUR CHILDREN TO LOVE THE WRITTEN WORD. If our children are taught to love the written word, they will always be in the LEARNING MODE. Blacks adults must educate themselves by reading books (like this one), and encourage the massive intellectual power of our children.
26. TEACH YOUR CHILDREN TO LOVE THE WRITTEN WORD. The reason slaves were punished for reading is the slave-owners knew READING led to THINKING. The same thing is true today. The average black public school deliberately makes LEARNING boring, humiliating, and painful. If our children hate to read (or learn), they will be forced to rely on their enemies for information -- and everything else they need.

27. DO NOT CONDUCT ILLEGAL AND DISHONEST ACTIVITIES IN FRONT OF YOUR CHILDREN or accept the reality that your children will not respect you even while they IMITATE you.
28. STOP FUSSING AND FIGHTING WITH YOUR CHILDREN'S MOTHER OR FATHER. Our children must take priority over our own selfish ego interests. We made the decision to have them (or didn't make the right decision to NOT have them). Our children did not ask to be born. We must NOT make them pay for our foolishness.
29. ADOPT THE 80% RULE FOR BUILDING STRONG MARRIAGES AND FAMILIES. Each partner giving 50-50 means BOTH are half-stepping. If each partner gives 80%, there will always be a SURPLUS (160% total effort) of love, care, empathy, support, and CONSTRUCTIVE ACTIONS. If your partner is willing to give only 50% or less, it may be time to get a new partner. If this applies to you, it may be time for serious self-analysis or to consider the OPTION of being alone).

Politics

30. HOLD ALL BLACK POLITICIANS TO THE HIGHEST POSSIBLE STANDARDS. Demand to know WHAT they are going to do for us, not what they think we should be doing for ourselves BEFORE they get our votes. Demand that all black politicians treat black voters with the same respect they give non-black voters.
31. UNDERSTAND THAT A POLITICIAN IS A POLITICIAN IS A POLITICIAN. A POLITICIAN IS NOT A PREACHER. We do not need them to preach at us, we need to know what they are GOING TO DO FOR US IF WE VOTE THEM INTO OFFICE. If, after ONE term, they cannot prove they are working in the black collective's best interests -- VOTE THEM OUT OF OFFICE.
32. BLACK CIVIL RIGHTS ORGANIZATIONS THAT ARE FUNDED BY OUTSIDERS (non-blacks) should be automatically suspect. Everyone has an agenda. Until we know what their agenda is, they should not be trusted.
33. DO NOT TRUST the "Showcase Blacks" who are used to wow and amaze us. Their "success" has NOTHING to do with progress for the black masses. Black progress can only be measured by what happens to the black masses, not to a few handpicked blacks. Even the cruelest master must throw his starving dog an occasional bone to keep it loyal AND to keep the dog from attacking its tormentor. (Yes, we are the starving dogs, not the masters).

STRATEGY #13: BECOME A "LEADER OF ONE"

1. **BECOME A LEADER OF ONE.** Once the INDIVIDUAL is empowered, they do not depend on other people to do the right thing.
2. The empowered individual raises EMPOWERED CHILDREN. This also ensures that a "movement" does not rest on the shoulders of one man or one woman. An empowered individual is spiritually CONTAGIOUS – if their actions are just, constructive, and righteous. The empowered individual can spread the gospel in a way a so-called national leader cannot.
3. The empowered individual leads by example; the national leaders CANNOT because most have already been purchased, bribed, or threatened into cooperating with our enemies. They are the wily foxes in sheep's clothing and the false prophets who will lead the (black) sheep to slaughter.
4. Most civil rights organizations are like sprinters. They start off running at full speed and are out of steam – and ideas -- before the end of the race for justice. The empowered individual is a marathon runner; in the race for the duration. The empowered individual is a LEADER OF ONE and does not get frustrated as easily as those whose power comes from a group, because he (or she) is NOT totally dependent on what a GROUP does OR does not do, and is not disabled because a so-called "leader" is disabled.
5. By choosing NOT to participate in those things that demean or degrade black people, we increase our PERSONAL POWER and SELF-RESPECT.
6. You cannot control anyone but yourself. By making more self-respecting decisions, you will influence others around you – even those that try to make you look or feel foolish.
7. BECOMING A LEADER OF ONE means you are making a powerful change from low to HIGH SELF-RESPECT. This may frighten and intimidate those who are still locked into self-disrespecting behavior. Do not let them discourage you. Before you know it, they will be singing your praises.
8. If you have children, teach by example. When your children hear you say you refuse to do X or Y because it is disrespectful or harmful to black people – ***they are listening to you.*** We must plant the right seeds in our children if we want to grow flower gardens instead of weeds.
9. **STUDY THE SYSTEM OF RACISM/WHITE SUPREMACY** so you will understand how it works. You cannot defeat racism if you do not understand how racism/white supremacy works.

10. STOP ASKING (BEGGING) for inclusion into a club (the White Supremacy system) that does NOT want you as a member. If you become a "token member," you become part of the problem, NOT the solution.
11. POOL OUR SKILLS, RESOURCES, MONEY, AND TALENT to benefit and enrich the black collective instead of making other communities stronger and richer with our dollars.
12. STOP TRUSTING SHOWCASE BLACKS simply because they are black. Being a black "first" does not mean they will work on our behalf. Pay MORE attention to what they DO (or don't do) and LESS on what they say.
13. STOP HATING ON OTHER BLACK PEOPLE. When we pull someone UP, we pull ourselves UP. Encourage the CONSTRUCTIVE efforts and ambitions of other black people because those efforts help the entire black collective.

The Power Of Universal Karma = The Universal Boomerang

The **Universal Boomerang** is the most powerful force in the world. It is GOD-FORCE. Karmic. Universal. What good we put out into the universe will be returned to us. If we are just and morally correct, what our enemies put out into the universe against us will be turned ***against*** them.

We Will Attract The Kind Of Justice We Deserve

We must not make the mistake of imitating those who abuse their power. Once the black collective regains our sanity and self-respect, only then should we seek unity with the non-black masses to fight for a more peaceful, and God-loving planet ruled by *Universal Man, Universal Woman, and the Law of Universal Justice.*

Each ONE, teach ONE
Do what YOU can, where you can
Become your own LEADER OF ONE
Pass this book along

If God is for us, who can be against us?

Romans 8:31

Resources

Recommended Reading/Viewing

BOOKS

Trojan Horse: Death Of A Dark Nation by Anon

The Isis Papers by Dr. Frances Cress Welsing

The United-Independent Compensatory Code/System/Concept: A textbook/workbook for victims of racism (white supremacy) by Neely Fuller, Jr.

The United-Independent Compensatory Code/System/Concept: A Compensator Counter-Racist Codified Word Guide by Neely Fuller, Jr.

Enemies: The Clash of Races by Haki R. Madhubuti

Asafo: A Warrior's Guide to Manhood by Mwalimu K. Bomani Baruti

Homosexuality and the Effeminization of Afrikan Males by Mwalimu K. Bomani Baruti

Mentacide by Mwalimu K. Bomani Baruti

The New Jim Crow: Mass Incarceration in the Age of Colorblindness by Michelle Alexander

Brainwashed: Challenging the Myth of Black Inferiority by Tom Burrell

The African Origin of Civilization: Myth Or Reality by Cheikh Anta Diop

The Destruction of Black Civilization by Chancellor Williams

How Capitalism Underdeveloped Black America by Manning Marable

The Conspiracy to Destroy Black Boys by Jawanza Kunjufu

What They Never Told you in History Class by Indus Khamit-Kush

Africans at the Crossroads: African World Revolution by John Henrik Clarke

The Spook who sat by the Door by Sam Greenlee (a novel)

The Golden Age of the Moor by Ivan Van Sertima

Your History J.A. Rogers by J.A. Rogers

The Secret Books of Egyptian Gnostics by Jean Doresse

Message to the Blackman in America by Elijah Muhhamad

Return to Glory: The Powerful Stirring of the Black Race by Joel A. Freeman, PhD, and Don B. Griffin

Black Man of the Nile and His Family by Yosef Ben-Jochannan

No Disrespect by Sister Souljah
Midnight: A Gangster Love Story by Sister Souljah

Recommended Internet Radio & TV Shows

Gus T. Renegade and Justice
(C.O.W.S. at www.contextofwhitesupremacy.com)

Edward Williams - Counter-Racism Television Network
(www.counter-racism.com/c-r_tv/)

Recommended Websites

- www.trojanhorse1.com
- www.counter-racism.com
- www.racism-notes.blogspot.com (Gus Renegade)
- www.justdojusticetoday.blogspot.com
- http://nonwhitealliance.wordpress.com
- www.drafrika.com (Dr. Africa)
- www.waronthehorizon.com
- www.ebonynewschannel.blogspot.com
- www.cree7.wordpress.com
- www.thecode.net
- www.mindcontrolblackassassins.wordpress.com
- www.facebook.com/umarthepsychologist
- www.finalcall.com
- www.blackagendareport.com

Black-Owned Bookstores:

- www.azizibooks.com
- www.TWPBooks.com
- www.counter-racism.com
- www.akobenhouse.com
- www.houseofnubian.com
- www.houseofkonsciousness.com
- www.freemaninstitute.com
- www.afriware.net

AUDIO CDS

Racism & Counter Racism by Dr. Frances Cress Welsing

Maximum Development of Black Male Children by Dr. Frances C. Welsing

The Psychopathic Racial Personality by Dr. Bobby E. Wright, PhD

(above available at: www.houseofnubian.com)

No Sex Between White and Non-White People by Neely Fuller, Jr.
Racism and Counter Racism by Neely Fuller, Jr.

Racism and Counter Racism by Neely Fuller, Jr.

(available: www.counter-racism.com)

Return to Glory: The Powerful Stirring of the Black Race
by Joel A. Freeman, PhD, and Don B. Griffin

(available at www.freemaninstitute.com)

DVDS

Dr. Frances Cress Welsing on Phil Donahue Show

Dr. Frances Cress Welsing Debates Dr. William Shockley & The Analysis of The Bell Curve

The Isis Papers by Dr. Frances Cress Welsing

Racism and Mental Health by Dr. Frances Cress Welsing

Worship of the African Woman as Creator by Dr. Yosef Ben Jochannan

(above DVDs available at: www.houseofnubian.com)

A White Man's Journey Into Black History
by Joel A. Freeman, PhD

(available at www.freemaninstitute.com)

Index

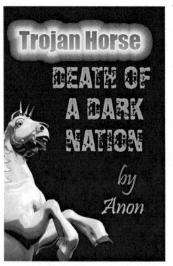

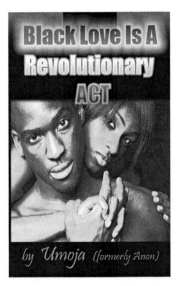

CPSIA information can be obtained at www.ICGtesting.com
Printed in the USA
BVOW081300110712

294909BV00002B/123/P

9 780982 206126